Spanish
New Orleans

Spanish New Orleans

An Imperial City on the American Periphery
1766–1803

JOHN EUGENE RODRIGUEZ

Louisiana State University Press
Baton Rouge

Published with the assistance of the V. Ray Cardozier Fund

Published by Louisiana State University Press
www.lsupress.org

Manufactured in the United States of America
First printing

DESIGNER: *Mandy McDonald Scallan*
TYPEFACE: *Whitman*
PRINTER AND BINDER: *Sheridan Books Inc.*

Cover illustration: *The Family of Dr. Joseph Montegut,* by Salazar. Courtesy of the Collections of the Louisiana State Museum.

Library of Congress Cataloging-in-Publication Data

Names: Rodriguez, John Eugene, author.
Title: Spanish New Orleans : an imperial city on the American periphery,
    1766–1803 / John Eugene Rodriguez.
Description: Baton Rouge : Louisiana State University Press, [2021] |
    Includes bibliographical references and index.
Identifiers: LCCN 2020029008 (print) | LCCN 2020029009 (ebook) | ISBN
    978-0-8071-7489-0 (cloth) | ISBN 978-0-8071-7500-2 (pdf) | ISBN 978-0-8071-7501-9
    (epub)
Subjects: LCSH: New Orleans (La.)—History—18th century. | New Orleans
    (La.)—Politics and government—18th century. | New Orleans
    (La.)—Economic conditions—18th century. |
    Spain—Colonies—America—Administration—History—18th century.
Classification: LCC F379.N557 R63 2021 (print) | LCC F379.N557 (ebook) |
    DDC 976.3/3502—dc23
LC record available at https://lccn.loc.gov/2020029008
LC ebook record available at https://lccn.loc.gov/2020029009

~

For my daughter Kelly and my son Alex,

that they may keep alive, in some fashion, the legacy of being a Rodriguez,

no matter what their last name may be.

. . . and the others, tributaries
and lesser streams,
joined together and equal
are those who live by their labor
and wealthy men.

I forsake the invocations
of orators most renowned
and famed bards;
I leave behind their fictions. . . .

—JORGE MANRIQUE
Verses Written on the Death of His Father

CONTENTS

ACKNOWLEDGMENTS

I have quietly mocked academic acknowledgements for years. Reading them is a little like closely examining the liner notes for a new music album (in my day) to learn which session musicians, backup singers, and perhaps even stars may have assisted.

And so I've decided to be a little different and give credit where it is truly due—to a number of dead and rather rambunctious people and a few alive—mostly on the Gulf Coast. Only a handful are teachers: Dolores Sumerall, my no-nonsense high-school history teacher who simply let me read and ramble, Dr. Martha Biles and the late Dean William Laforge from my years long ago at Delta State University, and my advisors at George Mason University, Dr. Joan Bristol, Dr. Rosemarie Zagarri, and Dr. Matthew Karush, who were extraordinarily patient with a much older but still rambling sea dog and his historical trivia show.

No, the people to whom much credit is due include a group of long-dead old men, a realtor turned amateur historian, a willing archaeologist, a gracious southern lady, a kind computer programmer, and, more predictably, several members of my immediate family. But such are likely the people who truly force history and continue it, beyond and perhaps despite books and professors.

I grew up in the company of sailors, men who drank and made machinery run or shrimped and fished, and occasionally went to war. They were the Elizabethan sailors of their day, but their poetic moments were simple lines said on porches to boys like we were. My grandfather Walden told of Casablanca and Atlantic convoys, my godfather Harold Houk of slipping into the Pacific from the burning hulk of the USS *Astoria* in the battle of Savo Island, my father of fleeing the exploding beach at Hungnam and night-boat patrols along the rivers of Vietnam. Eugene "Zany" Tiblier told me of a French colonial wreck discovered by his family in the bay, Adolphe Seymour of my great-grandfather Miguel's pride and silver watch chain (without a watch), and Schuyler Poitivent of my grandfather Rodriguez's kindness, although others told of his firmness (he killed three men in the line of duty). And Adolphe's son, a gentle and loyal man named Irwin Seymour, told me of baseball and, when he was sad, of bombing runs against Japanese cities. These are the "tributaries and lesser streams" to which Jorge Manrique referred, "joined together and equal" to any university, who in their stories and musings and character keep history alive. I thank them from the depths of my heart, and I wish I could speak again with each, and look forward to the day when I will.

In about 1973, Bobbie Davidson Smith, a local realtor turned amateur historian, was surprised to find that the newspaper letter writer so opposed to the reconstruction of a historic fort was a mere sixteen-year-old boy. She took me under her wing a bit—the door of her elegant home was always open, and it was through her that I was hired for my very first job, as an archaeologist's assistant with the team looking for Fort Maurepas, the first French settlement in the lower Mississippi Valley. That team was led by Sam McGahey, a red-haired and very kind state archaeologist who spoke to me for hours as he taught me to scrape. We never found the fort, although we found clues, and it has never been found since. Perhaps I will do so yet, for Ms. Smith and Sam.

In 1991, unexpectedly divorced, I turned myself back to history in my empty times, and researched and wrote a long, unpublishable book on early American New Orleans. I found a very willing research companion in my then ten-year-old daughter, Kelly, who spent much time in the libraries with me and a little digging in slave quarters and walking the battlefield of Chalmette. I was also encouraged by the late Mrs. Betty Pendley, a most gracious southern lady, who remained a lifetime proponent of historic archaeology and preservation in New Orleans and the state of Louisiana. Sharon Webster-Wileman loaned me her computer for my late-into-the-night typing; so did my cousins Wanda and Dieter Bartschat as I continued my research and restarted my life in Virginia. Throughout all of these years, I also had two other women in my life who were genuinely interested in history, especially genealogy, to encourage me—my mother, Bobbie Jean Walden Rodriguez, and my aunt, Maxine Walden Ramsey. So I suppose one could say that, while it was men who told me of history, it was women who later encouraged me in its pursuit.

No small debt must also be acknowledged to my son Alex, who was sometimes ignored while I took classes, but who is also a tough guy and greatly appreciated my trips to GMU because I routinely returned with barbecue for him, so perhaps there is no debt owed there at all!

Of course, despite all my irreverence here, in the end, I must acknowledge one final debt—the support of my wife, Jaewon, who permitted me to complete my MA and PhD at a much later age than is normal and encouraged me with food slipped onto the desk while I worked until very early in the mornings. Beyond the tales of old men and artifacts to be discovered and reshaped, Jaewon, my children, grandchildren, nephews, nieces, and innumerable young cousins represent the better angels of why men—and women—feel compelled to tell and write history and pass it on.

Spanish
New Orleans

Introduction

The Bourbon family ruled a vast global empire in the eighteenth century, an empire where, although the sun set, it was not dark long. The first Spanish Bourbon king, Philip V, who ascended to the throne in 1700, ruled an empire that sprawled across the Atlantic and the New World, extended west to several small Pacific islands, on to the Philippines, around to Spanish Guinea in Africa, then north to various North African ports, Italy, the Low Countries, and finally back to Spain itself.[1]

The most famous Bourbon colonies were those in the Western Hemisphere, most of which broke away after the temporary fall of the Bourbons in 1808. Much has been written on the tensions and opportunities that Bourbon rule presented these Western Hemisphere colonies, especially the tensions that arose as Charles III and Charles IV attempted to enforce their own philosophies, plans, leadership, and reforms on recalcitrant populations and officials. Much has also been written on the impact of the Bourbon rule on colonial transitions to independence. Historians have also explored, in less detail, the impact of Bourbon rule on those few colonies that most famously remained within the Spanish imperial grasp—Cuba, Puerto Rico, and the Philippines (formerly a province of Mexico). However, historians of Bourbon Spanish history have rarely focused upon the Spanish colony of Louisiana, in part because of a popular perception of it as really a French colony, albeit under Spanish rule.[2]

However, mere mathematics, demography, and political history belie the perception that Louisiana, and especially its capital, was really French. Louisiana was only founded in 1699, and it was not founded in Louisiana at all, but in modern-day coastal Mississippi and then Alabama. Modern-day Louisiana was only founded with New Orleans in 1718. The entire colony was poorly populated and even more poorly funded. French rule in the city only lasted forty-eight mostly miserable years; Spain occupied the colony via treaty in 1766. Spain ruled another thirty-seven years, until 1803—but, counterposed to the French era, the Spanish era was one of dramatic demographic and economic growth in both the city and the colony, led by some of Spain's most capable imperial governors. Spain formally retroceded the colony to France on 30 November 1803, but France in turn formally ceded the colony to the United States of America on 20 December.

The "French" New Orleans now so beloved by historians and tour guides had lasted only nineteen days, and it was somewhat of a sham. The ceremony was in the presence of the former Spanish governor and his troops, in a Spanish-built new city thriving under Spanish commercial rules and actually still under Spanish-appointed judges and Spanish law. Everyone in the city had known for weeks that the United States had already purchased Louisiana. By insisting on a formal ceremony before the arrival of US troops, the pompous French governor Laussat was merely attempting to score gratuitous political and personal points of no particular value. From a practical view, Louisiana was Spanish, and then it was American.

Louisiana, admittedly, did begin as a dismal French colony, quite late in Atlantic history. The small colony was managed as a mere periphery of a mercantilist economy and struggled to survive on the Gulf Coast, dependent upon and sometimes battling indigenous tribesmen, perhaps more deprived of metropolitan resources than the English colony of Jamestown was in the much earlier 1600s. The frustrated colonial governor moved to a new site on the Mississippi River in 1718; he labeled the shabby wooden town he constructed there "Nouvelle Orléans"—New Orleans. New Orleans, the colony's economic high point, was actually below sea level, and hunched behind a natural mud levee, next to a great river from which the French mostly extracted furs and limited agricultural goods. The colony remained semi-dependent upon trade with indigenous tribes.

However, with the conclusion of the Seven Years' War in 1763 via the Treaty of Paris, the Spanish Bourbon king Charles III acquired the vast Louisiana colony, which stretched on colonial maps from New Orleans north and northwest until the mostly unknown edges of the North American continent. The territory was immense, mostly unexplored, and almost completely populated by indigenous peoples. For the Bourbons, the Louisiana colony was seen as a logical march—a middle ground to hold between the British colonies in the most eastern quarter of North America and the rich and populous Viceroyalty of New Spain.[3]

But how to hold that middle ground? The previous Spanish conquistador model would have involved the use of allies to eject, enslave, or eliminate all of the peoples in the new colony, but such a model was unlikely to meet the needs of the Bourbons for an effective geographic march. Louisiana was not unpopulated—the Spanish found about 5,700 Frenchmen there, about 1,700 (30 percent) of those in New Orleans, and millions of indigenous peoples divided into many tribes. Ejecting most of the French would have been militarily feasible—the British did the same in some of the northeastern provinces of Canada they acquired in the Treaty of Paris, but the Spanish determined to permit the French, their homes, farms, skills, and connections with the upriver trade to remain in place, as did the British with the French already in Quebec, Montreal, and the then-western portions of Canada. The thought of attempting to eject, enslave, or eliminate the numerous indigenous tribes was simply too daunting for the limited Spanish resources available after the Seven Years' War. Consequently, Charles III was forced to instead adopt a model of accepting, suborning, and dominating the existing residents in the new colony of Louisiana.[4]

Charles III had been ceded Louisiana and its capital of New Orleans in 1763, but the emperor did not plan to govern Louisiana like other Bourbon imperial colonies. Rather than appoint a military officer with experience in fighting indigenous peoples or the French, Charles III instead appointed a famed explorer and scientist, Antonio de Ulloa y de la Torre-Giral. The emperor's choice of an explorer-governor was rational for a huge colony requiring so much exploration, and Ulloa had previously managed a district in Peru. However, in reality Ulloa was weak, conciliatory, and ill prepared to govern; he only arrived in New Orleans in 1766, and a short-lived junta of French planters forced him from the colony in 1768.[5]

Charles III was doubtlessly not amused: he appointed General Alexander (Alejandro) O'Reilly, a tough veteran of the European wars, as the new military/political governor. (Ulloa returned to the Spanish Navy and would never govern again.) O'Reilly sailed from Havana to New Orleans in the following year, 1769, with thousands of troops meant to overawe the populace and completely crush the revolt. Once he arrived, the new Bourbon governor actually abstained from using his considerable army against the populace. Still, he was in little mood for compromise: he quickly identified the leading dissidents, executed five by firing squad (a sixth died in custody, perhaps violently), and exiled several more to the foreboding Morro Castle, which still overlooks the entrance to Havana. Charles Gayarré, an early historian whose grandfather was a senior officer with O'Reilly, reported that the condemned men were "taken out of prison, and with their arms well-pinioned . . . to the place of execution, which was occupied by a large body of Spanish troops forming a square. . . . Rodriguez, the clerk of the Court, read to them their sentence in Spanish, and it was then repeated to them in French. . . . It was said that they met their fate with unshaken fortitude."[6] The prisoners were read their sentence first in Spanish, and only afterwards in French. O'Reilly's message was clear—Louisiana was now Spanish.

O'Reilly's brutal handling of the failed revolt would later become a touchstone of how Spanish rule was perceived in New Orleans, and he would be labeled then as "Bloody O'Reilly." But that would be after the Spanish had departed.[7] A successor, Governor Bernardo de Gálvez, proved to be much more popular, using the opportunity of the American Revolution to seize British West Florida. The expanded colony generally then prospered under a succession of Bourbon governors, most military officers, until 1803, when most of it was ceded to France and then almost immediately sold to the United States. Louisiana, then, was not merely a miserable French colony—it was also a successful Spanish colony, and indeed, the last large colony Spain would ever acquire.

This work is divided into three historic issues: demography, trade, and political administration and discourse. These three topics should not be seen as mere aspects of New Orleans—rather, they were layered stages, near-simultaneous steps in the colony's evolution. Each of these evolutionary steps provided the Spanish Bourbons with both challenges of governance and genuine opportunities to effectively expand imperial citizenship and actual imperial territory, profit from trans-imperial trade, and broaden political discourse, if the Bourbon ruler truly wished to expand his geographic, commercial, and political power.[8]

The choice of Charles III to Hispanicize a French colony and town rather than empty or even annihilate it required his governors to accept migrants, short-term residents of many ethnicities, and free people of color not as imperial *sujetos* (subjects), but as imperial *vecinos* (something much more akin to citizens), although this was also done, to some extent, in other Bourbon ports. However, his governors could not fully Hispanicize New Orleans precisely because of this multiethnic, multiracial, and multilingual population and, more subtly, by the shift in the city's women's more syncretic "American" tastes and material culture, largely built upon trade with the United States.

This trade in turn helped undermine Bourbon attempts to control the colony's economy via the critical chokepoint at New Orleans; the governors found themselves forced to normalize trans-imperial free trade in New Orleans and became almost entirely dependent upon trade with the United States. This economic dependence was steadily fueled by not only changing demographics and expectations for material goods, but also by frequent political and environmental disasters and the need for capital investment. This dependence in turn encouraged the Bourbon governors in New Orleans to negotiate both economic and political discourse in a city in which the populace was increasingly literate in three European languages, had its own information networks via trade, and was shaped by continuing flows of migrants, printed material, and political concepts from revolutionary United States, France, and St. Domingue. In the end, the Bourbons found that the colony they envisioned as a defensive march for Mexico was moving demographically, economically, and finally politically closer to the new and burgeoning United States.

The purpose of this book, then is not to merely reinsert New Orleans into Spanish imperial history—it is to consider what Spanish New Orleans reveals about the challenges and opportunities for the larger Bourbon empire. That empire, of course, faced many challenges worldwide and many challenges in North America alone, including relations, alliances, and wars with nearby empires and indigenous tribes, as well as its use of slavery. However, these particular issues have been much studied with reference to New Orleans.

Instead, this book will focus upon three less-often detailed issues in the history of Bourbon New Orleans—demography, trade, and political discourse—using a full spectrum of original sources and innovative methodologies. These issues—these challenges and opportunities—demonstrate how the Bourbon empire responded in its newest colony and its capital, New Orleans, and therefore might have responded elsewhere within the empire to the coming nineteenth century. That coming century, which arrived in New Orleans with the American annexation in December 1803, would be incredibly filled with geographic, economic, intellectual, and political expansion by other empires. The Spanish empire, however, would not expand again, and now would only shrink. The Bourbon Spanish empire reached its geographic zenith in New Orleans, and everything to follow led to nightfall.

A City of Chameleons

Withdrawn into the peace of this desert,
along with some books, few but wise,
I live in conversation with the deceased,
and listen to the dead with my eyes.
—FRANCISCO DE QUEVEDO, *"From the Tower"*

By 22 November 1803, when Spanish authorities formally ceded Louisiana, and a mere nineteen days later, when France in turn ceded the colony to the United States of America, the city of New Orleans was no longer French— at least demographically.[1] Census rolls and mountains of notarial and court documents clearly indicate that less than half of the city's populace still bore French surnames by 1803. Most residents still spoke the French language routinely, but most also had little reason to consider themselves "French" and were bilingual. Instead, the percentage of non-"French" residents increased year by year during Spanish rule, and the city became more multiethnic, multilingual, and multiracial, even as it became more "Spanish." By 1803, New Orleans was a city of chameleons.

However, unlike elsewhere in the Spanish empire, this demographic increase was a double-edged sword, because many of these residents, white and of color, had come from other empires—those of France, Great Britain, and the United States. All of these new residents, consequently, could work within multiple imperial structures and with multiple languages, beyond those of Spain. And most of these residents had not come to New Orleans at the invitation or instigation of the Spanish king and his governors—they had either been born in Louisiana, or they had come on their own.

6

THE CENSUS TAKER

In 1791, a census taker walked through the muddy frontier city of New Orleans, writing the names of the living. He was conscious of rank—he labeled dozens of the residents as "Don," and a few key officials not by their name but their position—"El Senor Assessor," for example, rather than "Dr. Nicolas Maria Vidal," who then filled that post. The census taker required that every male head of a family and every single or married female present both a first and a last name; he did otherwise only with widows, substituting the words *la viuda* for their first name. He was probably Spanish with reasonable French language skills, for he spelled most of the Spanish and only some of the French names wrong—and even some of those "incorrect" names he may have actually spelled correctly, for free people of color in the eighteenth century would often modify their names only slightly from the name carried by their white relatives. But in his written work, this census taker made no note of ethnicity or race. And when he was done with his compilation, he forwarded it to the governor and the *cabildo*.

It was important to the Bourbon kings and governors that they enumerate and know something about the peoples they sought to rule and, not coincidentally, tax, and this was certainly true of the new colony of Louisiana and its capital, New Orleans. Charles III had made a choice between using brute force or working with the people he had been given in the new colony, and he had chosen the path of acceptance, limited accommodation, and, presumably, eventual dominance. But he needed to understand exactly who was encompassed in this colony.

The 1791 census taker was actually following a time-honored procedure in both the Hapsburg and Bourbon Spanish empires. The Spanish had conducted their first censuses (*censos*) in the New World in the 1500s. However, it was only in 1776, during the reign of Charles III, that the Spanish royal court requested standardized, annual population data on its worldwide colonies. Given the size of those colonies, it was difficult for colonial governors and viceroys to comply, and certainly not on an annual basis. Puerto Rico was a notable exception, and issued aggregate population tables (*padrones*) every year from 1779 to 1802. Instead, most cities and towns only compiled detailed *censos* once or twice during the late Bourbon era.[2]

The Spanish first compiled aggregate population numbers for Louisiana in 1763, soon after Bourbon administrators arrived in the colony. The *Récapitula-*

tion generale des recensements ci-joint faits a la Nouvelle Orléans et dans tous les quartiers was prepared by a French resident, in his own language. The Spanish compiled similar tabulations (*padrones*) in 1766, 1777, 1788, and 1800. However, only two detailed *censos* of the city were compiled—one in 1778 and another in 1791.[3] Governor Carondelet conducted a subsequent "chimney census" in 1795–96, but, because it was meant primarily for taxation purposes, that census was only prepared piecemeal and then only of the city's core.

As the census taker walked through New Orleans in 1791, most of the buildings he saw were Spanish in construction, for most of the city had been destroyed only three years earlier in the Good Friday Fire of 1788. Although he would not have known, a subsequent fire in another three years, in 1794, would complete the task of destroying the city's wooden buildings, leaving a single French building to survive to this day—the Ursuline convent at the eastern end of the city.[4] The Spanish architecture taking shape inside the city included the use of stone, tiled roofs, iron railings on balconies, and cool inner courtyards and was presumably of little surprise to the census taker—for Spain had already ruled the vast Louisiana colony and this small but humming colonial capital of New Orleans for a quarter of a century.

True, some French planters had forced out the imperial governor long before, in 1766, but now in 1791, a quarter of a century later, the planters were older and wiser, their sons served in the Spanish militia, some of their daughters were married to Spanish immigrants, and those who had disagreed with the rule of Charles III, the longtime Bourbon King of Spain, and now the rule of his admittedly less competent son, Charles IV, remained quiet. Those executed by the Spanish governor had been dead and dust for an entire generation, and none were interested in following their predecessors' example. New Orleans was undeniably Spanish.

Historians have generally minimized the Spanish role in Louisiana and its capital.[5] However, the historians were wrong, and the census taker was right. Like Quevedo, we must "listen to the dead with my eyes"—but *not only* to the voices of one or two or ten. Rather, we must hear if not *all* of the voices, *most* of the voices in colonial New Orleans during the Spanish era, using the documents of not only the census taker, but also those of public notaries, tax collectors, a judge, a priest, a sergeant, a nurse, merchants, and even two artists. To do so, we will listen to the dead in lists of chimneys, ledgers of debts owed, internment and baptismal registers, military musters, hospital registers, and voluminous notarial, judicial, and military archives.[6] We will also use a large and comprehensive database, compiled by the author, of notarial business transactors in New Orleans from 1780 to 1799. Such a large database has never been used in colonial Spanish American history. To minimize miscalculation and inconsistency, I have used this comprehensive database of 10,000+ New Orleans residents in late Spanish New Orleans to ascribe a single ethnic background to each name based upon their surname and any additional historical details immediately available. This database permits a researcher to determine how both first names and surnames are initially spelled and misspelled throughout the two decades from 1780 to 1799.

POINTS IN TIME—1791 AND 1795

The census taker reported that 1791 New Orleans contained 5,037 residents; by way of comparison, the city was probably a little larger than the nearest US city—Savannah, Georgia—half the size of Montevideo in the Rio Plata, about 40 percent the size of Baltimore, Maryland, and only one-fourth the size of Charleston, South Carolina.[7]

The 1791 census listed 829 individuals (roughly one-quarter of the free population) by name, although four were actually not named but instead identified by their government titles (the gentleman governor, assessor, auditor, and bishop). The census taker assigned honorific titles to 90 individuals among these 829: the 4 government officials, a priest, and 85 men referred to with the title *Don*.[8]

The men with formal titles or considered as a *don* may be the city's male elite. Such an elite, captured by a single man at a single moment in the city's history, is admittedly subjective and presumably somewhat inaccurate, and it would not have remained static. But the title *Don* is a useful tool for evaluating which residents were perceived to be worthy of recognition in that moment. These men represented, at least in the eyes of the census taker, an elite of 15 percent of the free male population. Half of these "elite" males had Spanish surnames, another third carried French surnames, and a handful were of northern European ancestry. Based on their street listings, these men lived intermixed throughout the city; there was no elite neighborhood or street in the city then. However, none were free people of color—the census-taker had a limited view of who could be a respectable *don*.[9]

Ancestry and ethnicity are clearly social constructions, but analysis of the building, revision, and even dismantlement of those social constructs provides useful historical insights into how a society reshapes itself. The residents of

New Orleans were, like many societies, very busy with social construction, and the era of Spanish rule was no different. Consequently, I use surnames to determine probable ancestry—dividing those surnames into three categories: French, Spanish, and northern European, while setting aside a fourth category for those identified in the archives as being free people of color. Surnames do not determine the ancestry or ethnicity of any individual, if such could ever be delineated—but surnames can provide hints, and those hints are especially useful in tracking migration and the fusion of societies.[10]

Surname identifications are also not precise. People in the eighteenth century moved across imperial borders—or those borders themselves moved—quite often, and inevitably their names metamorphosed, for example from Seymour to Zamora, from Ryan to Raillen or Riano, and Rodriguez to Roderick. Despite the inevitable imprecision, surname identification very clearly indicates the changing demography within New Orleans and how it may have varied from other Spanish imperial cities. How much that demography indicates about cultural dominance is subject to discussion.

The 1791 census was only a single moment, a single portrait of the city in a specific year. Fortunately, another census was conducted only four years later, although it is not well remembered as a census of people. Instead, at least in public discourse in 1795, the next census was of chimneys. This census was officially meant by Governor Carondelet to provide data for taxes for street lighting, based on the numbers of chimneys in the core of the city. However, given that the "chimney census" not only carefully chimneys but also counted and named the residents in each building, the intent of someone in the government, perhaps Carondelet himself, was clearly to take the opportunity for a second census.[11]

The 1795 chimney census was divided into three imprecise age groups: Group 1 (ages 0–14), Group 2 (ages 15–50), and Group 3 (over age 50). It was also divided into free people and slaves, each further divided by sex and racial heritage—white, mixed, or African.

The division of residents by age group in table 1.1 was imprecise: Group 1, for example, was meant to count children from birth to puberty, while Group 2 was meant to capture the number of men able to serve in the militia. Similarly, the census taker and even the residents themselves probably made mistakes or lied a little about ages; the modern historian can only hope these errors were relatively uniform.

This census, however, reveals quite a bit about the heart of New Orleans,

TABLE 1.1

The Chimney Census of New Orleans, 1795

Age Groups	Free White Male	Free White Fem.	Free Mixed Male	Free Mixed Fem.	Free Afr. Male	Free Afr. Fem.	Slave Mixed Male	Slave Mixed Fem.	Slave Afr. Male	Slave Afr. Fem.
0–14 (Grp 1)	150	113	21	26	7	5	13	17	51	59
15–50 (Grp 2)	229	148	12	28	8	12	7	26	192	259
50+ (Grp 3)	38	29	0	4	4	8	0	3	6	5

Source: De Ville, *The 1795 Chimney Tax of New Orleans,* v–vii.

which can eventually be compared with other Spanish imperial cities and their statistics. One immediate revelation is that New Orleans society was not always divided into three groups (whites, free people of color, and slaves) or even four (dividing free people of color as *pardo* or *moreno/negro*, as was done in ecclesiastical records), but rather sometimes by racial divisions even within the slave populations. In New Orleans, at least on paper, the population was divided into five social and racial groups: white, free mixed, free African, enslaved mixed, and enslaved African, in a very clear social hierarchy, based upon the order of their listing in the census.[12]

Thus the 1795 chimney census indicates that, for the census takers and presumably the governor, slaves also required division and categorization. Planters of the time worried greatly about *bozales*—slaves newly arrived from Africa, who were believed to be more willing to revolt but also to be hardier for agricultural work, and perhaps the division of slaves into categories of mixed and African (in the actual text, *negro*) partly reflects that concern. But the division in the census is not by *bozal* or native-born: the division in the 1795 census seems to have been strictly based upon color. Given that the Spanish authorities were already statistically subdividing the slave population based upon shade of skin, one must wonder if free people of color and even slaves themselves were not also doing the same, in a manner consistent with Bourbon concepts of racial and social caste.

Another revelation is in the emerging geographic division of the city by race and social category. The city's heart could almost be divided into a baker's dozen—4/13 white males, 3/13 white females, 2/13 enslaved male, 3/13 enslaved female, and only 1/13 free people of color, male and female. The city's heart was, that is, almost all white or enslaved as of 1795.

One reason for the high percentage of enslaved Africans in central New Orleans in 1795 may lie in the continued slave trade through the city. A closer analysis of the actual census would probably reveal that most of the enslaved males in the city were residing on properties owned by merchants. Most of these slaves, then, would not be considered residents of the city save for the period of the census; instead, they were in sad transit to plantations. Others, however, would have been employed in warehouses, construction teams, and the like.

Although free people of color were counted as 6 percent of the city's population in 1791, they conducted 13 percent of the city's business transactions in 1795. While many of these transactions were actually their own manumissions, this doubling of transactions in only four years indicates that the free population in the city had grown considerably in size and economic power in the intervening four years. However, given that the 1795 census counted only 135 free people of color residing in the Vieux Carré—that is, only 9 percent of the population—it is likely that some free people of color were already living outside the Quarter before the creation of the Faubourg Marigny, which is often associated with free people of color. Consequently, although racial segregation was not required by the Spanish authorities, it may have already been at work in the city's core.

This likely segregation is illustrated by figure 1.1, which recreates a portion of a 1780 map of Spanish New Orleans (admittedly drawn by a French engineer), overlaid with dark lines indicating the streets on which most free people of color in the early American era (1805) resided. As can be seen, the free people of color were mostly living in the blocks away from the river, to some extent bounded by Bienville and St. Ann, that is, occupying only portions of about one-sixth of the inner city. This residence pattern comports with the 1795 census and the implication that many free people of color were already living outside the inner city in the Spanish era.[13]

Another form of hierarchy, of gender, is also notable in the discrepancies in the number of males versus females in the 1795 census, both among whites and among free people of color. Within whites in Group 2 (aged 15–50), the sex ratio was a little more than 3:2; within the free mixed and African population, the ratio was very opposite, at 1:2. Such sex ratios were consistent for New Orleans throughout the Spanish era.[14] Only two years after the American annexation, in the 1805 City Directory, roughly half of the 297 free families living in the

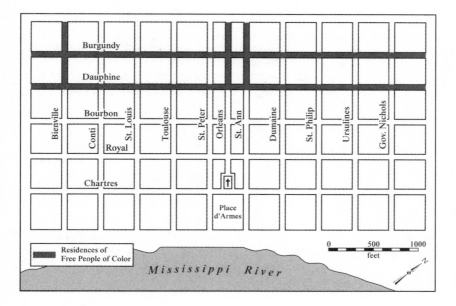

FIGURE 1.1. Central New Orleans in 1780 with overlay of residences of free people of color (*New Orleans City Directory and Census*, 1805). Map by Mary Lee Eggart.

city were headed by women.[15] Such a demographic mixture complicated both gender and racial hierarchies within the city, providing opportunities for male dominance over white, mulatto, and African females, and enforcing white male dominance over mulatto and African free men and slaves.

A final consideration is the age of the city's population. Although comparison with other Bourbon records is difficult due to a lack of their compilation and publication, comparison may be made with the US Census of 1790. The comparison indicates very clearly that the city's population, especially its male population, was considerably older than the overall population in the United States.[16] Bourbon New Orleans was clearly, first and foremost, a city for work and trade—not for raising a family.

Only a very few of the city's residents were indigenous. This lack of indigenous residents was not completely unusual within the Spanish empire: although many cities had very large indigenous populations—as in Mexico, Guatemala, and Peru—a few imperial cities did not. For example, the 1806–7 census of Buenos Aires reported that only 1.4 percent of that population was indigenous,

TABLE 1.2

Comparison of Count of Named Individuals, 1791 and 1795

		Named Individuals Only							
	Total	Free Male	Free Fem.	French	Spanish	N. Eur.	Total White	Free Ppl. of Color	Slaves
1791	829	589	240	400/414	304/306	73	776/793	53/34	Unknown
1795	1,480	469	373	485	219	108	707/808	135/128?	638

Sources: De Ville, *The 1795 Chimney Tax of New Orleans,* v–vii; New Orleans Census of 1791.

and both that percentage and the actual number of indigenous residents in the city dropped precipitously by the census of 1810, only three or four years later.[17]

The 1795 census also provides detailed information on the types of occupations in the city, the numbers of those practicing those occupations, the number of militiamen, and, as one would hope, the number of taxable chimneys. But compare this census with the 1791 census.[18] That census identified 1,480 residents in the city, but many of these would not be counted in the more limited 1795 census, which was, after all, focused on taxing central city residents to pay for central city improvements. However, the 1791 census listed the streets on which the residents lived, and when only the residents on those streets also counted in the 1795 census are counted,[19] the two censuses may be compared, as depicted in table 1.2.

This comparison evidences how much categories like race and social status may be socially constructed, even by a single census taker. For example, the 1795 census taker did notice race, but his perceptions differed from those of the 1791 census taker. Of 128 individuals on the 1795 census who appear elsewhere in Spanish notarial archives as free people of color, the 1791 census taker only noted 34 as such within his list of names. Among the then well-known free men and women of color who appeared in the 1795 census, for example, Charles Brule, Marie Laveau, Jacques Leduf, and Vincent Populus all had no notation of their racial status. The census also included at least five slaves, most owned by the convent or the king, but all living separately from their masters.

The 1795 census taker was also, at first blush, rather uncaring about social rank; he only identified eighteen men, almost all Spanish, by their position. Instead, he referred to many males as "Mr.," in this case, *Monsieur*.[20] Comparison

TABLE 1.3

Comparison of Named Individuals Given Titles, 1791 and 1795

	Percentages of Total Named Individuals Given Titles							
	Title French	Title Span.	Title N. Eur.	Title FMC*	Mr. French	Mr. Span.	Mr. N. Eur.	Mr. FMC*
1791	41%	51%	8%	0%	n/a	n/a	n/a	n/a
1795	6%	83%	11%	0%	58%	28%	11%	3%

*FMC = Free men of color.

Sources: De Ville, *The 1795 Chimney Tax of New Orleans*, v–vii; New Orleans Census of 1791.

TABLE 1.4

Comparison of Individual Groups Given Titles, 1791 and 1795

	Percentages of Individual Groups Given Titles							
	Title French	Title Span.	Title N. Eur.	Title FMC*	Mr. French	Mr. Span.	Mr. N. Eur.	Mr. FMC*
1791	9%	14%	10%	0%	n/a	n/a	n/a	n/a
1795	0%	3%	2%	0%	18%	19%	16%	3%

*FMC = Free men of color.

Sources: De Ville, *The 1795 Chimney Tax of New Orleans*, v–vii; New Orleans Census of 1791.

with the 1791 census, as seen in Tables 1.3 and 1.4, indicates a paradoxical shrinking and expansion in the elite of New Orleans—at least within the mind of the census taker—a small number of overwhelmingly Spanish elite (2–3 percent) and a much larger number (20 percent) of French-surnamed men deserving the simple title *Monsieur*. In this latter group, the census taker included three free people of color—Noel Carriere, Louis Daunois (Daunoy), and Louis Nicolas, at least two from prominent white families. Perhaps the 1795 census taker was a closet French republican, or perhaps title and race were mutually constructed by both the census taker and the individual being counted and named, as well as any official who reviewed the draft census. Finally, perhaps the city genuinely was stratifying, and the best a Frenchman now could be labeled was *Monsieur*.

Like the 1791 census, the 1795 chimney census also made no notice of ethnicity or status as a *vecino* (a term of arguable definition, somewhere between a royal subject and a royal citizen)[21] or foreigner. Unlike the 1791 census, however, the chimney census did not collect data on slaves, and therefore the data did not apply a five-level social/racial hierarchy to the city. However, when taken together, the two censuses of late Spanish New Orleans indicate that the city was structured according to a social and racial hierarchy, not only separating whites from free people of color, but also further subdividing free people of color and slaves via concepts of "mixed" and "negro." Such a social/racial hierarchy was the norm within both Spanish and French societies in the Caribbean, in those regions or islands in which there was no substantial indigenous population. The censuses also indicate that official titles meant something—there was clearly an elite—and there was further subdivision between men and women in the hierarchy, although that subdivision was left a little unclear in the data.

A NEW DEMOGRAPHIC METHOD: ECONOMIC POPULATION ANALYSIS

As recent North American history has shown, governmental policy and initiatives on immigration do not always reflect reality. Similarly, in the eighteenth century, Spanish policy and initiatives never reflected actual immigration. Despite serious Spanish concerns, US residents continued to flow into Louisiana and adjoining Mississippi/Spanish West Florida, and the Bourbon colonial governors seemed perplexed and resigned to their arrival. But the historical record is uncertain: what was the actual flow of immigrants into Louisiana during the Spanish period?

At least two modern historians have implied that immigration into Louisiana, especially into New Orleans, stagnated during the Spanish era.[22] The Spanish *padrones* and *censos* provide historical waypoints for understanding the overall demographic changes in Spanish New Orleans in terms of white/ free people of color/slave and male/female ratios. However, these sources do not provide enough data to permit serious charting of ethnicity ratios or immigration. For the latter chore, only the *censos* of 1778 and 1791 and the chimney census of 1795 provide surnames from which the changing ethnicity of the city's residents may be estimated.

Fortunately, while there are no Spanish records on immigration during this period, notarial records provide a gauge of the flow of immigrants into Louisiana and especially New Orleans. The Spanish-era New Orleans notarial archives, which comprise at least 20,000 pages of handwritten documents, represent

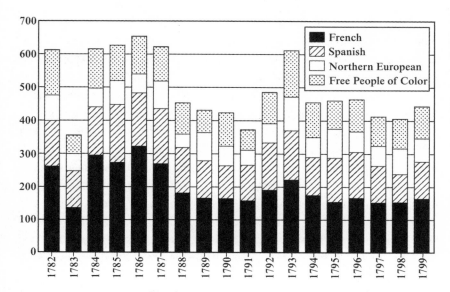

FIGURE 1.2. New business transactors in New Orleans, notarial entries, 1782–99.

the routine business transactions—sales, purchases, leases, powers of attorney, marriage contracts, wills, and manumissions—of at least 10,000 indexed individuals who lived, worked, or simply conducted business in Spanish New Orleans. This vast number of *vecinos* and visitors is certainly not comprehensive—many *vecinos* and visitors did not use the notarial system to document their routine or occasional business in the city, and the documents themselves contain sometimes dozens of unindexed names, including those of slaves, minor family members, and witnesses. Consequently, it is impossible to hear the voices of all the residents of the city, or even know their names.

However, the notarial archives provide broad perspective and great detail into both the demographic composition and the economic development of Spanish New Orleans. The total number of individuals conducting notarial transactions in New Orleans fluctuated over the years, as demonstrated in figure 1.2. These fluctuations not only serve as indicators of economic growth or stagnation, but also as indicators of the ethnic and racial makeup of the identified individuals who conducted these transactions.

Of the notarial transactors during the Spanish period, the largest single group was French. However, after 1786, the French never represented a majority of transactors. Instead, the other three groups combined formed a majority of notarial transactors; the French were replaced within the percentage of notarial transactions by the Spanish (27–29 percent of all transactions) and, to a lesser extent, by a very steady, uniform number of northern Europeans and free people of color conducting another 26 percent or so of transactions.

Among the new transactors (those who had not conducted business in the previous two years) from 1782 to 1799, the French also were the largest group, but as with total transactions, only exceeded 50 percent one year, in 1786, and after 1787 never had more than 40 percent of the new transactions. Instead, they were supplanted as new transactors by Spaniards and free people of color, although the latter statistic actually reflected the continued growth of that community via manumissions—which, it must be remembered, appeared as notarial transactions involving two parties, just like any other business deal.

Doubtlessly many new business transactors were *not* new immigrants to New Orleans. Instead, many were sons coming into their majority, daughters securing protected dowries, and men and women making their first notable purchase or contract, freeing slaves, or making their wills. Others were merchants and planters from within and outside the region, conducting their first business transactions in New Orleans, signing powers of attorney, purchasing or selling property, and then departing. Some, however, would have been immigrants, conducting not only routine transactions, but also conducting what might be considered start-up transactions—selling or purchasing slaves, purchasing or leasing property, and marrying their children into local families. These categories, of course, might well overlap, as when a son came into majority and purchased property on his own, but they would still be represented by only one transaction. Some of these new business transactors, especially incoming Spanish merchants, military and administrative personnel, and northern European/US subjects or citizens, may be readily identified from the historical record as they arrived in the city.

Historians have previously used Spanish censuses, militia rosters, and cathedral registers to estimate the population and demographics of colonial New Orleans.[23] Of these, the census records are perhaps most accurate, because they reflected the people counted both voluntarily and involuntarily in other records. The cathedral registers, on the other hand, are surprisingly inconsistent and inaccurate in spelling and terribly incomplete in their coverage of the city's population, especially when compared to the notarial archives. The archives were much more consistent and accurate in spelling names: the notarial documents were signed by the actual transactors, unlike the church records, which

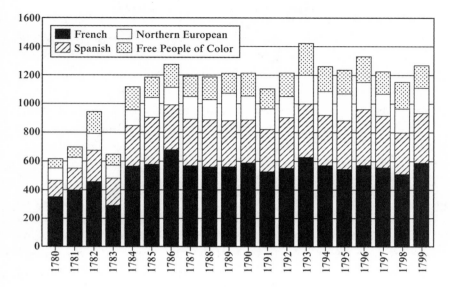

FIGURE 1.3. Total business transactors in New Orleans, notarial entries by
ethnic/racial groups, 1780–99.

were written by clerics, and were also much more comprehensive in capturing
the city's adult population, whether white, free of color, or slave. For example,
the notarial archives indicate at least 201 new business transactors in 1792, but
cathedral records for the period of 1791–99 only list 33 (16 percent) of these
individuals.[24]

This is where a fourth method of analyzing notarial records—focusing on the
number and type of transactions conducted each year by discrete demographic
groups—may prove useful to the historian. Figure 1.3 depicts the total number
of transactions conducted by Spanish/Spanish colonials/Italians, French/French
colonials, northern Europeans/US subjects or citizens, and free people of color
during the period 1787–92 recorded by notaries Perdomo and Ximenes, providing clear evidence that many Spanish immigrants settled in New Orleans.[25]

The percentage of Frenchmen and French colonials in the colony was perhaps
even lower than the percentages of total business transactors might indicate if
one focuses instead only upon new business transactors and compares those with
sacramental records. For example, there were 200 new business transactors in
1792; 31 of these later appeared, with clearly identifiable names and birthplaces,
in cathedral records from 1791 to 1799. Of these 31 individuals, only 58 percent

were French (some born in Louisiana); another 42 percent were Spanish. Such percentages are clearly inaccurate: they do not include free people of color and northern Europeans (often Protestant), but they do indicate that the French were not as numerous in the city as presumed by Francophone historians.[26]

Instead, close study indicates that new *vecinos* were constantly arriving or being recognized in New Orleans. These were mostly Spanish colonials, southern and northern Europeans (the latter often from the new United States), and free people of color. New Orleans was clearly being Hispanicized until 1803.

A FAILURE OF SPANISH IMMIGRATION POLICY

The Spanish Bourbon governors of Louisiana faced a dramatic set of demographic challenges: when they occupied the colony in the 1760s, the populace was almost exclusively of French, Native American, or African origin. In addition, the British colonies of Jamaica and West Florida were within sailing distance—and therefore within easy military striking range. If Great Britain attempted to seize Louisiana, such an attempt would not only be supported by the growing British Navy but also by the growing population of Jamaica.

The first Bourbon governors of Louisiana, then, were required to both subdue and perhaps convert the French population by force, persuasion, and migrants more loyal to Spain, and to ensure that Great Britain was discouraged from attempting to seize Louisiana, perhaps with support of the former French. Facing the internal challenge first, Governor Ulloa unsuccessfully attempted persuasion (1766–68); his successor, O'Reilly, used brute force and select executions and exiles (1769), and Unzaga unsurprisingly used persuasion with far more success than Ulloa (1769–77). Governor Gálvez focused upon the external threat first and foremost; he discouraged the British by marching into British West Florida, seizing Baton Rouge, Mobile, and Pensacola, and ethnically cleansing Pensacola by removing almost every British resident from that small town.

However, in the following years, Bourbon governors like Miró, Carondelet, and Gayoso faced a much more dangerous challenge: an extraordinary and prolonged wave of Americans south and westward into the Louisiana colony, who as they came forced the Native tribes allied with Spain, including the Chickasaws, Shawnees, Delawares, Cherokees, and Creeks, out of the eastern marches and toward the west side of the Mississippi River.[27] The Bourbons in New Orleans did not know how to respond to such a demographic and cultural challenge and struggled within their own administrative and racial paradigms to encourage the immigration of people they considered acceptable, that is, Catholic, white, and loyal to the Spanish king. In these efforts, although New Orleans and the southern portion of the colony was being steadily Hispanicized, the governors of Louisiana failed, because most of the Americans who came to the colony were decidedly republican, white, and Protestant. The Bourbon governors watched as their colony and its capital changed, not because of Spanish immigration policy, but despite it.

As in other Spanish colonies, the essential requirements to be *vecinos* of Spain or its colonies were to settle in one location or marry local women, obligate themselves to civic contributions and responsibilities (including militia duty), swear fidelity to the Spanish king, and to profess the Catholic religion.[28] In this, being Spanish was a constructed rather than an inherent identity. The last two of these requirements, however, considerably limited the Spanish search for acceptable migrants. It was not difficult for migrants to determine to move to a new, fertile land with economic promise; some may have chafed at the prospect of militia duty, but this, too, was not a dramatic burden. Rather, it was the requirements that they be royalists and Catholics, as well as the inconsistency of Spanish economic policies, which doubtlessly concerned many potential migrants from the United States and British colonies.

The requirement that migrants swear fidelity to the Spanish king implied a willingness to acknowledge one king or another, but many potential migrants to Louisiana from the United States, France, St. Domingue, and Guadeloupe were republicans, opposed to any king at all. In addition, many potential migrants were disenchanted royalists, frustrated with the unkept promises of their own kings, especially the inability of either George III or Louis XVI to protect their supporters in North America and the Caribbean or to assist royalist refugees. The final requirement, that migrants also be Catholic, further filtered potential migrants to Spanish colonies to those from other Catholic populations, including Ireland, western France, the Netherlands, Italy, French colonies, and from elsewhere within the Spanish empire.

It was within these strictures, then, that the Spanish governors of Louisiana first sought Acadian refugees. At first blush, it may seem surprisingly shortsighted that Spain sought to populate a former French colony with French-speaking immigrants. However, the Acadians had special reasons to be aggrieved with French rule. They had been brutally rounded up by British troops following the Seven Years' War, placed in camps where hundreds died, and then expelled to France. The French Bourbon king made no significant preparations for the refugees: consequently, the Acadian refugees had struggled in western coastal towns and on sterile agricultural land in France, been required to pay high rents, and had been made pawns in political machinations. Some Acadians had been resettled by their king, not in France, but in two extremes of climate, French Guyana or the Falklands; many of these died, and many others returned to France in frustration.[29]

Consequently, for the Acadians who managed to reach Louisiana, the opportunity for free, fertile land in an improved, stable physical and political climate meant a genuinely better life than before. For the Spanish, the Acadians, who bore an undeniable hatred for the British king, ambivalence and even bitterness toward the French king, and gratitude to the Spanish governor, and were decidedly Catholic, were perfectly acceptable immigrants.

Consequently, the first Spanish governor, Antonio de Ulloa, expanded a previous French open-door policy for Acadian immigrants during the period 1766–68, and even his feared successor, Alejandro O'Reilly, facilitated the establishment of Acadian settlements in the colony. In late 1785, Governor Miró followed precedent by accepting almost 1,600 more Acadian immigrants, many from failed colonies in Poitou. The transfer of these immigrants had been proposed by a Louisiana planter, Henri Peyroux de la Courdeniere, and an Acadian cobbler, Olivier Terriot (Theriot) to the Spanish ambassador in France, the Comte de Aranda. However, this last wave of migrants constituted a full 70 percent of France's remaining Acadian refugees;[30] after 1785, there were very few Acadians available for resettlement in the Spanish empire or elsewhere.

Inevitably, some of the Acadians chose to remain in New Orleans rather than work further up the rivers and bayous of Louisiana; others were attracted to the city later, often for work. Many Acadian surnames appear in the city's Spanish-era notarial records, including Bergeron, Boudreau, Broussard, Guidry, Hebert, Landry, and Melancon.

Some royalist immigrants also reached Louisiana from revolutionary France and St. Domingue during this same period, and they, too, would have been acceptable to the Bourbon Spanish. For example, Lieutenant Colonel François Agustin de Montault, a knight of St. Louis, arrived in New Orleans sometime before February 1794, when he married the widow of the city's former treasurer, Gilberto Leonard. He was a royal officer with an immediately marketable military skill and thus would have been welcomed by the Bourbon governor. However, the numbers of St. Dominguan refugees were never significant in Spanish New Orleans.[31]

Governor Miró had worried that the colony's economy was not going to improve; nor would Louisiana be secure from military intervention by another European power or slave revolt unless many more immigrants came to the colony. Louisiana's population had jumped dramatically in only three years between 1785 and 1788—from roughly 31,000 to 42,000—but the population of New Orleans lingered around 5,000 residents. By comparison, in 1790, only two years later, the state of South Carolina numbered 249,073 persons, and its largest city, Charleston, had 16,359 residents.[32]

Bourbon governors throughout the Spanish empire had no further access to more Acadians, and other colonial refugees migrated instead to the new United States or eastern Cuba. Given recent royal policy on tobacco and an ongoing economic slump in Louisiana during this period, Miró's choices were even more limited than usual. He therefore attempted to recruit from a mixture of migrant sources. He brought in numerous *Isleños* (Canary Islanders), settling them below New Orleans to guard the city's southern approaches. Although his predecessors had already expelled most British from West Florida, Miró attempted to convert some to Catholicism, probably with little success, to avoid ejecting them from the colony.[33] He also may have, perhaps unconsciously, encouraged the immigration of free people of color, although how many free people of color arrived in New Orleans remains uncertain.

While Miró could be reasonably certain about the loyalty of Isleños and free people of color, he had even more serious reasons to doubt the assimilation of republican, mostly Protestant Americans—already labeled *los Americanos*—into a royalist, Catholic colony. Nevertheless, he made several attempts to attract immigrants from the United States via the French chevalier Pierre Wouves d'Arges, the American general James Wilkinson, Colonel George Morgan, and Bryan and Peter Bryan Bruin, all of whom pledged to lead families from Kentucky. D'Arges, for example, hoped to lead 1,582 German–United States families, for example, about 5,000 immigrants.

None of these attempts were successful, in part because of the limitations of the Spanish economy and Miró's lack of authority. Most would-be immigrants desired financial assistance and/or large land grants, but Miró did not have adequate funds to bring immigrants, nor did he have the authority to make large land grants. He could not officially establish New Orleans as a free trade port or protect the profitable tobacco agriculture or the sale of slaves against royal policy; he had little influence, if any, on maritime taxation. In a word, Miró had little, if anything, to give immigrants, and nothing to withhold as a means of immigration control. Consequently, any migrants remained far north of New Orleans.[34]

Miró's plans for increased but controlled immigration failed by 1788. The Louisiana colony had grown by 35 percent, and Natchez was approaching the size of New Orleans, but that growth was upriver, and Miró simply did not control who came or why. In addition, the residents upriver in Kentucky, within the newly formed United States of America, already numbered 73,677 in the 1790 census—almost twice the size of the Louisiana colony. Miró made a final effort to bring the immigrants under Spanish control, issuing a blanket proclamation encouraging settlers from the United States in April 1789, under the standard Spanish conditions for *vecindad*.[35] But the settlers were already arriving, with or without his invitation.

Miró's replacement, Carondelet, took swift action to improve the economy and strengthen Spanish control by March 1792. In the next two months, he focused upon public security, improving police service, installing public lighting in the city, reorganizing the colonial militia, and beginning the work of fortifying the entire city. All of these steps, in theory, would have been attractive to would-be immigrants, but they were also steps indicating that Carondelet intended immigrants to be firmly under the control of the Spanish authorities. Carondelet's views on immigration per se are not well documented in Louisiana histories but, only two months into office, he opposed attempts by US residents to colonize in Natchez and elsewhere in Louisiana. When he did try to attract migrants, it was a lackluster attempt: an American, William Murray, claimed to serve as Carondelet's agent and offered potential American colonists four hundred acres of land in 1796, but the attempt fell apart.[36]

If Carondelet had wanted to attract US immigrants, Spanish royal policy did not help him. A royal decree in late 1792 permitted Protestants to exercise their faith in Louisiana and West Florida—a necessity for attracting large numbers of mostly Protestant US and British residents into the colonies. However, the decree also required that Protestants be married and/or baptized by Catholic priests, and so discouraged the very Protestants it was claiming to attract. Like Miró before them, Carondelet and the Spanish Crown failed to directly attract US immigrants to Louisiana, and in fact discouraged such immigration—at least within Spanish control. In this, Carondelet was even less successful than his predecessor, Governor Miró.

Carondelet, in the end, was a military man and an engineer—a man who knew how to defend the colony only with rules, negotiations, and walls. Before he departed, he wrote a letter to the royal court, requesting permission to assume his next assignment as the president of the Real Audiencia de Quito. He wrote that in four years he had defended twice against hostile French plans, deterred a French-inspired conspiracy of blacks to kill whites, contested "las incesantes tentativas de los Americanos paras separas las naciones salvages" allied with Spain, and augmented the king's dominions by fortifying the capital and other locations and building public works, including a navigable canal with the lakes, all with limited funds.[37] He said nothing of immigration as a counter-weight to the onrushing tide of "los Americanos."

But Carondelet and the other Spanish governors of Louisiana did have another option to increase immigration—by bringing mestizo and indigenous immigrants from Mexico. The Bourbon empire used such immigrants to colonize Texas, New Mexico, California, the short-lived Spanish colony near modern-day Vancouver, and even the Philippines during this very time period. Roughly 250 Mexican soldiers, in the Second Battalion of Mexico, were already serving in New Orleans,[38] and more Mexican militia units were probably available to settle in the colony. A less desirable source of migrants was the Mexican prisons, but the Spanish had indeed sent over a thousand convicted vagrants, military deserters, and criminals to the Philippines in this era, with a much smaller number instead shipped to New Orleans.[39] Receiving criminals would not have been a first for Louisiana—France had previously sent "cassette girls," including prostitutes and the fictional Manon Lescaut, to Louisiana.[40]

However, there was a much larger potential source of immigrants: the entire ocean of indigenous peoples in Mexico and Central America, especially those from regions with limited economic resources such as the Yucatan, where indigenous populations often moved to avoid Spanish demands and environmental disaster. Even the major cities of Mexico might have supplied migrants to Louisiana: famed scientist Alexander von Humboldt reported serious overpopulation of that viceroyalty, especially in the urban areas; he wrote, "Millares de hombres y animales pasan su vida en los caminos reales de Veracruz a Megico [sic]," a comment less on the road being busy and rather that the roads were filled with homeless vagrants.[41]

Mexican immigrants were indeed used to found and populate new colonies in California and New Mexico. However, most Spanish authorities clearly had concerns about relocating indigenous peoples, certainly for economic reasons and perhaps for racial and security concerns as well. In Guatemala, according to Miles L. Wortman, after the Treaty of Paris in 1783, Spanish authorities "ordered the establishment of new colonies in Trujillo, Roatan, Rio Tinto, and other coastal towns, to be populated by immigrants from Galicia, Asturias, and the Canary Islands. The treasury of Guatemala was to pay the transportation for the colonists' upkeep until they became settled." Carondelet himself, as governor of El Salvador in 1789, had recruited Spanish workers for the indigo industry in that region, rather than indigenous workers from other regions.[42]

Such plans could hardly have been cost-effective. Rather than using indigenous peoples to colonize their own territory, Guatemalan and El Salvadoran officials were choosing—or being directed—to pay for the substantial costs of recruitment, outfitting, transportation, and feeding of European and Isleño immigrants to a disputed coast. In addition, given the difference in diseases and climate, it would be expected that numbers of the colonists would expire in the first years of the new towns. Yet such were the plans.[43]

In any case, Carondelet and each of his successors—Gayoso de Lemos, acting military governors Colonel Bouligny and the Marqués de Casa-Calvo, acting civil governor Nicolas Maria Vidal, and Manuel Juan de Salcedo—seem to have merely fretted about immigration from the north. They did little to actually bring in new residents from elsewhere, and certainly not from indigenous populations elsewhere in the Spanish empire.[44] Whether the Bourbon decision to forego indigenous migration to Louisiana was driven by racism, a desire to "whiten" the existing population, economic utilitarianism, or bureaucratic inertia would require further research.[45]

THE IMMIGRANTS THEMSELVES

The general demographic statistics for Louisiana during the Spanish era indicate an ethnically mixed populace. Beyond these statistics, however, the individual lives of this populace also reveal insights into which immigrant groups came to Louisiana and why. Some key individuals may be considered representative.

The Spanish who came included colonial administrators, soldiers, and even convicts, but many came to the New World, and New Orleans in particular, to create new lives—and some were very successful, indeed. Bartolomé Bosque may be the best documented and most successful of these Spanish immigrants. Bosque (often spelled Bosch) first appeared in notarial records in 1789. He was thirty years old when he arrived, a native of Palma Mallorca, from a prominent family and a member of Bofarull, Bosch i Comp., of Barcelona, Spain. He probably was sent by his family and/or company to make money in New Orleans; he quickly became a successful and respected merchant—he married in 1793 at the age of thirty-four, built a still extant home in about 1795, owned four houses and five ships registered in New Orleans, and owned four more houses and three more ships in Pensacola, Florida (then part of the Colony of Louisiana and the Floridas). When he died early in 1810, he left behind a home filled with crystal, silver, linen, a piano, a harp, sheet music, carriages, and twenty-two slaves. He sent at least two sons to school in France; one became a notable merchant as well. His home bordered that of the first US governor of Louisiana, W. C. C. Claiborne, and after Bosque's death and the death of Claiborne's second wife, Bosque's daughter Cayetana Sophronie "Susana," "a famous beauty," married the governor.[46]

However, it was not only Spaniards and Spanish colonials who brought non-French culture and the Spanish language to New Orleans. A wide variety of Irishmen, Scots, Englishmen, US residents, Germans, and other immigrants of north European ancestry also brought their own ethnic cultures to the city. Based on the notarial archives, the percentage of northern European immigrants remained steady throughout the late Spanish era, occasionally increasing significantly, as they did in 1789, almost doubling from the previous year to represent 19 percent of new transactions.

The Spanish colony of Louisiana was clearly attractive to Catholics from Ireland and Scotland. Many of the names appearing in the notarial records are transparent in their origin: Antonio Barragan, Mitchel O'Hagan, William Fitzgerald, and the very prominent planter Augustin Macarty (whose family had also lived in France). A few others require a little more teasing out from the historical record, such as Joseph Aurion (O'Ryan) and Francisco Garic (Garrick)—these may be Irish or, in the case of Garic, of Irish ancestry but long-time Spanish and even French residents.[47] Many Irish and Scots had migrated to France and Spain in the seventeenth and eighteenth centuries, often fleeing British repression or seeking economic opportunities; Irish and Scottish troops and officers (like Alexander O'Reilly) served throughout the Spanish empire. Other business transactors in New Orleans of north European ancestry, including Baltimore merchant John McDonough, who made an appearance in the notarial record as early as 1787 but seems to have returned on a more regular basis in 1791, and Brigadier General James Wilkinson, were demonstrably US citizens—and there is no evidence they were Francophone.

Like the Spanish, the northern Europeans and US subjects or citizens who immigrated to Spanish New Orleans were primarily motivated by economic opportunity. Among these, James (Santiago) Carrick and Jairus Wilcox were probably the most typical. Neither was particularly successful upon their arrival in the city. Carrick, however, was Catholic, at least bilingual, married the daughter of an important shipowner in the city, and did then rise to prominence.[48] Wilcox, on the other hand, was Protestant, monolingual, and did not marry into local society.[49] Such choices, of course, were not limited to merchants in New Orleans—they were the same choices made in many other imperial ports, including those of the Spanish empire. A difference, however, was that many incoming would-be merchants of New Orleans were not *españoles* marrying into *españolé* families—they were instead foreigners marrying into Creole families, and were required to learn not only Spanish but also French.

A third portion of the populace that may not have been Francophone was that composed of free people of color. The number of free people of color in New Orleans grew dramatically during the Spanish era, in part because of Spanish legal protections that permitted free people of color and slaves alike to petition, file legal suits and criminal charges, and testify in court, and for slaves to petition for their freedom via the process of *coartación*, and in part because of the Spanish use of free men of color as valued soldiers and officers, organized into their own militia units. By 1800, the free people of color had been under Spanish rule for thirty years, and despite some tensions, there is no indication that most saw themselves as Frenchmen; they do not seem to have rushed to declare their loyalty to the incoming French governor, Laussat—he makes no mention of them at all. On the other hand, in January 1804, when fifty-five men of the free community petitioned the territorial governor to be recognized as full territorial and US citizens, they explicitly and proudly referred to their military service for Spain: "We were employed in the military service of the late Government, and we hope we may be permitted to say, that our Conduct in that Service has ever been distinguished by a ready attention to the duties required of us."[50]

The free people of color in Spanish New Orleans were not necessarily Francophone, but rather bilingual or multilingual.[51] The use of the French language within the city, then, only increased dramatically in 1808–10 with the arrival of the former St. Dominguan refugees—several years after the end of the colonial era. This demographic shift greatly problematizes any attempt to assess a "French" linguistic or cultural continuity from the Bourbon Spanish era into early American New Orleans.

The French population was admittedly still large, roughly half of the city, and certainly were an important part of New Orleans society. However, these residents had limited opportunities to reject Spanish culture. Spanish authorities controlled the governorship, administration, priesthood, and military, and upper society was increasingly dominated by Spanish administrators and American merchants.

The city's French residents could have rejected Spanish culture via endogamous marriage, geographic isolation, the retention of French modes of architecture, cuisine, and dress, and, perhaps most importantly, the continued use of the French language. However, they intermarried frequently with the new Spanish residents, shifted their architecture and cuisine to Spanish styles, and changed their dress to something more British and American.[52] Some probably isolated themselves on plantations and small farms, but such moves may have been less a rejection of Spanish culture and more the result of economics, as families like the Beauregards relocated to individual plantations when their children grew older and their agricultural and business endeavors evolved. Many residents did continue to use the French language, but their usage was variable.

Indeed, there is good reason to believe that the Francophone linguistic unity assumed by later historians was simply a myth in Spanish Louisiana. As Braudel pointed out so well in *The Identity of France*, the French language and culture were not a cloth of one piece in the 1760s,[53] when Louisiana was lost to the Spanish—and many of the original Louisiana residents were of Provençal ancestry. The French immigrants who did come to the colony after 1763 spoke different dialects, if not languages—the Acadians spoke one patois and the Bayonnais (often remarked by French editors in New Orleans) spoke another. Others spoke multiple languages on a routine basis. Probably the most prominent French member of New Orleans society well into the US period was Juan Bautista Labatut—who hailed from Bayonne and spoke very fluent Spanish and French, and probably spoke Basque. Similarly, Pedro (Pierre) Pedesclaux, the city's best-known notary, hailed from the Basque region just south of Bayonne, on the very border between France and Spain. To label such men as merely "Francophone" ignores their multiethnic, multilinguistic backgrounds. Letters, notarial archives, sacramental records, and early newspaper articles well into the US period normally cited the region from which a "French" person hailed—Bearn, Bayonne, Bordeaux, Paris, for example—rather than an amorphous "France."

Many of the "Frenchmen" in Louisiana, it should also be remembered, had immigrated to Spanish Louisiana for economic, political, and religious motivations. Of these immigrants, the Acadians were aggrieved with French rule;[54] royalists had fled the French revolutionary terror, and the few St. Dominguans

were fleeing an all-consuming civil war/slave revolt. By 1793 an entire generation of "Frenchmen" of all origins had been born and raised in Louisiana as
Spanish, not French subjects or citizens. The Beauregard family, for example,
often remembered as the essence of French heritage, provided enthusiastic
officers for the Spanish government—not for France.[55]

A fine example of this disunity of "French" immigrants can be glimpsed in
the life of Gilbert Sosthene Andry. He was born in 1763 in New Orleans; his
father, Louis Antoine Andry, was the French engineer, surveyor, and soldier who
led the Acadians to found the town of St. Martinville, Louisiana, in 1765. By
1793, he had spent his entire life under Spanish rule and was almost certainly
in the Spanish militia. That same year he contracted to marry Mary Taylor
Farrar—a bride from the United States. In 1803, when French commissioner
Laussat prepared to use the local militia to formally take possession of Louisiana,
he was surprised to learn that Gilbert Sosthene Andry, "the *Spanish* colonel of
the militia [*emphasis added*] and a brave and gallant gentleman" had discouraged
his men from serving France, telling them, "See if you want to serve the French
Republic in two weeks." Andry, French by birth, the son of the man who had
founded the largest new French community in North America in four decades,
was not considered by Laussat as a Frenchman, but instead as a Spanish officer,
and certainly no friend of "the French Republic." It is logical to wonder what
Laussat thought of the many other Louisiana natives of French ancestry who
routinely served in the Spanish militia.[56]

It is not only transactional, demographic, and notarial transactional statistics
which indicate that, as early as 1791, French colonials no longer constituted a
majority within New Orleans. Instead, the life experiences of the full spectrum of
all immigrants to New Orleans, including those from modern-day France, indicate
that the city's population was much more complex than being merely "French."

THE DEMOGRAPHIC JAMBALAYA

By the American annexation in 1803, French demographic—and thus likely
cultural influence—was waning in New Orleans. Instead, the colony was a
genuine jambalaya as early as 1793, a blending of nationalities, languages, and
immigrants: fragmented Frenchmen born in the colony or in distant Acadia, or
else forced to flee revolutionary France and St. Domingue; Spanish and Italians
from Catalonia, the Balearics, and the Canaries; Basques; Irish and Scottish
soldiers and merchants; independent residents from the new United States; free

people of color; and many slaves. The ancestry of New Orleans' free population by 1793 was probably about 3/6 French, 1/6 Spanish, 1/6 northern European/US subjects or citizens, and 1/6 free people of color.[57]

New Orleans's demographic, cultural, and linguistic mix was further complicated by intermarriage and interrelationships, especially during the Spanish period. The intermarriage is especially evident in the notarial records. Within the business transactors from a sample group for 1788–92, 308 females or males had double surnames listed, with the maiden names for females and primary surname for males clearly identifiable. Of these, 22 percent were married to a person of another ethnic and linguistic group and/or was the child of ethnically mixed parents. Over half of those with a northern European surname were actually women of French and Spanish heritage.[58] Remembering that many residents did not marry and that spousal relationships between whites and free people of color were very rarely formalized, it seems possible that the actual number of interethnic and interracial relationships might have been closer to 33 percent of the population.

The miniscule group of Jewish merchants in colonial New Orleans is an intriguing example of how intermarriage complicates our understanding of New Orleans demographics. Bernard Korn detailed how Governor O'Reilly expelled the successful merchant Isaac Monsanto and two other merchants, Mets and Brito/de Britto, in 1769 because of their religion and their commercial connections within the Caribbean. Monsanto and his family relocated to British-held West Florida but eventually returned to Louisiana. The notarial records show that at least four members of the Monsanto family continued to travel to New Orleans for business and probably resided there for periods of time. Isaac Monsanto's daughters, Spanish by birth and upbringing, married non-Jewish businessmen: Eleonora married Pierre Tessier, Graciana (Grace) married Thomas Topham, and Angelica married George Urquhart and, following his death, prominent doctor Robert Dow. Angelica's son, Thomas Urquhart, the grandson of an expelled Jewish merchant, would become a well-known merchant and financier, the Speaker of the House in the Louisiana territorial legislature, a cofounder of a Masonic lodge, and the husband of a French bride. As can be seen by the example of the Monsanto family, the ethnic composition of New Orleans was complicated.[59]

Free people of color had also continued to expand their role within Spanish New Orleans. The number of free people of color increased nearly 900 percent during the period of 1771 to 1791, and would almost double again by the start of the US period. Intriguingly, the ratio of males to females increased significantly during the period 1788–91, from 22 to 33 percent, indicating that the Spanish may have encouraged the immigration of some free black males, perhaps former soldiers from St. Domingue, into New Orleans during this period, or that a significant number of male slaves were being freed by the process of *coartación*.

Finally, the large enslaved population in Louisiana must be addressed. Although the number of slaves continued to grow in Louisiana, that number declined 16 percent in New Orleans from 1788 to 1791.[60] The decrease in slaves within the city may indicate that the Spanish actually restricted the importation of slaves into Louisiana, but at least 7,452 slaves were brought to Spanish New Orleans from 1783 to 1792, mostly from English-held Jamaica and French-held Dominica and Martinique. These imports decreased dramatically as England, France, and Spain fought imperial wars.[61] Consequently, the decrease in slaves in the city of New Orleans may simply be seen as meeting the growing labor needs of Louisiana plantations, despite political turmoil. This economic imperative would have encouraged slave owners to siphon their slaves, especially black males, out of the city and to their own plantations. The imperative may have also ironically created more work opportunities for free people of color and white immigrants in the city.

The demand for more slaves, despite any Spanish or wartime restrictions, also probably encouraged slave importation from the United States downriver directly to plantations, rather than through New Orleans. Many of these slaves would not have appeared in New Orleans notarial records because they were sold elsewhere. Like many of the slaves sent to New Orleans from English-held Jamaica, the slaves coming down the Mississippi River from the United States would have spoken English—not French or Spanish.[62]

What is clear from this jambalaya of nationalities, races, ethnic cultures, and languages is that the people of Bourbon New Orleans and the larger Louisiana colony were becoming something other than mere competing ethnic and racial minorities: they were becoming cosmopolitan, with significant numbers of foreign immigrants even during economic slumps and stagnation and legal protections and *coartación* encouraging the growth of the free populace of color. There was no significant mestizo or indigenous population in New Orleans (unless one counts the governor's Mexican infantry unit), and the Bourbon governors did not encourage mestizo or indigenous immigrants.

Therefore, New Orleans became a quite different city than perhaps any other in the Spanish empire. It was not a predominantly indigenous or mestizo city like those in the imperial Spanish interiors. More notably, New Orleans differed significantly from other major imperial ports like Havana, Veracruz, Cartagena, and Buenos Aires because, unlike those cities, New Orleans was not fully Hispanicized: much of the free population still spoke French, and the city had much more ready access to North American goods, information, financial capital, and political ideas than any other Spanish imperial port. To this extent, New Orleans was *sui generis* within the Spanish empire.

Perhaps the best word to describe a free resident of New Orleans by 1793 would be "chameleon." In this case, a typical free resident might speak French and Spanish capably, an increasing bit of English, and might even be familiar with a few words of one or another African language. If a male, he might have a relationship with a woman of color or a woman of another nationality. If a female, she might be married to a husband of another nationality, another language, and/or even another religion. Neither a male nor a female resident would have had reason to think of France or Spain as their true and future home—most males had intentionally left their native lands, and most females had been born in the New World. All of them, male and female, native and immigrant, free and enslaved, were rapidly becoming, in the broadest sense of the word, American.

On 20 December 1803, just a few days before Christmas, US troops marched in the city of New Orleans; the French flag was lowered, and the US flag was raised. The editor of a French newspaper wrote that "sorrow and emotion were depicted in almost every countenance, and tears flowed from almost everyone" when the French flag was lowered. But a US editor also present immediately labeled his counterpart's mournful account to be a "pathetic . . . partial representation" of the truth. He reported that those cheering as the US flag was raised obviously numbered more than the city's US residents and included the native-born Louisianans, as well as some French and English. The editor wrote that, instead, "joy was the predominant sensation."[63] Based on demographics and notarial records, the US editor's account of that cold day in New Orleans was probably closest to the truth.

CONCLUSION

New Orleans evolved from a French colony into a simultaneously much more Hispanicized and multiethnic, multilingual, and racially mixed populace during Bourbon rule. This demographic evolution was the result of trans-imperial, multiethnic, multilinguistic, and interracial immigration and intermarriage, and not because of Bourbon Spanish immigration policy. In fact, Spanish immigration policy was short-sighted. Instead, immigration into New Orleans produced a people "of, from, and knowing many parts of the world," to use the *Oxford Desk Dictionary*'s definition of "cosmopolitan."[64] By 1803, the people of Louisiana, especially New Orleans, were already becoming truly "cosmopolitan" and, given their separation from Europe, "American" in the broadest sense of that word.

In retrospect, what happened in Bourbon Louisiana is also a timely historical model for analysis of the postcolonial and postmodern Atlantic world. Spain restricted immigration from French colonies but could not check the flow of US immigrants into Louisiana.[65] But other Spanish imperial lands would experience similar migration, long after Louisiana was submerged into the United States. Within this hemisphere, Mexico, Peru, Brazil, and the United States have seen waves of Asian migration, and the United States has experienced mass migration from the Caribbean, Central America, and Mexico. The Louisiana immigration model indicates that, while immigration flow is always contingent upon a multitude of historical factors and events, the flow of immigrants cannot be effectively stopped over even a short period of time without at least the threat of coercive military force or a countering flow of immigrants from elsewhere. Even an economic downturn, as occurred in Spanish Louisiana, did not stop the flow of immigrants into Louisiana and the resultant realignment of the colony's culture into something new and increasingly independent of imperial control.

The Merchants of Spanish New Orleans

Merchant: Twenty-five, and not a penny more! That's already more than he's
worth! Is it a deal?

Judah: Not on your life! He's a very good servant, and he cost me more than that.

    Merchant: Spare me! Anyone could see that he's not even broken in. What's
the kid's name?

Joseph: Joseph, for my misfortune.

Judah: And, by God, a very loyal slave he is!

    —Miguel de Carvajal, *The Josephine Tragedy*

Merchants of every nation are often remembered only for their presumed
cleverness and avarice, and were often not even named in early drama, as in de
Carvajal's play, *The Josephine Tragedy.* However, it was the merchants of New
Orleans who built the Spanish city. These men (and some women) actually
planned, paid for, built, and modernized much of the city's famous physical
infrastructure, including piers, warehouses, roads, and even the cathedral.
Beyond this accomplishment, they also created a commercial infrastructure,
an edifice of business practices and law that would long outlast Spanish New
Orleans. They were led by a core group of leading merchants, labeled here
"foundational," who epitomized the opportunities to seize and challenges to
overcome in Spanish New Orleans.

Elsewhere in the Spanish empire, the term "merchant" was much less encompassing, divided into a hierarchy, with *comerciantes* (wholesale merchants) and
lesser *mercaderes* (retail merchants) supported by a foundation (and potential recruiting pool) of apprentices, clerks (*cajeros*), supercargoes, and ship
captains.[1] In New Orleans, however, merchants demonstrated more flexibil-

ity and served as wholesalers, retailers, and their own clerks simultaneously, and brought in apprentices from multiple economic centers who could do the same. A prosopographical study of key merchants of Spanish New Orleans will represent the broader community of the city's merchants. These elite merchants never coalesced into any resemblance of a formal group, but they were the most active in the city, and their very different but flexible approaches to commerce illustrate how they and the city's other merchants carried New Orleans through the geopolitical and economic storms of the late eighteenth century and laid the foundation of the robust American-era economy.

THE FOUNDATIONAL MERCHANTS

Economically, the sixteenth, seventeenth, and first half of the eighteenth centuries were marked in the Atlantic by European mercantilism, an economic imperialism in which the metropolitan centers were fueled by raw materials shipped from subservient colonies, which received some level of manufactures from the metropolitan in return.[2] French mercantilist practices, in particular, had ill suited the struggling colony of Louisiana; the colony's primary resource for trade was furs from far upriver, and these were more easily acquired by French merchants in their colonies in New France (modern-day Canada). The colony's agricultural commerce was especially limited because it failed to attract many settlers and had no capital for slaves; such crops as were grown, such as indigo, cotton, and corn, were not particularly competitive with other Caribbean sources, given that the French colony of St. Domingue (modern Haiti) had more impressive agricultural resources and was much closer geographically both to other French colonies and to France itself. The colony of Louisiana was a commercial and military burden upon the French state.

However, Spanish rule completely transformed trade in the colony of Louisiana and its capital of New Orleans. This transformation occurred largely because international politics, war, economic exigencies, and rational financial theories all drove the Spanish kings of the late eighteenth century—Charles III and Charles IV—and their ministers to experiment with and sometimes even permit complete free trade among the colonies with the merchants, ships, and ports of other empires. The merchants of New Orleans now had practical trading partners for their then meager goods—the often mountainous Spanish colonies and Spain itself for their furs, but more importantly Cuba and its busy port of Havana for wood and maritime products, as well as for some foodstuffs, cotton, tobacco, and so forth.

If they had stayed so limited, the city's merchants may have, nevertheless, perhaps continued working on an imperial periphery. Instead, they branched out with a vengeance, traversing unexplored territory northwest of the city to acquire hides, furs, and horses from indigenous tribes, building commercial connections far up the Mississippi River for minerals and agricultural produce, and consequently meeting and building commercial ties with the rebellious Americans slipping across the Appalachian Mountains and down the Ohio River. The latter step was the most important, for in doing so, the merchants of Spanish New Orleans eventually created a commercial system that was utterly dependent upon trade with another empire—the new United States of America. That system became remarkably circular—it flowed from the upriver United States and was shipped out of the Louisiana colony on US vessels to US ports. In return goods and produce were shipped from or at least via US ports to Louisiana and then moved upriver—sometimes even reaching the opposite end of the circuit in the upriver United States. And all of this trans-imperial trade flowed through the merchants of New Orleans.

This transformation was driven by the merchants themselves, who, within the Spanish empire, may have best learned how to work within the new and constantly changing commercial rules of their kings. This learning, however, was based on their geographic location, demographic composition, and practical flexibility. These merchants were a heterogeneous group, only in theory divided by ethnicity and language, who often found themselves working around and past their own Bourbon governors. Although they were sometimes limited by royal and local policy, they assumed roles as important and loyal Spanish *vecinos* and officials, worked through restrictions, and established a pattern of commercial activity unlike that in most other Spanish imperial ports, save perhaps those in the Rio Plata. These men, knowingly or not, not only built a city, but also a lever by which free trade in New Orleans would break apart Spanish mercantilism in the Gulf of Mexico.[3]

The merchants of New Orleans were bound, in an odd sense, by their differences—they were commercial and national chameleons. Whatever their ethnic origins and however they identified themselves (which remains uncertain), they and the Spanish officials who supported them typically spoke and wrote at least two languages, and often three, as reflected in numerous archives. They were all, in a word, already becoming American, or, if you prefer a term more often used in Spanish American history, *criollo*. However, these merchants were not the same as those in Spanish ports like Caracas and Buenos Aires. Consequently, it is important to study the city's early merchants and understand (1) how individuals rose to prominence in the Spanish era, (2) the extent, exercise, and limitations of their economic power, and (3) how they were supplanted by a new, American-era foundational group. It was, after all, these men, women, and their numerous associates and friends who most shaped the city's early history—what it would be and what it would not be.

According to the criteria of individual longevity, number and size of commercial activities, and political roles of individual merchants, the shorter list of the most important New Orleans merchants in the Spanish era consists of only fourteen names: Andres Almonaster y Roxas, Francisco Pascalis de La Barre Sr., Luis Toutant Beauregard, Daniel Clark Jr., Nicolas Gravier, Jaime Jorda, Geromo La Chiapella, Pedro de Marigny de Mandeville, Santiago/James Mather, Francisco Mayronne, Estevan Miró, Martin Navarro, Joseph Xavier de Pontalba, and Francisco de Riano.[4]

Six of these merchants were primarily of Spanish or Italian heritage: Almonaster y Roxas, Jorda, La Chiapella, Miró, Navarro, and Riano, although the latter may have been of Irish descent. Six were primarily of French heritage: de La Barre, Beauregard, Gravier, Marigny, Mayronne, Pontalba, although Beauregard and Pontalba were raised in Spanish Louisiana and served for years as Spanish military officers. Only two, Clark and Mather, were from northern European/American lineage. Even if the two senior Spanish officials, Miró and Navarro, are discounted—and, given, the Spanish role in managing its economy, discounting these very important officials may be premature—this would still mean four of the resultant twelve names would be Spanish or Italian.

Of the fourteen, ten men held governmental positions in New Orleans under either the Spanish or the first American regimes. That most of the foundational group would gravitate into political roles is hardly surprising, given the Spanish government's directive/meddling role in the colony's economic affairs. Three others (de Marigny, Pontalba, and Mayronne) were also extremely influential; Marigny would remain a political thorn in the side of Anglo-Americans in early American New Orleans, Pontalba would move to France and become very active in politics there, and Mayronne was a founder and leader of the city's Masonic movement. Indeed, that Gravier did not participate in politics is more surprising.[5]

This group of fourteen merchants was linked to each other and to other merchants and planters by multiple economic, governmental, personal, and familial relationships. Jaime Jorda, for example, was the son-in-law and brother-in-law of two *regidores* (the de Reggios); his son Gilberto's godfather was Gilberto Leonard, the army and royal treasurer; and another son married one of the several daughters of prominent planter Pierre Denis de la Ronde, the younger.[6]

Although not of the same national origins, this group was relatively homogenous in language and religion: at least ten and probably all fourteen merchants spoke Spanish; similarly, at least six and probably at least ten spoke French. All fourteen were Catholic and appeared as such in archdiocesan records.[7] Given how many of the planters/merchants chafed against royal restrictions via formal petitions, actively supported other imperial powers, and remained in New Orleans after 1803, the merchant elite of New Orleans seem to have worked well enough, chameleon-like, within the opportunities they found in Spanish New Orleans.

HOW THESE MERCHANTS BECAME FOUNDATIONAL

Although these fourteen merchants worked in the same city and often were connected to each other by trade and location, they may be divided into roughly three subgroups, with one outlier, based not upon ethnicity but how they became wealthy. Almonaster y Roxas, de La Barre, Beauregard, Gravier, and Marigny were probably planter/merchants. Jorda, La Chiapella, Mayronne, and Clark were not only merchants/sometime planters—they were also major slave traders. Miró, Navarro, and Riano were in the city mostly to govern it, and their business transactions reflect that emphasis. Mather may have been the only one of these focused on exclusively mercantile interests. He began not as a planter, merchant, or governmental official at all, but as a silversmith.

Among the planter/merchants, Almonaster was probably the most important, given that he was active throughout the Spanish era, served as *regidor*, and donated to the city's infrastructure, including the St. Louis Cathedral, beneath which he is buried. He was a middle-aged, widowed, Andalusian notary when he arrived with General O'Reilly in 1769. He became wealthy through land speculation, construction, and property investments, was promoted to and/or bought the positions of royal standard bearer, militia colonel, and *regidor*, and at the tender age of sixty, married a twenty-nine-year-old heiress.[8] His son-in-law, de La Ronde, also served as *regidor*.

Beauregard, Gravier, and Marigny were less active in the notarial records, and of these three, only Beauregard also served as a *regidor*. In fact, Gravier and

Marigny were placed on the foundational list not for longevity or position, but because of their large number of transactions in limited periods of time.[9] In 1786, Marigny jumped into the list of most active notarial transactors, selling numerous slaves; in 1788, he was still delivering numerous receipts and was again very active from 1794 to 1799. Nicolas Gravier only appeared on the scene in 1793–94, as the purchaser of numerous properties from Beltran Gravier Sr., who had been active in business for at least a decade before but died in 1797. Nicolas Gravier was involved in at least seventy separate transactions in the three years of 1794–96.

Jorda, La Chiapella, Mayronne, and Clark made the list by slave trading. Jorda, from the northeastern Spanish coastal town of Calella, was in New Orleans by 1782, but did not become truly prominent until the years 1786–90, when he conducted at least 160 transactions, mostly slave sales. Mayronne did likewise in almost the exact same period (1786–91), conducting at least 109 transactions; La Chiapella conducted 273 transactions from 1786 to 1792, although he was also often the official auctioneer rather than the owner.[10]

Miró, Navarro, and Riano were not merchants in any modern sense, but they were the highest colonial officials and routinely conducted numerous and notable royal business transactions, an important stimulus in the colonial capital. Miró was governor. (Felix) Martin Antonio Navarro, a Galician, arrived in 1765; his wife, Adelaide Gayoso de Lemos, was presumably related to the future colonial governor, given the uniqueness of her surname, and Navarro himself became the colonial intendant in 1780. His report that year, "Political Reflections on the Current Condition of the Province," urged increased migration and free trade to Louisiana and played a role in the royal decree of 1782 liberalizing trade for the colony. Francisco de Riano de Guemes was more closely connected to the Bourbon colonial regime than Navarro. His father was Juan Manuel de Riano, a mayor, judge, knight in the Military Order of Malta, and governor of the Spanish-governed provinces of Montalto and Modica in southern Sicily, and his brother (or perhaps close cousin), Juan Antonio de Riano y Barcena, was one of Governor Gálvez's most battle-hardened lieutenants and the governor's brother-in-law.[11]

Daniel Clark Jr. and James Mather are probably the best known to American historians among this foundational group and deserve a bit more attention than the others because of their transitional roles in the New Orleans economy. The two men were quite different: Clark was well educated, politically active on the national level, often mean-spirited, and managed a diversified portfolio of warehouses, ships, slave trading, plantations, and land speculation. Mather was perhaps less educated, focused on local issues, and primarily a merchant/ planter, although he conducted some slave trading.[12]

Daniel Clark Sr., a former senior British officer in Pennsylvania in the Seven Years' War, was active in New Orleans from at least the 1770s until 1790, and was the city's most active business transactor in 1780. His young nephew and namesake, Daniel J. Clark Jr., born in Sligo, Ireland, and reportedly educated at Eton, emigrated to Germantown, Pennsylvania, building connections there, and then moved to New Orleans in 1786 at the invitation of his uncle. The younger Daniel Clark burst into the New Orleans economy, bringing a slave ship into the port and conducting at least sixty-four transactions that year—more than double the amount of transactions ever conducted by a New Orleans *vecino* in a single year. In the following year, he conducted another thirty-one transactions, again mostly sales of slaves, and in 1788, twenty-eight more transactions, now including property.[13]

The Clarks invested much of their slave-trading profits into land, includ- ing a large tract south of Natchez. They almost disappear in the years 1791–93, perhaps because of losses caused by new Spanish restrictions on tobacco imports from Louisiana, but in 1793 the younger Clark acquired a well-funded distant partner, Daniel W. Coxe, whose brother, Tench Coxe, the assistant treasurer of the United States, worked directly for Alexander Hamilton. An infusion of capital into the partnership was very useful in cash-short New Orleans, but the Clarks were now more careful, and their only significant appearances in the New Orleans economy between 1790 and 1799 were in numerous protests for debts due.[14]

The other well-known "American" merchant of Bourbon New Orleans, James/Santiago Mather, was born in Great Britain. He appeared in the notarial archives in the 1770s, then every year from 1780 to 1798.[15] Mather and his frequent associate David Ross were the most important merchants conducting business upriver from New Orleans. In fact, Mather was listed as a resident of Natchez in 1792 and Ross as a resident of both Baton Rouge and Natchez; both men were probably "trusted agents" for upriver planters. Wherever Mather's formal residence may have been, he was eventually selected as the fourth mayor of New Orleans, serving during most of the crises of the early American period: the great Haitian/Cuban immigration, the Deslondes slave revolt, the hurricane of 1812, and the British blockade.

The two Americans, Clark and Mather, were certainly not cut from the same cloth. Clark was muscular, of dark complexion and "dark and penetrating eyes . . . temperate, if possible to a fault; as it has a tendency to segregate him from social intercourse." He loathed General James Wilkinson and correctly accused him of treason; he led the political revolt against Jeffersonian control of the city; he shot Jefferson's governor, W. C. C. Claiborne, in a duel (Claiborne lived).[16] Clark, however, appears in only a single engraving by Charles Fevret de Saint Memin, now in the National Gallery of Art, labeled "Clarke." He is only drawn in profile, but Clark seems in this drawing not only successful, but confident, energetic, robust, and surprisingly cheerfully focused, not forbidding or distant at all.

Mather, on the other hand, was described as "A very well disposed, hospitable planter, of Good understanding but unfortunate in his circumstances, his probity was never questiond [sic] but of late, his former partner accuses him of applying the joint capital to his own use, but such charges are frequently ill founded." And again he was depicted as "a native of England who has resided in this country a number of years on a valuable plantation; a sensible well-informed man highly respectable—Speaks French."[17]

Mather was painted by José Salazar in a deep red coat, a fine, frilled white shirt to the neck, and thin red hair curled around a confident young face, perhaps in his later thirties.[18] His clothing and demeanor are clearly that of an English gentleman. Clark was a man who had succeeded, failed, and succeeded again. On the other hand, Mather looks somehow like a man who had never failed, although the characterization provided to Thomas Jefferson implies that Mather actually had done so.

These brief personality sketches, especially those of the best documented Anglophones, Clark and Mather, illustrate the importance of researching each of these merchants—and other foundational personalities in New Orleans and the Spanish empire—at an individual level. It is only by understanding individual familial and business connections, the ebb and flow of individual mercantile or official activity on at least a yearly (if not monthly) basis, and any available personal data that the historian can fully understand the intricacies of shaping or governing an economy, a colony, or an empire. In this case, the available data on these merchants indicates that they may have been similar in outlook but were quite disparate in their motivations and approaches. One need only compare the relatively old planter/merchant Almonaster with the perhaps shady slave-trader/planter Mayronne and the man-of-all-skills Clark to recall that empires are made by men and women.

Comparison of the New Orleans merchants with those in other cities, including those in the Rio Plata and in Mexico, reveals intriguing similarities and differences between Spanish imperial cities. For example, while the presence of American merchants in New Orleans is unsurprising given the city's proximity to the United States, data from the Rio Plata indicate that other Spanish imperial cities were also being courted by American merchants. The 1804 census of Buenos Aires listed twenty-nine Americans and only fifteen English residents in the city; the British fleet's arrival at Montevideo in 1806 found sixteen American ships already there and only eleven from Portugal (then including Brazil).[19]

The merchants of New Orleans, however, had an edge over their counterparts in the Rio Plata and even nearby Mexico. In Buenos Aires, middle-aged men from northern Spain who had come much earlier (twelve–fifteen years) dominated that city's trade. Similarly, in Veracruz and Guadalajara, there was an "unusual sociology" in which immigrant men, again mostly from northern Spain, "enjoyed preferential rights in the marriage market." Many of these young *peninsular* merchants aspired to a long apprenticeship with another merchant, from whom they would one day inherit that merchant's wealth and debts, and often that merchant's daughter. By contrast, in New Orleans, incoming young peninsular merchants such as Jorda and Bosque (although Bosque was actually Minorcan) found themselves in competition for both wealth and wives with Frenchmen like Mayronne and Labatut and Anglo-Americans like Clark and Mather.[20]

Another notable difference between the merchants of New Orleans, Buenos Aires, and Mexico was in the versatility of work done by New Orleans merchants,[21] who demonstrated more flexibility and did not divide themselves into a formal hierarchy. This flexibility permitted them (at least the Americans) to survive changes of business ownership, because they worked within wide, informal networks of expertise, capital, and trust.

By comparison, the merchants of Buenos Aires officially had "only one form of commercial partnership, the *sociedad colectiva*," as mandated by the commercial ordinances of Bilbao (1737), typically trading with a limited number of trusted merchants, and perhaps via only one port in Spain. Consequently, commercial firms in Buenos Aires did not survive the death of one partner. Similarly, in Mexico, "The successful merchant was hence confronted with the good probability that after his death his business would be terminated, its stock auctioned."[22] In New Orleans, however, informal commercial partnerships could survive because, even long after a well-respected merchant like Clark Sr.

died, other partners (in this case, Clark Jr., Chew, and Relf), and a wide network of ties in numerous ports could sustain the remaining partners.

A final difference was in the range of investments made by New Orleans merchants. The merchants of Buenos Aires only began investing in land, agriculture, and livestock when British trade and merchants assumed a dominant role in the mercantile trade in the early 1800s.[23] The multinational merchants of New Orleans, however, had often gained their wealth as planters and continued investing in land or, like the Clarks, plowed their mercantile earnings into plantations and land speculation as early as the 1780s.

In summary, the New Orleans merchants became foundational within their Spanish city in three different ways—by originating as planter/merchants, coming to the city as merchants and building ties and capital via the importation of slaves, or working within the Spanish government. However, the incoming merchants did not fit into the Spanish mercantile paradigms in Buenos Aires, Veracruz, or Guadalajara—that is, northern Spanish merchant families continuously renewed by younger peninsular merchants. While some New Orleans merchants did come from northern Spain, many came from elsewhere in Spain, France, and the United States, and they generally did not assume junior roles in another man's personal mercantile business. Instead, they worked in every level of the merchant business, from ship to warehouse to store counter, certainly unlike their counterparts in Buenos Aires. Finally, the merchants in New Orleans invested in land early and often, diversifying their sources of income, in a manner more similar to the merchants in Mexico (who especially invested in mining and mining support) than in the Rio Plata.

THE TRANSITION INTO THE AMERICAN ERA

New Orleans was a city built upon trade, but within the context of the broader Bourbon Spanish empire—and that empire was in crisis. However, just how much of a crisis the Bourbons faced in the late eighteenth century is a matter of academic disagreement. There are at least two schools of thought, which may be labeled the "continual crisis" and the "crisis with opportunities" schools. The first school argues that continual war, changing alliances, overexpenditure, convoluted economic policies, and generally bad governance by Charles IV led to a never-ending series of financial crises and a greatly weakened Bourbon empire, and implies that the Bourbon empire was eventually bound to collapse.[24] The second school, however, sees opportunities within crisis; one historian of this school reported, "At once, the 1790s gave rise to a peculiar imperial prosperity, fueled by the shocks on rival French and British Atlantic mercantile networks. Iberian colonies flourished in part because they faced less competition."[25]

The Spanish New Orleans economy provides strong evidence to support the "crisis with opportunities" school, and the New Orleans economy was not driven by the Spanish wars. Instead, the city's economy seems to have been driven by trade with the United States, diverted into US vessels and through US ports. In this, the colonial economy of New Orleans and Louisiana may well be compared to that of Buenos Aires/Montevideo and the Rio Plata during the same period—a trans-imperial trade that continued despite any royal strictures or concerns.

Indeed, New Orleans may have been the most prolonged and open partic-ipant in the Bourbon experiments in free trade, in part because American merchants were able to subvert and dominate that trade years before the Amer-ican annexation in 1803. The foundational merchants in Spanish imperial New Orleans, however, were not only Americans, but rather an ethnic mixture of merchants who continued to push their own interests no matter what restric-tions the Bourbon government might attempt. These "crisis with opportunities" merchants worked within "one complex, interconnected, and interdependent Atlantic World,"[26] and so it may be said that the economy of Spanish New Or-leans clearly supports both the "crisis with opportunities" academic school and the broader "Atlantic World" camp of historians. The city's foundational merchants created prosperity and stability by skirting and even violating the Bourbon king's own restrictions on trans-imperial trade. Most of these same canny merchants, however, would be quickly eclipsed after 1803 by better-cap-italized American newcomers.

The key merchants who laid the foundations of the New Orleans economy, then, were a disparate ethnic mix of planter/merchants, slave traders, and government officials. However, they were a relative stable group, who moved in a broader but equally stable set of merchants. At least thirty-four Spanish-era merchants in New Orleans conducted business throughout the twenty years between 1780 and 1799 (that is, participated in notarial transactions for at least eighteen of the twenty years during this period). Many more aspiring merchants worked in lower levels within the city's mercantile sector.

Many of the numerous merchants in Spanish New Orleans simultaneously owned stores, ships, plantations, slaves; conducted export and import for their own purposes or on commission; negotiated notes and letters of exchange; and served as overseas agents. Such practices were, however, particularly notable to the city's North American merchants, for very practical reasons. The North American merchants had more access to a wider variety of produce and manufactured goods; they had connections to the shipyards and sailing captains of the US East Coast; most importantly, they had the capital to purchase produce, goods, ships, plantations, and slaves. Furthermore, they worked within a trans-imperial system of finance, mostly unhindered in their investments by Spanish law.

The American period brought two important new opportunities for the merchants of New Orleans to grow wealthy and/or prominent: corporate capitalism and membership on an elective city council.[27] These opportunities especially revolved around eight corporations—six banks, an insurance company, and a water company—and many merchants were financially stable or bold enough to join one of these corporations as a board member. Each of these corporations was dominated in turn by powerful founders who had almost all arrived before 1803 and worked in Spanish New Orleans. From 1804 to 1811, twenty-three men controlled 59 percent of all corporate board positions within the city's most important eight corporations. Each of these men also served concurrently on the city council. Of these twenty-three corporate directors/ city councilmen, an even smaller group of eleven men controlled 45 percent of all corporate board positions and 37 percent of all city council positions! These eleven men dominated the business—and the city—of New Orleans.

The city council clearly provided a political opportunity for New Orleans merchants to not only protect their own interests but also to effect necessary infrastructure changes in the city. In that, the elected city council was merely an evolution from the Spanish era, when the appointed *cabildo* members worked to effect change via the Spanish governor. A separate review of twenty-two elite merchants indicates not only that sixteen were in business before 1803 and that eleven served on the city council, but also that some served as territorial legislator, mayor, judge, and collector of US customs.

Partnerships played a major role in this new American elite. Three businesses—Kenner & Henderson (with Benjamin Morgan an inactive partner), Chew & Relf, and Amory, Callender & Company controlled 21 percent of the six non-navigation corporation boards. With Shepherd, Brown & Company, Winter & Harmon, the Urquharts, Pitot, Lanusse, Labatut, and McNeil, these partnerships controlled 54 percent of the boards between 1805 and 1811.[28]

A comparison of the foundational mercantile elite in Spanish New Orleans with the American-era elite is revelatory. This comparison indicates that only four family members of the Spanish-era elite, all of French origin, would have been considered as members of the early American–era elite. Stalwart and well-known men like Almonaster, Beauregard, Bouligny, Daniel Clark, Ducros, Marigny de Mandeville, Mather, the Oliviers, Pontalba, and de Riano were no longer in power. Instead, the few surviving members of the old elite were now the young sons: Antonio Cavalier Jr., Miguel Fortier, C. F. Girod's son Nicolas, and Santiago Livaudais. The only notable exceptions would have been Labatut, Lanusse, and Pitot. No merchants of Spanish origin appeared in the new elite depicted in appendix 2 of this work.

The American annexation represented a dramatic change in the New Orleans economy because it immediately empowered the well-connected, capital-rich American merchants already working in the city. The remaining Spanish, Italians, and even the still-prominent French merchants in the city began marrying their daughters to the newcomers, who after all were ambitious and had funds and grand visions; their sons continued building plantations outside the city. Certainly, there was much money to be made, and the economy boomed. The American era had come.

CONCLUSION

Although New Orleans was (and is) admirably placed to profit from trade with the very heartland of the North American continent, it was the Spanish-era merchants of New Orleans who pioneered that trade, developing the access to raw products and manufactured goods, shipping, information, and capital required to make the city into a maritime center within the Gulf of Mexico and the Caribbean. These merchants thus provided the Bourbon governors with the opportunity to make the colony and the city mostly self-sufficient (save for the high cost of military security) and, through fees, tariffs, and taxation, even potentially useful to the Spanish treasury. The planter/merchants provided an element of economic and political stability, while those heavily involved in the slave trade provided the necessary manpower to expand the Spanish plantation economy. Unsurprisingly, some of these slave-trading merchants, like Mayronne and the Clarks, became plantation owners themselves, thus diversifying their businesses more than merchants in at least Veracruz and Buenos Aires.

At least a few of these key merchants, however, may have been personally challenging for the Spanish governors. Almonaster was a bit pompous, Pontalba supported Napoleon, and Clark was clearly moody and ambitious—he would shoot the first American governor! Moreover, most of the merchants had commercial networks beyond the control of Spanish authorities, with counterparts in the Caribbean (Mayronne), the United States (Clark), and revolutionary and Napoleonic France (Pontalba). The foundational merchants of Spanish New Orleans would be mostly eclipsed by their American successors, but they had pioneered the city's growth—and they had further pushed the Bourbon imperial economic system toward completely free trade.

Trade in Spanish New Orleans

The treaty, Señor, . . . with the United States of America, concedes them a considerable portion of our establishments on this river, its free navigation, and likewise the free import and export of goods and agricultural products: it will prevent the National family from any real success in its mercantile operations.
—The merchants of New Orleans, August 1796, *to King Charles IV of Spain*

New Orleans coped with the twists and turns of Spanish mercantile policy reasonably well, once merchants like the Clarks, Fortiers, Jorda, and Mather, supported by trans-imperial capital, established themselves as *vecino* merchants. Spanish closures and restrictions of riverine trade did not crush the economy—statistics indicate that other policies and factors instead slowed the city's growth. Royal restrictions on the slave trade, tobacco purchases, and the use of silver certainly dampened the economy; so did bureaucratic impositions and taxation on goods arriving from the United States. However, the city's economy grew jaggedly but surely throughout the Spanish era, steadying from 1793 until 1802, and then swelling in 1803, based on expectations that the United States or France would soon be acquiring the colony.

In this trade, New Orleans bears similarity to that of the Rio Plata, which could often depend upon trans-imperial trade with nearby Brazil to weather changes in Spanish imperial policy and Atlantic war. However, New Orleans also differed significantly from other portions of the Spanish empire, such as Peru or even Mexico, because its economic fluctuations were not driven only by policy and war, but also by a steadily changing demography, chameleon-like merchants, and a truly trans-imperial trade.

DOCUMENTING TRADE

New Orleans was a Bourbon city built on trade—sometimes literally. The flat-boats from upriver were disassembled and converted into pieces of still extant buildings; the levees, if they were examined with multispectral analysis, would be found to be occasionally peppered inside with the hulls of wooden ships placed in crevasses or to build bulwarks. The New Orleans economy in the Bourbon era featured periods of boom, consecutive slumps, and slow growth before the American annexation in late 1803.

Documenting fluctuations in the New Orleans economy, however, is not an easy task: Spanish administrative records, even tax records, have survived only randomly, and bureaucrats of varying abilities did not keep the records uniformly. In addition, the city's trade flowed (and, in the Bourbon mindset, could therefore be taxed) in three different directions: from upriver, along the coast, and from overseas. Therefore, to compile comparative statistics, several varieties of records must be used: ship manifests, royal warehouse and shipping records, the city's more time-comprehensive notarial records, as well as private and official correspondence, newspapers, and contemporary accounts. These statistics and the resultant graphs, however, permit a better understanding of the economic impacts of natural crises (two conflagrations and a 1794 hurricane), royal and gubernatorial decrees (opening/closing free trade and limitations on the slave trade and tobacco exports), military crises (British blockade), and even mismanagement in government warehousing.

In turn, understanding the fluctuations of trade through New Orleans and even assigning preliminary periodization permits an understanding of the oppor-tunities and especially the challenges the governors in New Orleans attempted to balance during the Spanish era, and how those challenges were relevant to the larger Bourbon empire. The great conflagrations and hurricane of 1794 and limitations on tobacco exports forced those governors to perpetually ignore royal decrees and extend free-trade practices in the colony and city, and request permission afterwards. Royal limitations on the slave trade, despite the need for more agricultural workers throughout the colony, also encouraged Bour-bon governors to turn a blind eye toward enterprising slave traders like Jorda, Mayronne, and Clark. New Orleans, perhaps more than any other Spanish impe-rial city, was open for trans-imperial trade, especially with the new United States.

Two economic works on the Bourbon empire might seem, at first glance, diametrically opposed to each other. Carlos Marichal, in his masterful 2007 *Bankruptcy of Empire,* argued that continual "war demands and skyrocketing royal debts" created a "financial maelstrom" from which the Bourbon Spanish king could not recover.[1] However, he did not actually argue that this was a financial crisis from which individual colonies could not recover. In fact, Marichal may have left some room for individual colonies to prosper; he noted that financial crisis had a major impact on late colonial Mexico, but he also stressed, "The bankruptcy of the empire was even more pronounced at the core than in the periphery."[2]

More recently, Fabricio Prado has argued that trans-imperial trade and cooperation provided one means for Spanish colonies to actually thrive despite the financial and military difficulties of the Bourbon king. Prado reported that the trade between the Rio Plata and Spain continued throughout the 1780s and 1790s and prospered because it was simply diverted into Portuguese vessels and through Portuguese ports.[3]

As in the Rio Plata, statistics indicate that the New Orleans economy was not driven by Spanish wars, although the city's most notable merchants often refrained from economic activity then and never had access to enough capital. Instead, the city's economy seems to have been driven by trade with the United States, simply diverted into US vessels and through US ports. In this, the colonial economy of New Orleans and Louisiana may well be compared to that of Buenos Aires/Montevideo and the Rio Plata—a trans-imperial trade that continued despite any royal strictures or concerns.

There are at least five sets of documents that provide some level of detail on this trade—occasional ship manifests, correspondence, an administrative register of vessels arriving in 1789, another such register for vessels departing in 1798, and warehouse records used by the Spanish to control and tax trade from upriver. These records may be compared with the New Orleans notarial archives for the entire period of 1780–1803. These last records, although they do not capture significant amounts of trade except for that in slaves, do indicate the total amount of real estate, slave, powers of attorneys, and other business transactions in any single year (or even, if one breaks down the records further, by month, week, or day), and therefore provide significant insight into the general economic health of the city. These numbers can also be supplemented and compared to contemporaneous accounts on the city's trade, most notably that of a French mercantilist merchant, Jacques Pitot.

SHIP MANIFESTS AND CORRESPONDENCE

Ship manifests may occasionally be found in Spanish imperial records for New Orleans, as well as among the probate records that remain in the city. The manifest for a brigantine commanded by Archibald Harshaw indicates that, as early as December 1782, New Orleans was receiving quite large shipments of commercial goods and foodstuffs from Baltimore, which was still in a state of rebellion against Great Britain. The shipment included:

10 casks of earthenware
56 cases of glassware, divided between two different purchasers
100 barrels of bread
50 barrels of flour
56 barrels of apples
19 barrels of potatoes
140 bundles of hogs [probably smoked hams]
4 tuns [large casks mostly used for alcoholic beverages] of vinegar
10 pipes of gin
47 bales woolen goods, evidently for at least five different purchasers
3 boxes of boot legs and shivs [for shoemaking]
3 barrels of calf skins
200 boxes of soap
27 bales canvas
Cordage, bunting, and tar [for maritime purposes][4]

This manifest indicates that merchants in the rebellious American colonies, despite their own requirements at the end of a long war to import consumer goods for domestic American use, actively exported some consumer goods, including pottery, glassware, and significant amounts of foodstuffs, to a Spanish empire that was then their ally. It also indicates how much the Spanish in New Orleans desired foreign manufactures and foodstuffs, not only for themselves, but also for trade with the native American tribes far east, west, and upriver from New Orleans, and perhaps farther west to Veracruz and elsewhere in Mexico. While New Orleans can be quite cold and damp in the winter, it is likely that most of the forty-seven bales of woolen goods on Harshaw's ship were for resale upriver.

Another ship manifest indicates the continued market for North American foodstuffs and merchandise in Spanish New Orleans almost a decade later. The US-built *Dauphin* left Philadelphia on 6 May 1793, stuffed with 1,738 barrels of flour, fifteen barrels of beef, and nine boxes, eight casks, and one bale of "merchandise," the latter likely a mixture of clothing—skirts, pants, shirts, stockings, handkerchiefs, and the like.[5] The amount of flour being shipped into New Orleans on this single vessel is notable—if each barrel weighed only fifty pounds, the flour alone would have weighed 86,900 pounds—forty-three and a half tons. However, given that modern barrels of flour normally weigh four times that amount, 196 pounds each, the *Dauphin* may have been carrying as much as 170 tons of flour alone.

Even in the 1780s, there was significant correspondence on New Orleans trade—such was the private petition in 1789 of Enrique Darcantel, a merchant and later sometime Spanish port official, voicing some concerns on the city's commerce to the royal minister, Gálvez.[6] However, Darcantel's petition, and general Bourbon correspondence on the city's commerce, were light on actual statistics.

ARCHIVAL STATISTICS

A financial report in 1786 and an administrative register kept in 1789 provide the first solid statistics on trade through the city. The financial report, by the city treasurer, indicates that 124 vessels arrived in the port—72 from the French West Indies or France, 43 from Spain or its colonies, 8 from the British West Indies, and only 1 from the United States. By contrast, the 1789 administrative register reported only 45 vessels entering New Orleans that year, although it documented their contents in painful detail. Most arrived in February and July. Unfortunately, another such register does not appear to have been preserved until 1798. This register, for departures rather than arrivals, lists 98 vessels departing the city. The statistics from both of these registers, for 1789 and 1798, are depicted together in figure 3.1.[7]

The law of the sea is much like Newton's law—ships that enter a port must leave. There are some exceptions, as in times of great economic unrest (such as a gold rush, blockade, or full war), maritime disaster (hurricane, tsunami), complete commodity collapse (whale oil), or when a port contains a large construction shipyard. In addition, comparison of ship entries with ship departures will inevitably be historically imprecise: ships may be renamed, repurposed, or simply left to rot and sink, mostly without a paper trail. But, in general, the number of ships entering a port is close to the number departing.[8]

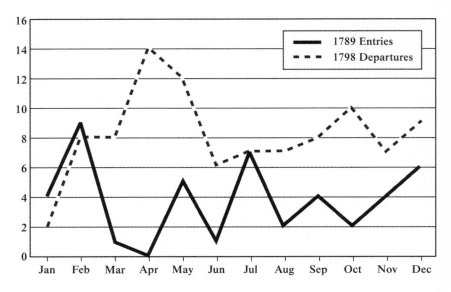

FIGURE 3.1. Ship entries (1789) and departures (1798) at New Orleans.

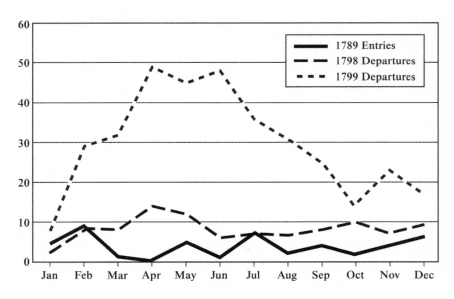

FIGURE 3.2. Ship entries (1789) and departures (1798, 1799) at New Orleans.

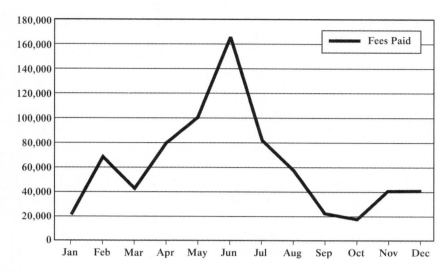

FIGURE 3.3. Export revenue fees paid in pesos at New Orleans, 1799.

A comparison of the 1789 and 1798 statistics, then, hints that the economy of New Orleans grew significantly between 1789 and 1798, doubling in less than a decade. This growth was occurring mostly in the months of March–December, that is, over the course of nearly the entire year, with perhaps a gap in July. It is hardly surprising that the most robust months were those when flatboats could most easily be floated down the Mississippi River, riding on spring flooding.

In 1799, the statistics indicate that trade passing through New Orleans suddenly exploded.[9] Ship departures from New Orleans climbed rapidly as early as February and increased as much as fourfold by April that year, reaching close to the previous year's monthly totals only in October. This export explosion is depicted in figure 3.2.

In evident confirmation of this trade explosion, the official who maintained the Spanish records on entries and departures, Manuel Gregorio de Texada, summarized the resultant revenue at the end of his records for 1799. As figure 3.3 indicates, the increase in export revenue in pesos was just as dramatic as the number of vessels departing would seem to indicate.[10] However, the actual revenues notably spiked from April through August that year much more sharply than the number of departing ships would indicate in figure 3.3. The spike in export revenues in mid-1799 may, however, have simply represented an increase in the number of American flatboats arriving and being assessed fees by Spanish authorities, as will be more evident in figure 3.4.

This trade was overwhelmingly with the East Coast of the United States, especially New York, Boston, and Philadelphia, but also Wilmington and Alexandria. One or two vessels departed each month for Havana; occasionally, one departed for Veracruz or even upriver Natchez, but such were the exceptions. The boom in the economy of Spanish New Orleans was based upon the US economy, and the central actors within the city were the planters, the merchants, and the Spanish authorities who could assist or hinder the first two groups. Of the ninety-eight vessels departing the city in 1798, most were speedy, thin brigantines, many built in shipyards in Baltimore and New England, and certainly owned and captained by North Americans. The brigantines were invaluable during the 1790s and early 1800s because of their speed—the Europeans powers were at war, sometimes changing sides, and sometimes enlisting privateers to their cause, and a well-captained brigantine had a good chance of outracing or otherwise eluding approaching warships, privateers, and pirates. The American brigantines, racing north with cotton and tobacco, were supplemented by larger, longer frigates and smaller goletas.[11]

By comparison, in Cartagena, modern-day Colombia, the entry book for the Spanish import/export tax known as the *almojarifazgo* in 1800 indicates seventy-eight vessels departing with taxed goods in that year, 20 percent fewer than from New Orleans. Many of these vessels from Cartagena were simply sailing to nearby Trinidad, while many other less-seaworthy bilanders sailed to Panama. Only four vessels were sailing from Cartagena on long-distance voyages; all four of these vessels were American and were all eventually returning to the United States.[12]

The fragmentary ship-departure records for 1798 and 1799 are fortunately supplemented by four documents: a list of anchorage fees in the city for 1801, an article in the *Moniteur de la Louisiane* that provided data on ship arrivals in the last five months of 1802, and two books in the Spanish archives that listed all of the produce and goods deposited by North Americans in the royal magazine, the Guarda Almacén, between April 1798 and November 1803.[13]

The 1801 anchorage fees indicate that almost half of the vessels then entering the city were American—80 of 181, but 49 were from the British West Indies and England, a similar number (44) from the Spanish colonies, and only 8 from the French colonies, France, or elsewhere in Europe. The 1802 statistics tell a similar story—76 of 172 vessels from the United States, 32 British, 38 Spanish, but

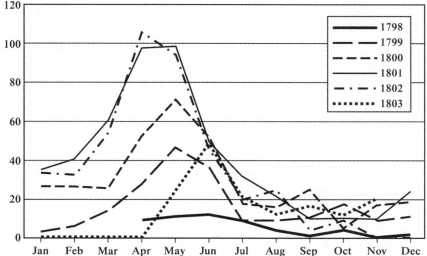

FIGURE 3.4. Entries for North American goods deposited in the Guarda Almacén at New Orleans, 1798–1803.

an expanded number of vessels from the French colonies and France (22) and elsewhere in Europe (4). Given this latter data is only for a five-month period, the implication is that a considerably larger number of vessels actually entered the port over the complete year.

The Guarda Almacén records, captured in figure 3.4, reveal that the most important economic bustle took place between March and June each year, peaking in April and May as flatboats arrived and goods were deposited in the Spanish warehouses. This pattern held true every year but one—1803. The ship departures peaked from April to June, and the Spanish export revenues peaked dramatically in June as well, as merchants paid their bills to the royal government, loaded their ships, and sent those ships away. However, as figure 3.4 indicates, some flatboats now continued reaching the city almost throughout the year.

The notable exceptions for this trade, at least as represented by the Guarda Almacén records, were from July 1798 to April 1799 (a rather flat period) and the period from November 1802 to May 1803, when Spanish authorities famously stopped the right to free trade to American traders. In the latter case, the Spanish records abruptly stop on 15 October 1802 and do not begin again until 18

May 1803. The deposit of North American produce and goods in the Spanish warehouses peaked in June and continued at a normal level until November, but the damage had been done in the earlier, vital trade months of March through May, when goods must be delivered, customers assured, and ships chartered. In the first half of 1802, the merchants had brought in 367 shipments—basically, flatboat loads—into the Spanish warehouses. In the first half of 1803, they brought in 73. The Spanish governor's decision to close the river had stunned the merchants of the city—and ironically devastated the governor's own revenue flow. By late 1803, the merchants of New Orleans—French, Spanish, and American alike—were presumably eager and glad to see American troops march into the city. Even Spanish trade officials may have sighed in relief and planned new careers under North American rule; several such officials, including Martin Duralde, did indeed remain. In any case, the last entry in the registers is 29 November 1803, the very day the Spanish administrators turned over their colony to their French counterparts, who already knew that they, too, were on their own way home following the US purchase of Louisiana.[14]

But there are other ways to use the Guarda Almacén records. If, for example, one extends the previously stated law (or at least theory) of the sea to riverine trade as well, the implication is that, if a vessel (in this case, a flatboat) brings cargo to a port, then that cargo will be departing on a ship. Given that a flatboat generally carried about thirty to forty tons of cargo and a brigantine carried about sixty tons, one would presume that most ship departures from New Orleans would represent about two flatboat loads, that is, two loads or entries in the Guarda Almacén registers. In fact, figure 3.5, which compares those statistics for the two available years, 1798 and 1799, indicates that the proportion was reversed, and that the number of ship departures was about three to four times more than the number of flatboats arriving (or at least of warehouse entries). Simple math indicates that the ratio of flatboats to ships should be two to one—not one to three or even one to four! Here the historian must face a mathematical conundrum—if the North American riverine commerce sparked an economic boom in New Orleans, why did so many more ships depart the city than American flatboats arrive?

The potential answers to this conundrum seem relatively simple—either North American flatboatmen diverted their cargoes around the Spanish administrators or the Spanish colony of Louisiana was much more productive than is assumed. The first possibility, that English-speaking merchants such as the elder Daniel Clark intercepted upriver produce headed downstream and labeled

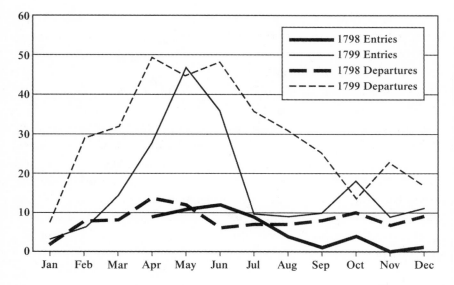

FIGURE 3.5. Entries for North American goods deposited in the Guarda Almacén (1798–1803) and ship departures (1798–99) at New Orleans.

it their own to avoid moving the cargo into Spanish warehouses and paying Spanish taxes, is certainly plausible. One must recall that the city's merchants in their August 1796 petition bemoaned the American proclivity for "clandestine" commerce—such clandestinity did not necessarily imply smuggling down waterways, after all, but probably simply meant "rebranding" cargo as "Spanish" to the detriment of Spanish revenue.

At the same time, it cannot be discounted that the Spanish side of the Mississippi River was already the source of significant produce. The expansion of plantations in modern-day Louisiana, Arkansas, and Missouri, matched with increases in agricultural and industrial expertise and the number of available slaves, resulted in considerable economic growth within the Louisiana colony itself during the Spanish era. Such success would not appear in the Spanish records because it was untouched by traditional Spanish means of taxation. The Spanish mercantilist system had been focused upon cash crops shipped to the Peninsula; now, in 1798, the Bourbons had not fully grasped one consequence of free trade, the ability of its subjects to sell cash crops *to* another empire. In 1790, the Spanish king had stunned planters in Louisiana and merchants in

New Orleans by ordering a reduction in tobacco sales to Spain, but by 1798, the planters could simply sell their tobacco to North American merchants for resale throughout Europe. But they now also sold cotton and sugar, both better suited for the Louisiana colony and more profitable.

In the end, then, the amount of riverine produce and goods arriving from North American sources and delayed by the Spanish probably amounted to about one-third—roughly 27 to 36 percent—of all trade going through New Orleans.[15] If some percentage was being diverted past the Spanish warehouse, this would still provide strong evidence that Louisiana and the merchants of New Orleans were prospering several years before the American annexation. However, the percentage of produce delayed in the Guarda Almacén was certainly important to New Orleans merchants for its profit margin, especially to those merchants closely tied to the planters/merchants on the US side of the Mississippi River.

THE NOTARIAL ARCHIVES

Beyond the Spanish archives, there is another set of economic statistics available on the New Orleans economy—those that may be compiled from the New Orleans Notarial Archives. These voluminous records do not provide an easy source of statistics—in fact, any such data have to be laboriously crushed and squeezed out of each document, then compiled into a different format. There are simply no tables of data in the notarial records. In addition, the archives mostly document the sale of real estate and slaves, not produce or goods, and can be skewed by emancipations, dowries, powers of attorney, mortgages, and the like. However, most such miscellaneous transactions—at least emancipations, dowries, and powers of attorney—can be linked to periods of economic prosperity. In addition, while the notarial documents themselves are difficult to digest, the WPA indexes of the archive are much easier to study, and can at least be quantified by not only numbers of transactions for a given year, month, or even day, but the number of pages for those transactions, which may seem frivolous, but is actually a useful checksum.[16] Best of all, the notarial archives are time-comprehensive, extending over most of the entire French and Spanish colonial era and through the American era until the present.[17]

Based upon overall business transactions in the notarial archives, figure 3.6 illustrates the general ebb and flow of business in Spanish New Orleans. Evidently no previous historian of colonial Spanish America has attempted

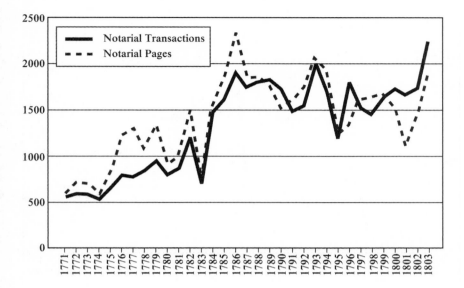

FIGURE 3.6. Total annual entries for notarial transactions and notarial transaction pages at New Orleans, 1771–1803.

to compile data on notarial transactions and graphically depict economic fluctuations.

If the methodology is correct, then figure 3.6 indicates a complex history of economic booms and slumps in the Louisiana and New Orleans economy, even perhaps a crash not previously noted in the historical record. The first complete indexes indicate a surge in the economy in 1776 as the North American colonists revolted, a surge that certainly fluctuated but then doubled again in 1784, when the independence of the thirteen former British colonies was more certain and North Americans began surging west. However, business transactions seriously slumped from 1787 to 1793, plunged 28 percent in 1795, rebounded, and then slumped yet again through at least 1799. This prolonged slump or stagnation was not precipitated by the French and Haitian revolutions, because it began before those great upheavals. Nor does it seem to have been precipitated by the reported closing of the Mississippi River to American shipping in 1784 or the associated failure of the US Congress to pass the Jay-Gardoqui Treaty or later negotiations permitting American shipping with a 15 percent surcharge.[18] Instead, the economic stagnation indicated by the New Orleans

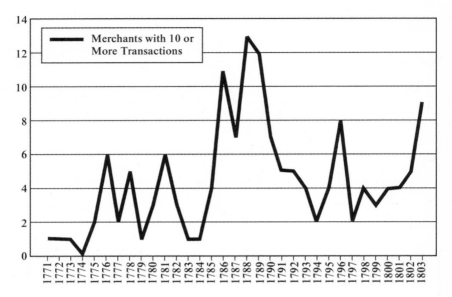

FIGURE 3.7. Merchants with ten or more notarial transactions at New Orleans, 1771–1803.

Notarial Archives ended dramatically and only during the last year of Spanish rule, probably because of expectations and then confirmation that the colony and city would be annexed by the United States.

Another useful method to study the notarial archives is to determine the major business transactors in a single year or group of years, and then study the patterns of their transactions. Large numbers of transactions in Spanish New Orleans did not necessarily suggest business success; they sometimes indicated failure and a subsequent sale of slaves and property to clear debts. Multiple transactions also sometimes indicated major life changes, such as sales to provide a dowry, to divide property to pay for a son's education, or preparatory to an anticipated death. However, the general number of these transactions reveals notable peaks and dips that closely match the economic flow of overall transactions. In other words, the major transactors in New Orleans were, unsurprisingly, making decisions to buy or sell slaves and property based upon where they sensed the economy was moving.

Figure 3.7 indicates that the major business transactors in Spanish New Orleans perceived some economic opportunities during the early days of the

American Revolution, became bearish until 1786, perceived much more opportunity until 1789, hibernated again until a brief period between 1795 and 1797,
and returned to sleep until 1803, when they notably revived again, perhaps not
only on expectations of US annexation, but also encouraged by a single shipment of slaves in early 1803.

A closer example of the actual transactions by the "major transactors" also
confirms the general direction of these statistics. Before 1776, most major transactors were making routine enough purchases and lifestyle changes, except
Braud and Braquier, who each sold notable numbers of slaves in a single year.
The number of major transactors notably jumped in 1776 but fluctuated for
years: slave sales continued to be important, and even two women appeared as
major transactors, based upon their sales of slaves. Ironically, the most active
slave trader during this period was Oliver Pollock, who famously was funding
the Continental Congress and supplying rebel troops. As the American Revolution ended and the business environment stagnated, Pollock and another major
transactor sold out their properties to pay bills, and a third such transactor died.

The increase in transactions from 1786 to 1789 were clearly based upon slave
trading, but those numbers began to slip in 1790 and plunged in 1791. Apparently the best business opportunity in the city itself was still to slip in with a
ship full of slaves and pray (or perhaps pay) for government authorization to
sell them. The government's role in stimulating the economy was probably
essential, although it was often based upon auctions, especially those of seized
slaves. Consequently, Governor Miró and the merchant/auctioneer Geromo
La Chiapella often appeared as "major transactors" during this period. Governor Miró noticeably reduced his own official transactions, from twenty-four in
1789 (nine with Americans, especially Jacob Cowperthwait) to fifteen in 1790
(two with Americans). Miró had less money to spend in 1790 than before, and
was less willing or able to spend that money with Americans. By the second
half of 1792, the most successful New Orleans merchant, Daniel Clark Sr., was
reduced to one transaction via the notary Ximenes—seeking payment of a debt.
Indeed, the only men in New Orleans who conducted more than ten transactions in 1794 New Orleans were the Graviers, as the father transferred various
properties to his son; the years 1797–99 were equally dismal, and almost all of
Daniel Clark's transactions in 1798 were protests against other merchants for
payment of moneys owed. Only 1803 brought new opportunities.

Another view of notarial activity in New Orleans is admittedly possible. This
argument would hold that the city's merchants and merchant/planters used the

entire period to acquire land, build plantations, and purchase slaves outside New Orleans itself, in other parishes including the German Coast and Natchez. These merchant/planters, as Spanish *vecinos*, would have then shipped their produce downriver without needing to stop at the Guarda Almacén, and their economic activity would thus be somewhat invisible to the modern researcher, except via shipping receipts in North American companies, few if any of which remain available. If this theory is correct, only a comprehensive comparison of the Spanish notarial records across the entire Louisiana colony would indicate if there really was an economic stagnation in New Orleans, or if slow waters actually hid a swiftly moving undercurrent. However, given that most if not all of the merchant planters remained in New Orleans and active in maritime trade, some percentage of their expenditures would have been in property and slaves registered in New Orleans—if they truly had funds to expend.

The number of merchants with ten or more notarial transactions took a dramatic leap upwards in 1803, from five to nine. The leap was in part by some new players positioning themselves ahead of political changes, and some forced by personal choices. The most dramatic reentry into the list of top merchants was Juan Francisco/Jean François Merieult, who conducted an astonishing 175 transactions in 1803. Almost all of these transactions were for the sale and receipt of slaves brought into the city between May and November that year.[19] (Merieult had sold at least 15 slaves in 1792, a much smaller number, indeed.)

However, Merieult was not the only merchant exerting himself in 1803, according to the notarial records. Antonio Pico, a newcomer to the archives, sold at least eleven slaves in mostly single sales; Gabriel Fonvergne, Vicente Rillieux, and Maria Tronquet each had spurts of activity, delivering receipts for property (including slaves) to multiple customers. George Pollock, a distant cousin of the better-known American merchant Oliver Pollock, formerly living in New York,[20] was very active in New Orleans, as was the longtime Spanish merchant Bartolome Bosque, who may have been profiting from his relationship with Daniel Clark.

US merchants were active but not dominant among the city's major transactors, and only until 1790 or so. Oliver Pollock was active in 1778, 1782, 1789, and 1790 acquiring and paying debts for the Continental Congress; Santiago Mather, the Clarks, Vaugine, and Hodge all conducted routine business (or in Clark's case, sold numerous slaves) in the late 1780s; but then only Clark appeared for a decade, suing for payment of bills in 1798, and Henry sold everything in 1802, perhaps because he was dying. The young merchants who would soon become so prominent in American New Orleans, including John McDonough and Clark's protégés Chew and Relf, barely appear in Spanish notarial records. They likely worked under the sponsorship of a Spanish *vecino*—Clark and Mather, for example—and therefore did not sign anything official in Spanish records.

The New Orleans economy during the Spanish era was only partially built upon a slave economy, and therefore only partially dependent upon external slave sources. Many people of every shade sought to buy slaves, especially when the economy improved. However, given the lack of capital available in New Orleans for outfitting slave ships and the unwillingness of the Spanish government to permit such activity, the vast majority of the slaves brought to New Orleans came from within the Caribbean and not directly from Africa. An estimated 12,000–14,000 slaves were brought to Spanish New Orleans—8,000–9,000 from 1783 to 1793. During this middle period of Spanish rule, forty-six vessels carrying 2,701 slaves departed Jamaica for New Orleans in the period 1783–89. Significant numbers of slaves were also shipped from Roseau in the French colony of Dominica to New Orleans, peaking at 916 in 1789. However, slave trading seriously contracted from 1801 to 1803, with only 1,200 slaves arriving during that period.[21]

These statistics are supported by the significant number of notarial slave transactions in New Orleans during this period. For instance, the notarial records indicate that most of Daniel Clark's sixty-four transactions in 1786 were related to slaves, and Pablo Segond, Hodge, Vincent, Dupuy, Herbert, Jorda, Sauve, Alva, Mayronne, LaChiapella, Merieult, Girod, and Fortier all sold numerous slaves from 1786 to 1792. Tribino did so in 1793, and Santa Cruz did in 1796 (thirty-one transactions). In sum, there is solid notarial evidence that numerous slaves were being traded in New Orleans long before the American era (and therefore, probably arriving by sea) in 1786–93. However, that funding then contracted, and slave trading became dangerous until 1803. Perhaps the only exception to this decade-long slump in large-scale slave trading was in 1796, when Santa Cruz received a slave ship for a doubtlessly eager market.

The *Trans-Atlantic Slave Trade Database,* sponsored by researchers at Emory and Harvard universities, lists only five voyages directly from Africa (more or less) to New Orleans during the period of 1780–1803. These ships were the *Thetis* in 1784, *Guipuscano* in 1790, and three ships in 1803, the *Africain* (arriving sometime in or after January, *Confiance* (11 June), and *Sally* (6 September). This level of maritime slave trade was very low compared to other parts of the Spanish empire; during the same period, for example, seventy-three ships disembarked slaves in the Rio Plata and five also disembarked at La Guaira, in modern-day Venezuela.[22]

Of the five slave ships that entered New Orleans in the late Spanish period, the French-flagged *Thetis* with 185 slaves, arriving in or about February 1784, does not seem to have left an impression in the notarial indices. Perhaps the slaves were sold in a few large groups, without showing up in many transactions. The arrival of the Spanish-flagged *Guipuscano* sometime in 1790 with another 197 slaves should also have left some mark in the notarial record, and is surely related to the transactions of La Chiapella (51, mostly slave sales), Mayronne (26, mostly slaves), Estevan Pedesclaux (24 receipts), and Jorda (24 receipts).[23] The ship was probably owned by a Basque—Gipuzkoa is a Basque port and therefore *Guipuscano* means a man from Gipuzkoa—but the database does not list a captain, home port, or owners for the ship. Probably not coincidentally, Pedesclaux was from San Sebastian, in Gipuzkoa Province. Jorda and La Chiapella, at least, were well-placed in Spanish society; Jorda was a military officer who hailed from Calella, a seaport northeast of Barcelona, and was seemingly connected to everyone in the city's leadership; Mayronne, although he was of French origin, was also from a seaport (Bordeaux).[24]

Spanish records also indicate that at least three other ships arrived directly from Africa that were not reported in the *Trans-Atlantic Slave Trade* database: the *Santa Catalina* (204 slaves) and *Feliz* (228 slaves) in 1788 and the *Amable Victoria* (307 slaves) in 1792. The *Santa Catalina* was commanded by John McDonough, presumably an older relative of the young Baltimore merchant of the same name who would arrive in New Orleans in about 1802 and become one of the wealthiest men in North America. The *Feliz* was commanded by Alexandro Bauden (Baudin), who conducted at least fifty-nine transactions that year, mostly the sale of slaves with Jaime Jorda; Geromo La Chiapella was involved in sixty-eight transactions that year, almost all slave sales, and the most of any New Orleans merchant that year, so it may be presumed that those were related to the arrival of the *Santa Catalina* and/or the *Feliz*, as well.[25] However, given that he often served as a public auctioneer, the Spanish governor might have seized some or all of the slaves from one of the vessels and auctioned them, with the proceeds going to the government itself.

Of the three slave ships that arrived in 1803, all three were French-flagged. Both the *Africain* and the *Sally* were co-owned by Guilbaud and Roustand, merchants of Bordeaux, and the *Confiance* was owned by another evident Bordeaux partnership, Ladurantie and Durecu. A petition was introduced on

24 May requesting to introduce the 143 slaves brought by the *Africain*, and Spanish authorities agreed to such a request "since Louisiana was indeed in the process of being retroceded to France." Similar intercession was made by the incoming French prefect, Laussat, for the entry of the *Confiance*. The *Sally* left its intermediate stop of Havana for New Orleans in August 1803 but detoured to Pensacola because of bad weather, illness, and storms. Given that Merieult's career began a slow ascent in March 1803, then surged in late May throughout November, it may be safely assumed that it was he who sold most of the slaves arriving on the *Africain* (143), *Confiance* (170), and *Sally* (110) in 1803. And indeed, Merieult was the consignee for at least the slaves from the *Sally*.[26]

COMPARING ALL SOURCES ON THE NEW ORLEANS ECONOMY

For comparison and summary, let us overlay all of the available data—the notarial transactions and pages, the "major transactors," goods deposited in the royal warehouse, and ship departures, to see if all of this conglomeration indicates a conclusive economic pattern for the city. To compare these apples and

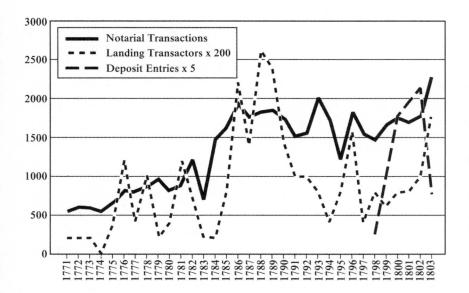

FIGURE 3.8. Notarial transactions (1771–1803) at New Orleans compared to weighted total annual entries for goods deposited in the Guarda Almacén (1798–1803) and transactions by leading transactors (1771–1803).

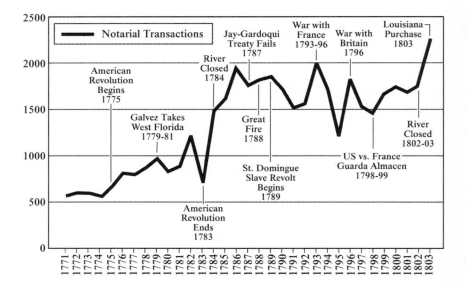

FIGURE 3.9. Notarial transactions in New Orleans compared to major historical events, 1771–1803.

oranges, of course, we will bend the numbers with general ratios. The resulting figure 3.8 indicates that there was indeed some unexplained drop in the New Orleans economy (or perhaps the economic statistics) in 1783, a retrenchment in roughly 1786, and a slow decline at least until 1799, then growth, especially in 1803. However, the number of major transactors did not always keep pace with the economy—in fact, it often plunged far lower than the economy would indicate, as can be seen in the deep troughs in major transactor activity for every year from 1791 to 1803, barring 1795.

Finally, let us compare these variations in the New Orleans economy with historic events—revolution in the British American colonies, the American colonist victory, an American constitution, a slave revolt in French St. Domingue, changing Spanish royal policies on the river trade and tobacco, along with wars, fires, and hurricanes. The resultant figure 3.9 indicates that the New Orleans economy remained at a very rough plateau from 1785 to 1803, based upon a confluence of events—some natural, but most tied to Spanish international policies. The city clearly could grow to another level only once freed from the needs of the Spanish military and expectations of the Spanish court.

Spanish mercantile policy has been aptly described as "convoluted"; that policy resulted, in Spanish Louisiana, in the opening of New Orleans trade in 1782, the closure of the river to Americans in 1784–88, the reduction of duties in 1793, and free navigation and deposit in 1795 (via Pinckney's Treaty) until 1802. Furthermore, the governors in Spanish Louisiana, at least, interpreted and enforced royal polices with a great deal of independence.[27] Figure 3.9 provides some evidence of how this "convoluted" policy could drive the city's economy up in 1782, down in 1784, up in 1793 with the reduction of duties, and steadily up in 1795 until 1802. However, it also demonstrates that these particular Bourbon policies were not at all decisive—the city's economy had already plunged in 1783 before any Spanish closure of the river, revived in 1786–87 before the river was officially reopened, continued to drop in 1793 despite the reduction of duties (partly because of war), and did not dramatically grow despite Pinckney's Treaty until 1803, when it grew based on expectations that the United States or France would be acquiring the colony. In summary, Bourbon policies clearly had something to do with the volatile growth patterns of the New Orleans economy, but other factors also drove and hindered that growth.

THE ECONOMIC SLUMP OF 1788-1793

From 1788 to 1793, New Orleans was struck hard by numerous physical and political-economic disasters. A major fire had already destroyed much of the city on 21 March 1788, but the economy recovered quickly, and the city's leading merchants remained very active, notably selling many slaves.[28]

However, peninsular Spain's inconsistent support of "free trade," frequent enforcement of mercantilist monopolies, and often burdensome taxes and fees were much more dangerous to the city than mere fire and flames. In June 1788, Spanish officials prohibited trade between Louisiana and neighboring Texas, presumably to ensure Texan dependence on goods from Spain and Mexico. A royal decree later in 1788 enabled Governor Miró to lower the tariff on upriver trade from 15 to 6 percent, but, in the following year, another royal decree prohibited the export of specie. Given that flatboatmen and sailing captains expected to be paid in specie for their produce and goods, rather than with goods or letters of exchange, this second decree vitiated the usefulness of the first.

In the same year, 1789, New Orleans was seriously rattled economically by the French Revolution and, much more immediately, by the chaotic civil war in St. Domingue. It is unclear if Governor-General Esteban Rodriguez Miró informally banned slave importation from the French colonies in 1789, but legal slave importation into New Orleans itself plummeted, with some notable exceptions, as indicated in the notarial archive. The plunge may have also been caused by market forces, including a shortage of slaves (unlikely), an increase in prices (also unlikely, given that average slave prices in Cuba actually dipped from 1792 to 1796), a fear of purchasing additional slaves during a time of revolt (possible), or the importation of slaves directly past New Orleans to upriver plantations, where their sale might or might not have been recorded in other parishes. In any case, it was probably then in 1789 that the city and the colony's overall economy slumped seriously. Whatever the reason for the reduction in slave sales, it was probably similar to the reduction in slave prices in Cuba, where the number of notarized slave sales decreased precipitously in 1791 and did not increase.

A decrease in the number of slave purchases/sales should not be confused with a change in prices, but the average slave prices in Cuba declined about 10 percent in 1792 and did not return to a similar level until 1796.[29] Slave prices in Cuba increased notably in 1798, especially for African males, and continued to remain high for the next decades, and it may be justifiably suspected that the slave prices in New Orleans, and perhaps throughout Louisiana, similarly fell and then rose in a similar fashion. If so, then the upriver plantations should have been competing for slaves, thus driving up prices and incidentally building the New Orleans economy in the years 1798 until at least 1803. However, figure 3.8 indicates that any economic growth in the city was not directly tied to slave prices.

The colonial New Orleans economy, then, seems to have been based on the flow of produce through the city, not slave sales, slave prices, or the sale of land. This is not to deny that the sales of slaves (when they occurred in the city) and the division of land by the Graviers and Marignys provided financial capital into the city, but it is to assert that such sales were not the waterwheel of the city's economic growth. Instead, the economy was based upon the flow of produce, admittedly grown and harvested and mined via a slave economy. However, the actual slave transactions within the city made only a sporadic difference during the colonial era.

It was at about this time, in March 1789, that New Orleans merchant Enrique Darcantel dared to write a frank letter to the minister of the Indies, José de Gálvez. Darcantel boldly addressed eight economic concerns, all of which might have angered one group of Spanish mercantilists or another. These issues were: (1) the requirement that merchants be actual Spanish subjects, (2) that trade with St. Domingue/Santo Domingo should continue in Spanish ships, (3) that trade with France and allies be permitted to continue without taxation, (4) that hard cash be retained in the colony and not spent on European slave ships or shipped elsewhere, (5) that Jamaican and other English ports should be considered neutral, especially for slave trading, (6) that hard cash acquired via slave trading should be documented, (7) that goods not included in existing tariffs be taxed at 40 percent over their cost, and (8) that an additional tax be removed from trade with French St. Domingue.[30]

Darcantel's issues above were especially centered on traditional planter concerns—limiting the power of French, British, and US merchants, acquiring slaves, and taxing competing goods. However, his letter was probably to little avail, because events were moving too quickly in the chaotic Atlantic world, particularly those involved in trade with France and St. Domingue. The city's major French firm, Vivant, Duclos & Soulie, disappeared from the notarial record after October 1789, perhaps a victim of lost St. Dominguan contacts and markets.[31]

In May 1790, whatever Miró may have done informally, the royal government issued a secret order that formally banned slave importation from the French colonies, in order to prevent slaves who had participated in revolts from being dumped on the New Orleans slave market. This order inevitably became public and dashed the hopes of French planters and merchants working in New Orleans. Only seven months later, in December 1790, the Spanish Supreme Council of State reduced the amount of tobacco to be purchased from Louisiana from two million pounds to a mere forty thousand pounds—effectively destroying the legal tobacco market for planters in Natchez and Baton Rouge. This decree was intended to protect tobacco growers in other Spanish colonies and manufacturers of tobacco products in Spain itself. However, the decree was crippling to the Louisiana economy. Governor Miró was simply unable to spur Louisiana's sluggish economy, and he was dismissed in March 1791.[32]

Francisco Luis Hector Baron de Carondelet, then the governor-general of El Salvador, was directed to replace Miró. For unknown reasons, it required nine months for Carondelet to arrive in Louisiana, in December 1791. However, once in New Orleans, the experienced Carondelet acted quickly to reshape the Louisiana economy. He formally banned the import of black slaves from French-held islands on 5 March 1792, although, as the notarial archives indicate, he was merely publicly formalizing the impact of the secret royal edict of May 1790. More importantly, he anticipated the potential economic impact of publicly limiting the importation of slaves, and took other steps to keep the economy viable. Only ten days after his decree on slave importation, Carondelet approved a moratorium on the debts of the Natchez planters, who were being ruined by Spanish policy and restrictions on tobacco sales. A week later, he proposed free trade for Louisiana settlers with other nations—including those from Great Britain and the United States. Carondelet's swift action spurred the Louisiana economy, as seen in the increase in notarial transactions in 1792, depicted in figures 3.6 and 3.8. In January 1793, a royal order lifted the ban on the importation of slaves into New Orleans. Five months later, in June 1793, a royal decree supported Carondelet's request and established free trade for the colony with countries friendly to Spain.[33]

The number of major transactors, however, did not noticeably increase during this period, as depicted in figure 3.7, above; in fact, the number of such transactors actually declined. Some of this decline may have been caused or offset by the movement and investment of capital outside the city. Daniel Clark Sr., for example, relocated to a plantation near Natchez; François Mayronne acquired a plantation on Barataria Island. With few major transactors, no one in the city may have possessed adequate capital to initiate new construction, to include piers, markets, and warehouses.

Carondelet worked to fend off royal prerogatives and decrees and improve the Louisiana (and New Orleans) economy, but he could not defeat nature. On 10 August 1794, a major hurricane struck the city and devastated shipping. Carondelet reported that the hurricane destroyed or seriously damaged thirteen ships, all but one commercial vessels. At least nine were still stranded aground, at least some presumably *inside* the levees, where they would have been very difficult if not impossible to move. Of the nine, three were frigates, much heavier than the packet boat and brigantines also damaged. One brigantine, previously very active and now aptly named *Nuestra Señora de los Dolores* (Our Lady of Sorrows), was "broken into pieces," and three light goletas were similarly destroyed. The only royal ship stranded and damaged was the postal ship *El Balahu* (Needlefish), but it was joined on the beach by two of Carondelet's military galleys, the *Luisiana* and the *Victoria,* and his felucca. The Customs Service felucca was somehow floating but nonfunctional.[34]

Given that only about a dozen commercial ships visited New Orleans each month in the early 1790s, the hurricane of August 1794 probably swept every ship *near* the city *into* the city. Carondelet would have sent a surviving vessel immediately to Havana to inform the Captain General of the disaster, but clearly delayed sending a more detailed account until he had something more definitive to report, and perhaps better news. He would have encountered a difficult time moving about: in his letter, written three weeks after the hurricane, he noted that all of the smaller vessels in the city—or at least, those he could find—launches, *yoenchas,* pirogues, and canoes—"had been completely lost."[35]

Any arriving ships would have found a waterlogged city—Carondelet reported the inundation extended over an expanse of ninety *toesas,* roughly five hundred feet into the city. Such a watermark would have not only covered the levee, it also would have flooded the warehouses closest to the levee and the *plaza de armas,* reached Chartres Street, and probably spilled into the ground floors of the *cabildo* and the cathedral, which both open onto that street, although Carondelet did not mention damage to those buildings. The *cabildo* requested a reduction of import duties to help defray the costs of the hurricane;[36] two of the city's cash crops, cotton and tobacco, would have been waterlogged and headed for ruination, if not swept away from levee warehouses or lost on destroyed vessels. The economic impact of this hurricane was probably quite serious for months afterwards, but was followed in December by the great fire of December 1794, which destroyed most of the wooden buildings that had survived the fire of 1788.

THE SLUMP OF 1795–1798: REAL OR IMAGINED?

Gayoso de Lemos, then commandant at Natchez, was promoted in 1796 to succeed Carondelet as governor of Louisiana; Carondelet was eventually assigned as the president of the Real Audiencia of Quito, where he again thrived from 1799 until his death in 1807. Pitot reported that Gayoso was partial to the United States, quarreled unnecessarily with the intendant, Juan Ventura Morales, lacked public confidence, and was corrupt ("poor and in debt, his needs often took precedence over his duties").[37]

The news was not all bad; figures 3.6, 3.7, and 3.8 above all indicate a genuine economic upturn in 1796. However, many of the merchants had little faith that the upturn would be permanent, and they banded together to draft a strikingly insistent, long petition to their king.[38] The merchants began obsequiously enough, but got to the heart of the matter immediately in the first paragraph:

Señor,
    The commercial sector of New Orleans, to Your Serene Royal
Majesty with the deepest respect with which it can convey . . . such
priceless advantages arrive wasted, as much because of the consider-

able burdens in gold currency to assist and subsidize the war expenses
which Your Majesty imposed . . . as by the well-known, disastrous
calamities of three violent hurricanes and a raging fire suffered in the
city during the last epoch, which nearly entirely ruined the fortunes of
laborers and merchants.

The colonial merchants of New Orleans bluntly told Charles IV: "The treaty,
Señor, established by Your Majesty with the United States of America . . . will
prevent the National family from any real success in its mercantile operations . . .
will render useless the many precautions taken to guard against clandestine
American commerce." They returned to flattery only for a moment, before
plunging into the remedies they sought: "To avoid such imminent damages
and those by which the Americans little by little lord over all Louisiana, they
flee to Your Majesty's paternal goodness, imploring for the indicated remedy,
which they entrust to your innate mercy. We do not only act, Señor, to obtain
from Our Señor's mildness the appropriate exemptions."

Those exemptions included permission to export silver, to freely purchase
and export American agricultural goods (presumably both to the United States
and within the Spanish empire), to ship directly from all European ports (and
not merely from two designated Spanish ports of limited utility), and the establishment of a local merchants council, a *consulado,* "as in the example of those
in Vera-Cruz, Lima, Cartagena, and la Havana."

Finally, before a gracious ending, the merchants pointedly noted the importance of their city and colony: "The said *gracias* will consolidate the security
and prosperity of these your dominions, so necessary for the conservation of
the Kingdom of Mexico, which serve as a barrier and without which it (Mexico)
will remain very exposed to the greed of our ambitious neighbors."[39]

The letter was signed by at least fifty-nine merchants, including, among
the more prominent, J. S. Merieult, J. B. Labatut, Nicolas Gravier, Geromo La
Chiapella, Wikoff and Garland, Viennes y Hamelin, Francisco de Riano, Louis
Darby Danycan, Michel Dragon, Christoval de Armas y Arcila, Daniel Clark,
Bartolome Bosque, Beltran Gravier Sr., Juan Bautista Poeyfarre, and Francisco
Mayronne. The merchants included Frenchmen, Spaniards, an Italian, and a
Greek officer in the Spanish employ, Scots, Germans, and Americans.

One must wonder how this petition was received by Charles IV—if he saw
it—and his ministers. Louisiana, its capital of New Orleans, and its merchants
were not sending Charles IV silver, gold, or contributions for his several wars

and grand projects; indeed, they were costing him funds for military defense and finessing their way around his customs system. And yet these merchants, most from other lands, were reporting that his war was costing them financially, that his recent treaty with the United States was a mistake, that they desired an expansion of their economic power within the empire, and that they considered themselves deserving to be granted a *consulado* and thus equivalent to the centuries-old cities of Veracruz, Lima, Cartagena, and Havana. Their warning that their colony was the only barrier between their "ambitious neighbors" and the silver-rich colony of Mexico, upon which Charles IV so depended financially, was meant to be economically unsettling—and perhaps not so veiled in its implications.

Another group of the city's merchants later drafted a second petition to the king, difficult to read but partly focused, like Darcantel's letter, on keeping hard specie inside the colony and also governing the use of paper currency. This petition was signed by at least twenty-two merchants, mostly with French surnames, including M. Fortier, Francisco Mayronne, and J. B. Labatut, but also including two prominent Spanish names, that of Geromo La Chiapella and Domingo de Lemos, and the Anglo James Kennedy.[40]

THE FINAL YEARS OF 1799-1803

Governor Gayoso died in the summer of 1799. As the ranking military officer assigned to Louisiana, colonial colonel Francisco Bouligny assumed the duties of acting military governor until the arrival of a formal replacement. Bouligny was hardly the perfect man for even a temporary position—Carondelet had assessed three years earlier that his colonel "has talent, zeal, but is beginning with the years to lose his activity,"[41] and as a Creole without title, Bouligny did not command the respect that any replacement would require. Bouligny only remained in his position for two months until a new acting military governor, the Marqués de Casa-Calvo, arrived.

Casa-Calvo, whose much longer full name was Sebastián Nicolás Calvo de la Puerta y O'Farrill, like Bouligny, was a Creole, but after almost two centuries in Havana, his family had become one of the most important in Cuba. He was a veteran of the American Revolution and the long series of Spanish battles in the Haitian Revolution. He was first and foremost a military man,[42] sent to New Orleans to measure and buttress the defenses of a vast colony threatened by a demographic wave of Americans, privateering French vessels, and hostile British warships.

And Casa-Calvo had genuine reason to focus on those colonial defenses, even before he arrived in the colony. Two corsair goletas of sixteen and eighteen guns, both presumably French, attacked a vessel accompanying Casa-Calvo's warship on 16 September. He was informed that British ships also were cruising off the entrance to the Mississippi at the Balize. However, at four in the morning on 17 September, Casa-Calvo arrived in New Orleans aboard the royal brigantine *El Saeta* (Arrow) and assumed command of Louisiana.

His arrival was not propitious. Two nights afterwards, on 20 September, Casa-Calvo and the entire city were awakened at three in the morning by the enormous explosion of the *repuesto de polvora* (a small powder magazine) in the San Carlos redoubt. The explosion killed four and wounded five from the Regiment of Louisiana, one gravely. It also destroyed the barracks of that regiment's grenadier company and broke windows throughout the city. Understandably, Casa-Calvo focused upon military issues in the following days, preparing a complete spreadsheet enumerating all military personnel available throughout the colony and appointing new sergeant-majors (the most senior enlisted personnel, especially entrusted with organizing and leading troops at the ground level) on 22 September. But even that week, he learned that a convoy of six Spanish merchant ships had only reached the city by escaping a British squadron outside the river.[43]

Casa-Calvo continued to focus upon military issues, but struggled with the acting civil governor, Nicolas Maria Vidal, over cultural/social issues. He was more fortunate in his dealings with the acting intendant, Juan Venture Morales, over economic and security issues. It was only two weeks after Casa-Calvo's arrival that the royal revocation of neutral trade reached the city. Morales asked for Casa-Calvo's advice, and the latter suggested that Morales resort to the tried-and-true Spanish formula to obey but not comply, while compiling correspondence from himself and local authorities, including the *cabildo,* to support a continuance of trade. Morales took this sound advice and forwarded the correspondence to the Council of the Indies.[44]

This duality of government between the acting military governor and the acting civil governor would only be resolved by the appointment of Manuel Juan de Salcedo into both positions as the regularly appointed governor of Louisiana. However, Salcedo, like Vidal a longtime Creole bureaucrat, leaned upon Vidal as his advisor, continued to argue with the *cabildo,* and played a decisive role in stopping the city's riverine traffic in 1802. The Marqués of Someruelos, governing Cuba, sniffed of Salcedo, "the governor lacks the necessary talent for that command"; Gilbert Din, the historian perhaps most familiar with the daily correspondence of the Spanish period, opined of Salcedo, "He was either grossly incompetent, inexperienced, or approaching senility."[45]

Only one contemporary narrator on Spanish New Orleans had a mercantile background—Jacques-François Pitot. Pitot's manuscript work details the city's trade as he saw it during the climactic years of 1799–1803. The work is worthy of detailed (and sometimes critical) study not only because of Pitot's facts, but also because of his personal perspectives, which were those of a traditional French mercantilist.

Pitot was born in Normandy, moved as a young man to Cap Français, St. Domingue, to seek his fortune, returned to France as the slave revolt began, fled France during its Reign of Terror, attempted to return to St. Domingue, but instead settled in Philadelphia from 1793 to 1796 and became a naturalized US citizen. After Spain opened Louisiana to US trade in late 1795 via the Treaty of San Lorenzo el Real (Pinckney's Treaty), Pitot relocated to New Orleans in 1796, at the age of thirty-five. He served as a syndic in the local chamber of commerce and was elected as a ward commissioner in 1802. He wrote a careful, short book-length (seventy-six pages) *Observations on the Colony of Louisiana from 1796 to 1802* in the latter year for the use of French business and government associates; this manuscript work remained in the company archives of Begouen, Demeaux, and Company in Le Havre, France, then in family archives, until it was finally translated and published in 1979.[46]

Pitot's work is very well organized and insightful, proceeding from chapters on "Government and Finances" through "Commerce," "Agriculture," "Trade with the Indians," and even an "Analytical Topography Based on Interrelationships Among Politics, Agriculture, and Commerce." Pitot's views in that work may be compared with contemporaneous documents and modern statistics. For example, the manifests indicated that, as early as 1782, the rebellious American colonies were actively exporting consumer goods, including pottery and glassware, and significant amounts of foodstuffs to Louisiana. This market (in the case of New Orleans, this importation) remained busy long afterwards and is reflected in the occasional manifests found one and two decades later. Pitot never used a ship's manifest as evidence but did provide an explanation for such busy importation from Louisiana: "It is well known that the manufactured products of Spain provide almost nothing for the consumer needs of its colonies . . . contraband trade in peacetime, as in war, provides nearly all the articles of luxury and essential needs for the large and fertile Spanish possessions in the New World."

Pitot also opined that this contraband trade permitted Spanish officials and foreign merchants to enrich themselves and actually discouraged foreign (that is, British and French) invasions because it was so profitable.[47] Indeed, he mocked "the scarcity of resources in the colony" throughout the Spanish era, and wrote:

> In order to try to cover up the barrenness of such a narrative, I would have enumerated with some emphasis the bolts of linen and wool, the assortments of foodstuffs, scrap iron, hardware, china, and various articles useful to the Indians; all the items, in fact, which the businessman or peddler of New Orleans could import from the three ports of France at which Spain, in her generosity, allowed them to call. I would have observed that through a coastwide trade still permitted by the mother country, Saint-Domingue furnished indirectly a part of these supplies, and I would not have neglected to say that the island of Jamaica, and others, were selling the miserable remnants of Negro cargoes which supplied the slave quarters."[48]

And again he wrote that New Orleans had probably not received more than 1,200 barrels of flour from the western United States in 1796 but had imported more than 50,000 barrels in 1801.[49]

However, in these representations, Pitot was providing his partners in the French business community, as well as potential partners in the French government, a rather skewed vision of New Orleans commerce. Although he was a syndic, presumably able to procure copies of some exemplary ship manifests, Pitot did not do so. The 1782 manifest contained not only "bolts of linen and wool, the assortments of foodstuffs, scrap iron, hardware, china, and various articles useful to the Indians," as Pitot would argue, but rather *many* casks and cases of consumer goods, hundreds of barrels of foodstuffs, and maritime supplies—and this was merely one ship. The *Dauphin*'s 1793 manifest included 1,738 barrels of flour alone—more than Pitot alleged were imported into the city (at least from the West) in the entire year of 1796, and this was only one of many ships.[50] Pitot was clearly playing fast and loose with his statistics and opinions.

Pitot also did not provide any statistics on ship entries and departures, including the nationality of those ships, but claimed that the goods arriving in New Orleans were "all the items, in fact, which the businessman or peddler of New Orleans could import from the three ports of France at which Spain, in her generosity, allowed them to call." He was ignoring a painfully obvious point. While French (or British or Dutch) merchants could in theory supply the needs of Louisiana commerce, those commercial needs were already being met by US merchants, geographically better positioned, with much faster ships and probably much lower prices. The ship entry records for 1798 make it clear that this trade was overwhelmingly with the East Coast of the United States. One or two vessels departed each month for Havana; occasionally, one departed for Veracruz or even upriver Natchez, but such were the exceptions.[51] Whichever French ports were designated for trade with the colonies, including Bordeaux (Burdos), Le Havre, or Marseilles, none of those were essential to the commerce of Louisiana; nor, for that matter, were the ports of Spain itself. The archaeological record of New Orleans provides additional proof that the only "essential" items received from France were various wines and liqueurs—and these may not have been essential at all to Americans and Spaniards alike.

Pitot was very critical of the Guarda Almacén system; he seems to have been aware of the diversion of commerce past the royal warehouses and accused the royal decrees of creating a "warehousing and contraband trade" and the customs house employees of gross corruption and pillage. He also fretted over the inconvenience of unpacking cargoes for customs inspection, noting that this practice, "by deteriorating the merchandise, would annoy both the foreigner and colonist." Given that he did not detail the process, extent, or names behind that diversion and corruption, it possible that, even as a *syndic,* he had no access to the actual Guarda Almacén registers.[52]

Pitot's actual emphasis throughout his *Observations,* especially in his final chapter, often seems to have been on trade with Native American tribes. He traveled far upriver, wrote in detail on the great logjams on western rivers and their impact on local navigation and flooding, and concerned himself for a few pages on the Alabama-area trade with Native tribes, a commerce that was then controlled by an English firm.[53] In these interests, Pitot almost seems to have been a merchant of the old mercantilist school, reporting to his French associates that Louisiana could have a robust economy but not realizing that it already did have such an economy.

Finally, Pitot's view of the city's overall economic trend must be compared with the available statistics. The notarial archives seem to argue that the city's economy was a complex history of economic booms and slumps, perhaps in 1783, but much more likely from 1787 to 1793, followed by an even more dramatic 28 percent plunge in 1795, a rebound, and a slump yet again through 1799. Pitot's cynical account, however, captures none of this likely volatility. Instead, he merely implies that the city's economy was stagnant throughout the 1770s and 1780s, only improving because the French-born Carondelet "had found only peddlers in New Orleans, and . . . wanted to established business-men there." He did argue that the economy was corrupted by a confluence of events, including the appointment of a corrupt governor (Gayoso), the Spanish concession of the east bank of the Mississippi River, and establishment of free trade with the United States without a similar concession to all neutral ships (in Pitot's reasoning, those of France), the inconvenience and corruption of the Guarda Almacén system, prohibitions against currency exports, and the exclu-sion of trade with Veracruz. Indeed, Pitot felt so strongly about these issues that he wrote a "Memoir to Communicate to the Commercial Interests of New Or-leans," a letter that he circulated within the business community and provided a copy to Governor Gayoso himself.[54]

Pitot's claim that the economy of Louisiana and New Orleans was stagnant throughout most of the Spanish era does not hold up to statistics—the ship arrival records for 1789 and the departure records for 1798–99 alone indicate that he was exaggerating greatly.[55] His explanation of why the New Orleans economy might have suffered slumps was more logical, but flawed. While the impact of corruption is difficult to measure, the Spanish concession of the east bank of the Mississippi River should not have resulted in less trade (or fees) coming into New Orleans, but in fact more trade, as North American planters flocked into the area and shipped their crops to New Orleans. Some may have even paid the required Spanish import fees, thus increasing Spanish revenues. The lack of a similar concession to neutral, that is, French shipping probably mattered little to the New Orleans economy, save the merchants with French connections like Pitot—the city was able to do quite well on its commerce with the United States.

Pitot did touch upon a financial point of serious concern to some New Or-leans merchants of French origin—their desire for permission to export silver currency out of the city. These merchants lacked ready access to capital for "mercantile speculations" or commercial improvements unless they became slave traders, which some of them were. There was no longer any French capi-tal available from revolt-wracked St. Domingue, nor from war-wracked France. Their competitors, the Americans, however, did have access to capital from Philadelphia, Baltimore, and even London and the Netherlands.

Pitot did report another restriction on the New Orleans economy—an exclusion on trade with Veracruz. He complained that the city was "the storehouse of the wealth as well as of the supplies of Mexico" and that the royal court had opened Veracruz trade to American vessels "to enrich foreigners rather than its own subjects in Lower Louisiana, who can ship there only by the particular favor of their intendant, or by contraband trade."[56] However, Pitot was incorrect on an actual exclusion of trade with Veracruz: tonnage duty records from Veracruz indicate that it did maintain low-level commerce with New Orleans during the very period in which Pitot claimed an exclusion was at work. Admittedly, these ship visits numbered only two or so a year from 1792 to 1799, a very small number. The number of visits increased in 1800 but only to four or five a year, then ended in 1803 until new regulations could be worked out in 1805. In any case, there seems to have been no formally declared exclusion of Veracruz commerce, but Pitot was correct in that there seems to have been a *de facto* exclusion of Veracruz commerce with Louisiana.

In any case, Pitot probably underestimated the resistance such trade would have encountered in Veracruz itself. Given that only nine other vessels arrived from non-Spanish European ports in the period from 1792 to 1799, ships from New Orleans, arriving with a variety of merchandise from both European and American ports, would have attracted great consumer interest in Veracruz and endangered the monopolies of the established Veracruz merchants. Little else can explain the "open hostility" with which Veracruz's merchants considered the arrival of non-Spanish vessels. The *Betsey* of Charleston, for example, was ordered to leave port without unloading.[57]

Finally, one must compare Pitot's views on economic success or failure with data that indicates the city's most active merchants were much less inactive in 1786–89 and 1795–97. Surprisingly, Pitot did not differentiate much between years of success or failure in his report; instead he merely emphasized "the precariousness of the colony's existence" to his French associates. Nor did he name any of the city's most active merchants. Instead, he only made an intriguing, rather backhanded allowance: "[New Orleans] owes all its local improvements to the courage of its inhabitants and its location; and that it is exclusively to foreigners, whom a beneficial chance brought to the upper reaches of the Mississippi's left bank, that Louisiana owes the inexhaustible flow of prosperity which will overcome, as it spreads in its course, all of the obstacles that they wanted to place in its path."

What Pitot never articulated was that the "foreigners" building the Louisiana economy had not been brought by "a beneficial chance" to the Mississippi River—they came, just as he did, in search of success, and they worked very hard to build plantations and businesses once there. Pitot also did not seem to accept that, on the east bank of the river, many of the most successful were not "foreigners" at all: they were all *vecinos*, often of French ancestry like him. Indeed, although he did not mention it to his French associates, Pitot himself was no longer "French"—he was a naturalized American citizen (yet arguably a Spanish *vecino*). What Pitot also did not admit to his French associates, perhaps even to himself, was that the "foreigners" were no longer foreign; they were home, and the land he saw and the river he explored were quickly slipping from Spanish grasp—they were becoming simply American.

Upon the annexation of 1803, Pitot accepted that the Americans were not very foreign at all. He became a member of their first city council, was appointed as mayor from mid-1804 to mid-1805, and then as the first parish judge, in which post he remained until his death in 1831.[58] Jacques-François Pitot, ardent French nationalist and rather prejudiced mercantilist observer, died as James Pitot. Like it or not, he, too, had become an American.

CONCLUSION

The available statistics on New Orleans indicate that Bourbon policies had something to do with the city's volatile economic growth, but other factors were also driving and hindering that growth. The statistics indicate that the slump of 1788–93 was driven by both natural disasters and policy restrictions on the sale of slaves; the slump of 1795–98 was caused by a loss of major merchant/investor confidence and a lack of capital (here more clearly driven by wavering Bourbon policy), and the slow growth of 1799–1802 may have been the result of the same lack of confidence and capital.

Bourbon policies and wars, then, did not necessarily prevent New Orleans from growth. As in the Rio Plata, Louisiana and New Orleans simply diverted produce and goods into another trans-imperial partner's vessels and ports—and it became the United States that drove the economy of the city and colony. The Bourbon governors in New Orleans attempted to tax and control that trans-imperial trade, but they ultimately failed. The colony was already slipping away into economic independence.

Spanish Attempts to Control Trade

Prince Ursino: You, my friend, are deaf as a post,
you cannot understand the fuss,
you are out of step with the world.
　　—Pedro Calderon de la Barca, *The Painter of Dishonour*

The Spanish authorities in New Orleans, like those in other imperial ports, attempted to control trade both to conform with imperial policy and to funnel tax revenue into the colonial coffers. Their attempts generally focused on regulating and taxing access to the city's riverine trade; controlling which nationality of vessels, sailors, and passports were used to conduct trade; monitoring which sources of news were used to shape local trade; and finally, controlling the source and nature of the capital, especially specie, coming into and leaving the colonial capital.

The merchants of Spanish New Orleans gradually overcame many of these restrictions with tactics based, in large part, on the de facto dual citizenship possible in *vecindad* and the power of their own trans-imperial trade, which undercut efforts to limit trade without seriously undermining the entire colony. In the end, these merchants slowly bent Spanish policy and restrictions in Louisiana, and especially in New Orleans, toward a more open trade in not only produce and goods, but also in current news and capital funding.

ROYAL CONTROL OF A CIRCULAR TRADE

The Bourbon Spanish emperors, it is generally conceded, were distinct from the Hapsburgs in their focus on centralizing power, especially financial power, within the throne,[1] and they clearly expected their colonial governors to control colonial trade to the betterment of the royal treasury. However, at least within the Atlantic world, Bourbon attempts to control colonial trade were challenged by both an increasingly trans-imperial trade and the expansion of rival empires, including the new United States. This trans-imperial trade worked, despite Spanish restrictions. In these practicalities, the resiliency in the Bourbon New Orleans economy bears comparison to that of Buenos Aires/Montevideo during the same period.

However, New Orleans was probably the most prolonged and open Spanish participant in trans-imperial trade, given that the United States so dominated the city's trade. Much of the produce reaching New Orleans from upriver was actually from the western United States; that produce and Spanish produce alike were then traded for goods mostly brought by US vessels and sailors and shipped to the rest of the world via US ports. The New Orleans trade, then, was almost circular, from the United States to New Orleans to the United States— and the Spanish city was merely a well-placed halfway point.

It is not surprising, then, that the Bourbon attempts to control the city's trade from both upriver and the Atlantic world were relatively unsuccessful. That world had been dramatically changed by the American Revolution and subsequent US expansion into both the North American heartland and, at sea, into the Caribbean and Gulf of Mexico. Like Prince Ursino's companion in *The Painter of Dishonour*, the governors in Louisiana found themselves "out of step with the world"—a world in which they no longer controlled trade or its most basic requirements.

The late-eighteenth-century trans-imperial Atlantic world can be viewed as might a merchant or a dutiful Bourbon governor—through the prism of four essential requirements for trade: access to raw produce and/or manufactured goods, a means of transportation, current information, and a source of capital. The governors in New Orleans, and perhaps other Bourbon governors in other colonies as well, attempted to control all four of these requirements to meet the political and financial needs of the empire. Consequently, the challenges they faced in imposing such control, their willingness to adapt to new economic realities, and the opportunities and dangers those adaptations presented to the larger empire may all be glimpsed in New Orleans.

ACCESS TO RAW PRODUCE AND MANUFACTURED GOODS

In order to trade, any merchant must have access to both raw produce and manufactured goods. However, such access may be impaired by vagaries of supply and demand, caused by drought, floods, pestilence, and even war. The merchants of Spanish America, like those of any other time, had no voice in such distant events. However, each day, they faced a much more mundane impediment to their access—bureaucracy and taxation. This impediment, at least, the merchants of New Orleans could—and did—work around, with perhaps more success than other Spanish merchants of their day.

Charles IV signed the Treaty of San Lorenzo, or Pinckney's Treaty, in 1794, permitting Spanish trade with the United States, including riverine trade, which would be funneled via a deposit system of warehouses and customs duties.[2] However, it was only in April 1798 that the Spanish authorities in New Orleans established a Guarda Almacén (a royal warehouse) into which goods from upriver (whether Spanish or American) would be transferred for purposes of taxation, then carefully controlled for proper exportation.

In theory, the Spanish warehousing of incoming goods from upriver provided an important service to the merchant community—it provided royal protection of goods, standardized weighing of those goods, and ensured some documentation in the event of fire or spoilage, both of which were certainly possible in New Orleans. The resultant documentation also meant that Spanish authorities would be cognizant of just how much potential wealth in raw materials and agricultural products was passing through the city, and where that wealth was coming from. Similarly, the warehouse records should have revealed the ebbs and flows of upriver goods into the city, in this case by date, owner, origin and composition of the goods (when noted), and the number of breakouts in any particular shipment.

In reality, the Spanish records themselves indicate that this Guarda Almacén system broke down immediately, with serious economic ramifications for the city and the Bourbon project in Louisiana. The Guarda Almacén system was simply too bureaucratic and slow, and it discouraged the very trade required by the city's merchants and desired by the Bourbon tax officials.

A single shipment from upriver, for example, was warehoused on 30 April 1798 for Guillermo Lintot, a merchant/planter in Natchez, an area only recently annexed into the Mississippi Territory of the United States. Lintot's shipment included forty-seven individual shipments (breakouts) weighing a total of 12,797 pounds—an average of 272 pounds each, mostly if not all cotton. The Spanish administrative system was built on such produce going out in only one lot, to a single company or monopoly in Spain. But Spain did not have cotton mills, and Lintot's cotton was instead split into multiple lots for multiple merchants and purposes, to at least three different merchants—Pedro Baylly, David Ross, and Daniel Clark. Some was meant for Clark's store but in the care of Bartolomé Bosque, implying that the latter merchant already had a customer, perhaps in Spain or Spanish America. Some was shipped on the *goleta Americana,* more on the *Dos Hermanos* (which was already carrying Clark's cotton from a previous shipment), some on the *Amistad* (with more of Clark's cotton, also purchased in Natchez), and some on the brigantine *Franklin* bound for Wilmington.[3]

The reader must imagine the time, effort, and paperwork required to unload, weigh, register, store, and then later ship so many individual shipments. To further complicate the work, of course, were these multiple breakouts of produce and goods once they were *in* the warehouse, as seen with the Lintot cotton. Loads leaving had to be broken apart in some cases and reweighed, renumbered, documented, and sent out of the warehouse. All of this would have seemed a bit maddening to American, British, and French shipowners and merchants who routinely shipped large consignments from eastern ports to European cotton and tobacco exchanges. The madness would only improve when merchants agreed to accept standardized evaluations of cotton, sugar, or tobacco—"common," "middling," "prime," "first quality," and so forth—and accept that the cotton or tobacco they received was not necessarily that of a particular grower, but rather merely that provided by the merchant. But that improvement would only evolve in the 1790s through the 1840s, long after the Spanish era in New Orleans.[4]

In the meantime, the Spanish had devised an economic net of paperwork from which the Americans both upriver and on the eastern seaboard seemed unable to escape. What is also astounding is how little of this paperwork was standardized by the use of printed forms. Almost all Spanish archives consist of documents that were laboriously handwritten, in a variety of cursive styles, some almost medieval in their lettering, and others flowing and clear. The Spanish bureaucracy simply could not—perhaps would not—stop writing, and quite unnecessarily. Rafael Perdomo, for example, in his 1789 register of vessel arrivals, insisted on spelling out even dates and quantities rather than using digits, and thus hiding key information in a cloud of text.[5] The resulting tension between bureaucratic desires (and probably job security) expressed in script and the commercial desires expressed in print and ledger books is palpable in the records of New Orleans. This was truly a tension within the Bourbon system—the many products and materials from the Mississippi River Valley flowing into New Orleans and being trapped for days and weeks in a paper net of Spanish script.

However, there were at least three other models for the Bourbon administrators in New Orleans to follow. One was the business ledger system used so assiduously by the American and British merchants in the city. These lined, printed ledgers were in simple, modern formats, with columns, rows, and asterisked notations. When a merchant died, his creditors often submitted the relevant pages from their ledgers to the probate court, and these ledger pages, which can be found in most probate successions in Spanish New Orleans, are the best evidence that Spanish officials in that city were aware of a much easier way to manage commerce and, for their purposes, taxation.

A second model was that of British and American port officials, who were already using printed forms for ship entries and departures. Clearly, Spanish officials were aware of these forms because a few may still be found in the archives from Louisiana and Cuba.[6]

Finally, a third administrative model was that of the Spanish colonial military, with which most Spanish officials were intimately familiar, given their often dual roles as officers and administrators. While customs, warehouse, and postal administrators spent long hours on lengthy, handwritten records, military officers assigned to New Orleans were already using printed forms and spreadsheet ledgers by 1795. Indeed, officials from New Orleans forwarded two samples of printed spreadsheets to authorities in Cuba to demonstrate how bookkeeping could be improved within the Americas.[7] The military service records compiled by Carondelet in June 1796 in a printed format demonstrate how efficient Spanish administrators could be when they used then-emerging business practices.[8] Dr. Antonio Sanchez de Mora of the Archivo General de Indias argues that the Bourbon-era military forms clearly provide evidence that "renovation of the Spanish system was coming from the colonies."[9]

In any case, it was not merely Spanish royal decrees, hurricanes, fires, and naval blockades that played havoc with trade in New Orleans—it was paperwork that also clogged the river. The Spanish insistence on unloading flatboats, warehousing and documenting every breakout of cargo, then reloading that cargo with additional documentation significantly burdened the city's merchants, shipowners, and upriver sources.

However, the American willingness to use *vecindad* as a tool to bypass the net of Spanish bureaucracy and taxation challenged the Bourbon concepts of absolutism and mercantilism that were so effective in ports like Veracruz. The merchants of Spanish New Orleans also sought their own economic goals by similarly bypassing Spanish controls over shipping, information, and capital.

ACCESS TO SHIPPING

Once raw produce and manufactured goods reached New Orleans, they required transport, whether downriver past the Balize ("the Buoy," a remote Spanish post) and on to the ports of the Caribbean, North America, and Europe, or upriver to Spanish and American plantations, farms, mines, settlements, and trading posts. The Bourbon Spanish, in their desire to control this transport, had some advantages—large shipments could only be brought in over a dangerous mud bar at the mouth of the river, guarded by the Balize. There were, however, at least two routes to move smaller cargoes to and even past the city, one via Lake Pontchartrain and Bayou St. Jean at the rear of the city, and the other via Grand Isle and the Barataria swamp. The Spanish generally succeeded in controlling these access points, but that success may have been less their own and more that of British prize cruisers and French privateers.[10]

Therefore, it was relatively simple for Spanish authorities to control shipping into the city. The difficulty was that the Spanish had relatively few ships of their own in which to transport produce and goods about the vast empire, much less to trade with the most logical customer, the new United States, or the most powerful economically, the French, Dutch, and British. Therefore, most of the trade of New Orleans—indeed, the overwhelming majority—was carried in vessels from the United States.

Consequently, the Spanish focused upon ensuring that only its imperial *vecinos* were permitted to conduct trade with foreign nations. Merchants in New Orleans were therefore sometimes required to prove that they were indeed *vecinos* of Louisiana. Such was the case with the well-known Miguel Fortier, who was ordered in 1783 to provide proof to Intendant Navarro "that he is a resident in this colony" before being permitted to land a vessel from France. Fortier cannily presented three Spaniards as his witnesses to testify that he had been "a resident and a merchant of this colony for about ten years," and Navarro approved the petition.[11]

Luis Depeaux had been in the city fewer years than Fortier and, perhaps because he was less confident than Fortier, brought five witnesses, including two Italians and the well-known planter/merchant Jean Gravier to testify that he was "a devout Roman Catholic, resident and merchant of this City." Dupeaux's petition reported that "he has resided and is established in business in this City for more than three years, which is the required period for legalization."

Dupeaux's petition clearly stated that the residency requirement to be considered a *vecino* was three years, as did similar petitions by Legret, LeMoyne, and Dousset. However, Francisco Gallart's petition reported that he had resided and worked in the city for only "more than two years," and he was duly recognized by the probate court as a *vecino*. However, a merchant might be resident in the city but still considered a *vecino* and a resident of somewhere else. Such a case was that of Lafita/Lafite, who the probate court considered to be both "a merchant of the City of Burdeos [Bordeaux] and a resident of this City [New Orleans]."[12]

Beyond restricting who could trade from New Orleans, the Spanish also attempted on numerous occasions to restrict trade from the city to a limited number of Spanish ports. However, the merchants of Spanish New Orleans, like many in other Spanish cities, often responded by simply diverting their ships beyond the imperial restrictions and asking forgiveness later, occasionally with rather unbelievable excuses.

For example, Juan Helay, the master of the brigantine *Hercules* sought to exonerate himself legally from liability in early 1785, after he diverted a ship filled with fruit bound from Havana to New Orleans (a northbound route) to Guárico (in Venezuela, and a decidedly southbound route). He reported that he had "encountered inclement weather and suffered other misfortunes on the high seas." The New Orleans Probate Court exonerated him. Three weeks later, the court exonerated Don Antonio Argote, the owner of the frigate *La Matilde*, and the vessel's captain, Agustin Crespo. *La Matilde* had sailed from Santiago de Cuba (on the southern side of the island) bound north for New Orleans, but "suffered heavy damages on the high seas, and its Captain was forced to approach land at the port of Philadelphia"—quite a long distance from Cuba or New Orleans! A perhaps more believable and much more detailed account is that of the captain of the brigantine *San Antonio,* who sailed from San Fernando de Omoa (a fortress in Honduras) on 19 July 1786 for San Fernando de Cádiz in western Spain. Captain Juan Bautista Albella reported that, well into the trip, "the wind increased violently causing said brigantine to drift a period of six days and that the navigator and other members of the crew became very ill with 'certain epidemic.'" However, they sailed the *San Antonio* until they reached what the crew believed to be La Tortuga (a small island north of Haiti), then turned north for St. Augustine, Florida, for food and assistance. Instead the crew found themselves at Barataria Bay, west of New Orleans, and arrived in the city on 28 August. Again, the New Orleans Probate Court exonerated the captain of all liability.

A final example of people getting around the rules is that of Juan Pedro Blanco, a merchant of New Orleans and captain of the corvette *La Petit Julia*. He reported to the probate court that he sailed from New Orleans to Bordeaux, France, but "through no fault of his own nor of the crew, went aground several times and encountered stormy weather, all of which caused considerable damage to said vessel and forced it to seek refuge in the port of Marseilles, where it was repaired and from whence it has returned to New Orleans." Once again, the probate court exonerated the captain of all liability.[13]

Clearly, the claims by ship captains that they had diverted south around Cuba to Venezuela, missed New Orleans but reached Philadelphia (thus bypassing most of the eastern seaboard of the United States), confused Florida with Barataria (a smuggler's haven), and somehow sailed past Spain and far into the Mediterranean to reach succor were simply fairy tales spun by captains intent on getting around Spanish trade regulations and accepted by Spanish probate courts/ governors in Louisiana to ensure such trade continued. These shipping practices, meant to circumvent royal restrictions on trade, were in fact similar to those used by the merchants and captains of the Rio Plata in the same period. Fabricio Prado reported that ships from Montevideo frequently used "the traditional right to emergency landing, referred to as *arribada forzoza* in Spanish law, as a pretext to admit foreign vessels in their ports and to enter foreign ports, mostly on the Brazilian coast." The ships from Montevideo especially began using this obvious ploy after 1777 to transfer goods and slaves between Portuguese Brazil and Spanish Montevideo, in what Prado has labeled "trans-imperial cooperation."[14]

However, "trans-imperial cooperation" was not always desired by Spanish authorities and, for whatever reason, ploys sometimes did not work and New Orleans merchants were found guilty of smuggling or trading in contraband. For example, in charges were filed in late 1787 to early 1788 against several unidentified merchants, probably American, accused of smuggling. However, two days after the great conflagration of 21 March 1788, a royal decree was issued to pardon all those found guilty of contraband, and this order was conveyed to the public in Louisiana by a Lopez Armesto letter dated 13 July that year.[15] Apparently the services of the accused smugglers were required again.

The Spanish government did exercise yet another form of control over shipping in New Orleans—it inspected vessels to determine seaworthiness. Such inspections, of course, seem to the modern eye to be for safety purposes, but meant much more to colonial authorities, given that the economy was so dependent upon reliable shipping. When ships or cargoes disappeared, sank, damaged, or were seized by pirates, a foreign navy, creditors, or Spanish officials, a Spanish probate official was expected to make a determination on fault and/ or reparations. Consequently, probate officials were also frequently to report on the seaworthiness of the vessel involved in any particular case. To speak authoritatively, Bourbon probate judges in New Orleans utilized Arnaldo Magnon as an official vessel inspector until 1783, when he was replaced by Pedro Visoso.[16]

Finally, for overland trade with the native American tribes, the Spanish required passports. Loison, for example, was granted a passport so that he might

> travel safely at will and . . . trade in the territory of Alabama, in the village to be assigned to him by the Commander of the post of Mobile, with the understanding that he will conform himself to the trade regulations in effect there concerning dealings with the Indians.
>
> He will see that the said Indians be devoted to the Great King of Spain, procuring by all possible means, to inspire in them the veneration and respect they owe to our Monarch and under no circumstances nor pretext will use, in the said dealings, the services of Englishmen or Americans, employing only Spanish subjects who are well known to this Province.[17]

Loison was restricted to trading "in the village to be assigned to him." He was also expected not only to obey royal trade regulations, but also to ensure that the Indians in his assigned village venerate the Spanish king and, of course, only employ Spanish subjects. In the Spanish empire, even overland trade was regulated, albeit not taxed, and it was a form of paperwork, the passport, that permitted that regulation. The New Orleans Probate Court also used passports as leverage over debtors, and could deny such a passport, as it did for José Boyoval, who wished to travel to Pointe Coupee for business but still owed money in the city.[18]

ACCESS TO INFORMATION

Merchants must have also quick and ready access to information, especially in a world of burgeoning free trade. In this, the merchants of Spanish New Orleans were no different from merchants in Baltimore, London, or Cádiz; indeed, they were in competition (or perhaps competitive cooperation) with those cities to get the best possible price for exports like cotton and tobacco and imported manufactured goods. The primary destination for most of the city's trade was not within the Spanish empire—it was to British North America or the United States. Accordingly, the merchants of New Orleans required the most speedy news available on markets not only on the eastern seaboard (where much of their cotton and tobacco were shipped), but also on the final markets for those commodities, that is, Great Britain, the Netherlands, and France. The merchants also required timely news from Spain and France, given the fickleness of Spanish economic and foreign policy in the later Bourbon period under Charles IV, whose *cédulas* could mean life or constriction to commerce, agriculture, and even a costly war.

The Spanish governors would have liked very much to control the flow of information and news into the colonial capital at New Orleans. However, the colony was simply too vast for such control and, more importantly, there were multiple paths for news into the city, from four primary sources—the new United States, Great Britain, France, and Spain itself.

Market information and news of potential economic impact (treaties, machinations, and war) could be quickly acquired by the city's merchants via their American shipping connections. American ships arrived constantly in New Orleans, and each presumably brought newspapers and letters. Correspondence could also be exchanged with merchants upriver, especially in Pittsburgh, but river traffic then was slow, and overland traffic, without post roads (such as the later Natchez Trace) and through tribal territories, was dangerous and unlikely.

British warships and merchant ships increasingly controlled the Atlantic and Caribbean, and many vessels traveled from Jamaica into or near New Orleans.[19] However, the British were often at war with Spain, and perhaps spent more time blockading or menacing New Orleans than actually reaching it.

French ships arrived with news, but such news was probably often dated and of limited use—ship captains from Bordeaux and Bayonne had limited access to or interest in news from London or the Netherlands, and often stopped at waypoints in St. Domingue, Guadeloupe, or other island colonies before arriving in New Orleans, thus delaying the currency of their information. Pierre Clément de Laussat, the incoming French governor of Louisiana, for example, received official confirmation of the Louisiana Purchase (and thus a rather sudden change in his career) only two months after he had heard rumors of the agreement and four months after the treaty was signed.[20]

Spanish officials needed their own reliable, official information system, and they received that information from Spain via the Correos—the postal service. Indeed, if the Spanish empire was likened to a human body, then the Correos was its central nervous system, and while the brain might (or might not) have been in Madrid, certainly all of the official nerves were centered in Havana. To this extent, New Orleans was not at all in the Bourbon periphery—it was actually quite close to the central nerve center of the empire in Havana—and it had its own unofficial system running back to Philadelphia, New York, and beyond to London.[21]

The archives in Seville fortunately hold all of Havana's postal records for the years 1765 to 1835,[22] and thus provide great and untapped historical detail on the flow of information throughout the Spanish empire. The central Correos in Havana was exceedingly busy; dozens of ships passed through Havana each month, dropping off and picking up mail packets. The Correos made 222,405 *reales* in 1795 alone, mostly in general charges (199,297 4/8), but also a notable amount from the sale of official seals and stamps (*sellados y franqueacon*, 21,757 4/8). The Correos also provided a minor service for certifying documents (*certificado*), similar to what a notary would provide.

From there, the mail was distributed to numerous cities in 1795. Only three of these cities were on the Spanish peninsula, and of these, only Cádiz received notable amounts of mail.[23] Within the hemisphere, Havana shared mail with twenty other cities; three of them (Peru, Lima, and Montevideo) were quite distant. Mail for Peru presumably actually was going to Lima and then inland, similar to how mail to what is now modern-day Mexico was divided into Mexico proper (certainly the city), Veracruz, and Campeche.

New Orleans, like about a dozen other Spanish cities in the northern empire, had its own *estafeta*, a sub-post office that in turn distributed mail to subsidiary towns in the province. New Orleans was certainly not on the empire's information periphery; the archives indicate that mail was delivered from Havana rather regularly, roughly every week. The postmaster for New Orleans in the 1790s was Pedro Marín Argote.[24] By comparison, Governor Carondelet, in his previous posting as governor of El Salvador, would have received mail from Havana or Spain only every two to four weeks, if that often, via ship to Veracruz, then overland (mostly by foot couriers) via Oaxaca and Nueva Guatemala.[25]

The Havana postal service also kept records of how many *gazetas* (newspapers) they received; by one accounting, 5,600 in 1796 and, by another accounting, 6,569. Oddly, almost half of those were of issues 71 through 77, evidently of the royally operated *Gaceta de Madrid,* which was published in those very numbers in September that year (1796), with more for October. The implication was that, for some reason, the *Gaceta* became more important to send to New Orleans in September 1796 than perhaps earlier. Other *gazetas* never reached the city, lost in a shipping accident in La Coruna. While the *Gaceta de Madrid* was an official newspaper, its receipt in Cuba and subsequent distribution was clearly a matter of some note, perhaps pride, in the postal service.

The postal authorities in Havana played a central role in the distribution of *gazetas,* in this case, the officially sanctioned news, throughout the Spanish empire. The account of postal fees earned for that distribution covered fourteen different key Spanish cities or regions, clearly the nodes for Spanish news: Puerto Rico, Santo Domingo, Campeche, Veracruz, Floridas/Louisiana (that is, New Orleans), Mexico (City), Guatemala (City), Panama, Portovelo (on the northern coast of modern-day Panama), Cartagena, Caracas, Santa Fe (on the central northern coast of modern-day Venezuela), Guayra (La Guaira, capital of present-day Vargas state in Venezuela and a key port for Caracas), and even distant Quito. The remainder were presumably handled via a postal office in Buenos Aires, which would have in turn handled Montevideo, Santiago, Lima, Asunción, and Potosi.

The distribution of these *gazetas* earned the Havana post office 2,362 *reales* in 1796. Of this amount, New Orleans, the capital of the Floridas and Louisiana, spent a startling 894 *reales*—38 percent of the total spent on *gazetas* in the northern Spanish empire. By comparison, Mexico City spent 638 *reales* (27 percent) and Veracruz, a much smaller port, 384 (16 percent). The other cities and regions spent far less, including Cartagena, 125 (5 percent); Guatemala, 93 (4 percent); and Santa Fe, 93 (4 percent).[26] While officials in New Orleans would have further distributed *gazetas* to Baton Rouge, Natchez, St. Louis, Mobile, Pensacola, St. Augustine, and other locations, clearly the printer's share were being read in the political and economic capital, New Orleans itself.

The annual postal report for 1798, however, reveals the inconsistency at the heart of the Spanish bureaucratic system. While the postal reports for 1796, for example, are relatively easy to understand and flow logically, the report for 1798 splits, intermixes, or even omits previously documented revenues, including those from Louisiana, without logical explanation. Nothing was missing from the individual *estafetas,* which continued their normal, exhaustive documentation process; indeed, the final, central report on top of those *estafeta* compilations is still bound together with the thick, now-faded blue or brown strings (like a modern-day wide shoestring) running through a single large hole in the top left of each page, tied together by a bureaucrat two centuries ago. But the overall report from Havana and its numbers simply don't make sense compared with those of previous overall reports.[27]

Fortunately, Pedro Marin Argote remained the postal officer in New Orleans, and his records remain in the same clear format as before, with overall and monthly reports. He reported that in 1798 he had imported 1,700 gacetas, 110 mercurios, and 31 guias "to benefit this administration and that of Pensacola" and that he drew a new profit from this importation, duly noted in his monthly reports. He had sent 200 gacetas, 4 mercurios, and 6 guias to Pensacola, an implication that New Orleans, however, remained the primary destination of incoming newspapers and consequently the source of his very small profit.[28]

There was no mail service to or from foreign ports in the Spanish Western Hemisphere, so New Orleans merchants were also forced to develop their own informal international mail routes via a loose network of ship captains or factors and partners in foreign ports. Among these, Bartolomé Bosch communicated via Bofarull, Bosch i Comp. of Barcelona, Spain, a company with long ties to his native Palma Mallorca, as well as with Bofarull and Carbonell in Cartagena. Pitot wrote his Observations for Begouen, Demeaux and Cie in Le Havre, France. Even the Americans had their own sources in Spain: the well-connected Beverly Chew returned to New Orleans in 1801 "from Bilbo [Bilbao, Spain] after a voyage of three years." Chew joined forces there with the Philadelphian Richard Relf, who was already working with Daniel Clark and who had married Gertrude Quinones, the daughter of a Spanish official.[29]

Often such routes were handled by the appropriate foreign consul. Given the importance of timely market data and international news to merchants, it is easy to comprehend why merchants greatly desired to have foreign consuls established in their capital cities, and why they were also willing to bear the burden (and some honor) of being a foreign consul. This reasoning helps explain why even French and Spanish merchants of New Orleans were so adamant in their 1796 petition that a US consul be established in that city and why senior Spanish officials in both Cuba and Louisiana opposed such a consul.

At least as early as 1796, the merchants of Spanish New Orleans feared that "los Americanos poco a poco señoreándose de toda la Luisiana" (the Americans little by little lord over all of Louisiana); official correspondence, even that written by the governor of Cuba, the marqués de Someruelos, referred to the migrants, merchants, visitors, sailors—indeed, the entirety of the United

States and other Anglophones as well—as "los Americanos." The Americans were extremely well placed for commercial domination of New Orleans; they were led by their merchants, including men like Daniel Clark and Evan Jones, who were both citizens of the United States and *vecinos* within Spain and thus enjoyed exemption from Spanish imposts. The export produce so vital for the city's life came downriver from the American farmers, some in US territory, some in Spanish political control—for the moment. Most of the city's imports now came upriver from the United States.

The Americans also had access to new sources of capital from both England and American seaports like Baltimore, Philadelphia, New York, and Boston. They had many vessels of every shape and size and dominated the levees in New Orleans; indeed, the Spanish authorities in Philadelphia probably had learned of former New Orleans merchant James Rumsey's test of a steamboat in 1787. The new United States of America had studiously avoided entanglement in the European wars (save for a brief naval fight with France) and could be seen as neutral or even as allies of every nation. The new US Constitution also encouraged a free-wheeling commerce across state lines without internal taxation—a substantial advantage over the Spanish empire and especially Spain itself, which was still contorted commercially by internal taxation between provinces and even cities. Finally, the United States also had a postal service that efficiently moved vast numbers of newspapers and letters.[30] In a word, the chances of Spain competing economically with the United States in its own colony of Louisiana were very quickly dwindling to nothing.

Now US-based merchants simply needed to establish their own representative, a formally recognized consul, in the port of New Orleans. Such a consul would not only ensure the quick communication of prices for both commodities and manufactured goods, but could also smooth over any difficulties with Spanish officials, assist sick or wayward citizens, encourage migrants to continue upriver to US lands, and provide invaluable intelligence to the US government. All of these purposes were exactly why Spanish authorities in Havana were so adamantly opposed to permitting such a consul in New Orleans.

Governor Carondelet had reportedly urged the establishment of "a consular court," which would be empowered to consider complaints by foreign consuls on business and maritime issues. Jacques Pitot, who supported such a court, wrote that "the dilatory tactics of lower courts cannot be tolerated" and was much frustrated by the lack of interest among merchants who "had acquired the habit of scheming in the midst of a monopoly system's impediments."[31] Daniel

Clark the younger evidently served as an informal US consul during this period, but in 1799, the US secretary of state nominated John Morton ("Juan Morton" in Spanish correspondence) as consul in New Orleans.

The Marqués de Someruelos wrote from Havana on 27 September 1799 to Acting Governor Vidal, warning of Morton's nomination. The marqués reported that he was contesting the appointment to the royal court on the grounds of precedent (there had been no consul before) and other reasons, and was insisting to the court that Americans in Louisiana would receive quick administration of justice by his own tribunals. He told Vidal to on no account permit Morton to conduct activity as a consul in that city, despite Morton's orders from the US president. Someruelos considered the Americans perfectly capable of diplomatic subterfuge, and so he added a note in his own writing, warning Vidal to not permit Morton or any other to serve as *vice* consul, as well.[32]

Someruelos wrote a month later to the royal court, reporting that another American claiming to be the consul in New Orleans, Evan Jones, was in fact a Spanish militia captain; Someruelos was concerned that Jones could not serve two masters—both the Spanish as a militia officer and the *Americanos* as a consul. Someruelos's concern was logical: permitting the American representative to lead Spanish troops certainly offered a threat of potential revolt. Moreover, Someruelos wrote that Jones was "ambitious, and so are the Americans—nearly all commerce is going in their ships." Someruelos consequently wrote that "he could not compromise regarding the resolution to obey the King literally on his order of 3 Sept 1799.[33]

It seems that, from the Spanish perspective, at least the Marqués de Casa-Calvo and Governor Someruelos in Havana de facto agreed to the establishment of an American consul, while perhaps not formally doing so. Subsequently, the Spanish also referred to "Don Diego" Murphy as the US vice consul in New Orleans, and Laussat reported that the US vice consul (at this time, perhaps Daniel Clark) attended a banquet on Easter Monday in 1803.[34] It is likely that the title of "vice consul," provisional as it might be, permitted both Spanish authorities and American merchants the opportunity to cooperate without Spanish royal approval, as Someruelos had hinted.

ACCESS TO CAPITAL

Finally, the Louisiana colony required capital for development—and there was sometimes precious little to be had for the Bourbon governors, not only in

Louisiana, but throughout the Spanish empire. The late Bourbon government spent huge sums for war, issued interest-bearing bonds (*vales reales*), assigned colonial revenues for war loans, requested and often required loans from elites, increased taxes,[35] manipulated trade policies, established and reassigned state monopolies, and generally complicated any efforts by merchants, miners, and other *vecinos* to accumulate lasting wealth and invest it in their own business infrastructure or opportunities.

This is not to say that the Bourbons did not spend their silver and gold in the American colonies; most American revenues remained in the Western Hemisphere.[36] Much of the revenue was not only spent on fortifications, soldiers, cathedrals, and *cabildos,* but also on market buildings and warehouses—logical investments for future trade. However, the Louisiana colony, repeatedly struck by weather and fire, may have been considered a poor environment for official Bourbon investment—and so it seems most of the imperial money spent there was for rather unimpressive fortifications, soldiers (including the regiment from Mexico), royal vessels, and administrative salaries. When Governor Carondelet wished to establish street lighting in New Orleans, he funded it not with existing Bourbon funds but instead with a tax on chimneys. It was a private donor, Almonaster, not a Bourbon governor, who built the still-extant St. Louis Cathedral.

Spain, England, and France were often at war with each other during the late Bourbon era; Spain, therefore, had limited funds for investment in Louisiana, and neither England nor France would divert scarce capital to support a Spanish colony. The French and Spanish merchants of Spanish New Orleans remained fixated upon acquiring capital, but none was to be had during this tumultuous era, and French and Spanish investors were much more inclined to invest in sugar on either Guadeloupe or Cuba, as did British investors in Jamaica. (All three nations invested in sugar in St. Domingue, and all three lost their investments in the long and painful course of that colony's revolution.) In any case, the Bourbon viceroys and governors throughout Spanish America had the political, military, and social authority to limit the source, amount, and nature of financial investment in their own colonies—except in Louisiana and its capital of New Orleans.[37]

What perhaps made New Orleans *sui generis* within the Spanish imperial economy was not the problem—the lack of capital for investment—instead, it was the pervasive presence of a solution outside the control of the Spanish governor—American capital. Through merchants like Clark, Mather, and Dunbar, American, English, and Dutch capital could reach both the plantations of Spanish Louisiana and the city itself, in the latter case not through the building of major government infrastructure, but instead through the construction of basic commercial infrastructure (such as warehouses and stores) and the funding, operation, repair, and eventual building of vessels to carry the produce of the river.

The American and British merchants in New Orleans had their own preferred investments (plantations and ships) and their own sources of capital. American merchants drew early upon prominent British and Dutch bankers, but the First Bank of the United States, proposed by Alexander Hamilton, was chartered in 1791 and physically completed in Philadelphia in 1797, and Americans like Clark and Jones could begin drawing on that bank (and other banks along the US eastern seaboard) as well. American capital admittedly only moved into the city gradually, because it was being spent instead in the movement across the Appalachians and down the Mississippi, especially for acquisition, speculation, and development of tracts sometimes far upriver from New Orleans. Merchants like Clark, probably wary of Spanish policy, albeit friendly with Spanish governors, were also probably wise to invest in their own properties, away from effective Spanish control.

The American ready access to capital came via letters of exchange, those indispensable eighteenth-century/early nineteenth-century equivalents to a modern bank check that could be transferred about as if real currency, albeit based upon a system of trust and mutual economic stability. These letters of exchange were extremely useful because they permitted easy spot purchases of commercial goods and produce on either end of the exchange. A merchant in Philadelphia, upon learning of a glut in cotton in the New Orleans warehouses, could easily and relatively quickly convey directions to an associate in New Orleans to purchase a shipload or two of cotton at low prices with a letter of credit, especially if he had previously entrusted that associate with the letter. At the same time, that associate in New Orleans could later sell an incoming cargo of foodstuffs, blankets, and farm tools to an upriver plantation owner in return for another letter of credit, perhaps a letter from the very same merchant in Philadelphia!

The French and Spanish were much more constrained in their use of such letters, given the unstable financial situation in both nations and the physical distance from their major associates in Bordeaux and Cádiz. Therefore, it is unsurprising that some wanted to ship currency back to Europe for new investments (including outfitting slave ships) and personal uses (education of children, for example) while others, especially those with American or British connections, wanted to keep currency inside the colony.

Jacques Pitot had noted the relative scarcity of silver in the city despite current Spanish restrictions, and blamed some of that scarcity on "the tacit consent of local officials and the court," claiming this prohibition was "advantageous only to the guardians of the customhouse who must be bribed." The merchants' petition of 31 August 1796 stated, "it would be worthwhile to grant the *gracia* solicited by these leaders and this body of commerce, to be permitted to export, based upon a modest contribution, the silver money so necessary to invigorate mercantile speculations."[38]

However, the merchants' petition of 22 February 1797, like Darcantel's 1789 letter, had focused on keeping hard specie inside the colony and better governing the use of paper currency. Both of these petitions were mostly signed by merchants of French ancestry.[39] The disagreements between French merchants on what to do about a currency scarcity are understandable—they had no ready access to capital for "mercantile speculations" or commercial improvements, unless they became slave traders (which some of them were indeed). There was no longer any French capital available from revolution-wracked St. Domingue, nor from war-wracked France.

What happened in the New Orleans economy after the American annexation provides a mere hint of how much capital the American merchants might have had access to during the Spanish era. In the nine years between the American annexation in late 1803 and 1812, the merchant/planters of New Orleans formed eight corporations, including *four* banks: the Bank of Louisiana (1804), the New Orleans branch of the First Bank of the United States (1805), the Bank of New Orleans (1811), the Louisiana Planters Bank (1811), as well as the New Orleans Insurance Company (1805), the New Orleans Water Company (1811), the New Orleans Navigation Company (1805), and the Mississippi Steamboat Navigation Company (1812). The North American merchants not only established new banks, but also insurance, transportation, and a host of major and minor infrastructure projects. Their capitalization alone was close to three million dollars. This capital was "unimpressive" compared to that enjoyed by American merchants on the East Coast such as Stephen Girard, but "as consequential in a small universe as a large input in a large universe."[40]

CONCLUSION

As in other imperial ports, although the Spanish government attempted to regulate the mercantile business of New Orleans, it faced serious challenges. Its attempts to centralize and tax foreign access to raw produce (via fees and an intrusive, bureaucratic, and clumsy warehousing system) and domestic access to manufactured goods (via tariffs) were subverted by dual-citizenship, Anglophone *vecinos* like Clark and Mather. Similarly, these merchants were able to skirt and even flaunt the occasional regulations on foreign shipping, because war and economic competition were slowly sweeping Spanish vessels from the Mid-Atlantic and Caribbean. Nor does it seem likely that the usual Spanish control of information via its postal system and officially sanctioned newspapers (*gazetas*) was effective; the Anglophones simply established a US vice consul, and the Spanish authorities found themselves obligated to concur. Finally, the Spanish exercised little control over the capital funds being expended in their own capital city—much of the silver in Mexico was being funneled to the Bourbon king and his wars. Consequently, it was the Anglophones, particularly US citizens, who controlled the flow of capital into the city, and quite possibly the flow of hard silver out as well. And because of the Anglophone merchants (and despite the governors), the northern march of the Spanish empire, managed in New Orleans, was a full participant in a trans-imperial, Atlantic world of interlinking merchants, trade, access, shipping, information, and capital.

Spain might have used this trade to its own imperial and economic advantage, by permanently establishing free trade (especially in Veracruz), reopening the slave trade, and encouraging an influx of American-British capital. Indeed, the merchants of New Orleans called for such moves in the merchant petition of 1797. But those merchants also recognized that Charles IV and the Bourbon monopolist economy would not change, and so they spent warily, even after the Mississippi River was opened. They temporized, working around the Bourbon system, acquiring Spanish *vecindad*, land, plantations, slaves, and distant business connections. In early 1803, it became clear that Louisiana would become French or American, and only then did the merchants throw themselves wholeheartedly into trade, and the economy truly begin to boom.

The opportunity was always there, in New Orleans, for the Bourbons to create a new, bustling economy within the Caribbean—but they could not exceed their own conceptual and political limitations. They still saw the Louisiana colony as a border area and not as a potential new center and model for a reinvigorated Spanish empire. In the end, the Bourbons saw only challenges, and not opportunities.

5

Literacy in a Spanish Imperial City

To travelers I'll be an epitaph,
since my face, lifeless, will declare to them:
"It was Love's triumph to make war on me."
—Francisco de Quevedo, *Surrender of an Exiled Lover*

The chameleon-like population of Spanish New Orleans understood the events that shaped their colonial world because many of them were literate and read about those events. Indeed, statistical and practical evidence indicates that New Orleans had reasonably high literacy rates among whites and probably free people of color long before the American annexation in 1803. These rates were reflected not only in basic literacy (as evidenced by signature analysis) but also in advanced literacy (as indicated in postmortem book lists).[1] The city's founders did not display significant scientific literacy, as displayed elsewhere in the Spanish, French, and British empires, but they did dabble in science.

Such basic and advanced literacy within the Spanish empire, as evidenced in New Orleans, greatly problematizes historical discussion of both literacy and political evolution in the Spanish empire. A level of literacy implies that political reading and discourse may have been more robust elsewhere in the Spanish empire than has been previously noted. New methodologies, however, may be used to develop further data on basic and advanced literacy within the empire. Only with such data can historians truly compare the impact of colonial and post-independence era education, the role of literacy in independence movements, the establishment of colonial and post-independence bureaucracy, and the spread of science and medicine.

LITERACY OR ILLITERACY IN SPANISH NEW ORLEANS:
A HISTORICAL CRITIQUE

The most frequently used evidence on literacy in Spanish New Orleans is found in the earliest official US report on the city, *An Account of Louisiana*, provided to Congress in 1803 following the Louisiana Purchase. That document claimed, "Not more than half of the inhabitants are supposed to be able to read and write, of whom not more than two hundred perhaps are able to do it well."[2]

This US government report was patently false—its source, merchant Daniel Clark, had only reported in his correspondence that "not above half the inhabitants can read or Write the *French* [*emphasis in original*], & not two hundred in the whole country with *correctness* [*emphasis in original*]." However, less than half the inhabitants were French, and the full question from the Jefferson administration and Clark's answer reveal something more complicated:

No. 22 What public Colleges and Schools have they, can the Inhabitants generally read & write; wht degree of information do they possess beyond that

Ansr There are no Colleges, & but one Public School, the Masters of this are paid by the King to teach children, the Spanish language only,— There a few private Childrens schools, not above half the inhabitants can read or Write the French, & not two hundred in the whole country with correctness—in general, their Knowledge extends little further, altho' they seem to have been endowed with a good natural genius & with an uncommon facility of learning any thing they apply to.

In the first sentence, Clark emphasized that public education was only in Spanish: he presumably did not expect the population would write French well. Indeed, having been taught Parisian French at Eton, Clark may have been a bit snobbish about the other "French" languages and colonial dialects spoken in New Orleans, which admittedly were not written "with correctness," according to his view.[3] Furthermore, Clark neglected to mention that the Ursuline nuns were also teaching children, and that the somewhat small city did not necessarily require a college at that time—college education was available in nearby Havana.

In fact, while some Spanish colonies presumably had low literacy rates, especially those with large indigenous or enslaved African populations whom Spanish colonial elites refused to educate, historians have presented little more than anecdotal evidence of such illiteracy among the populace of Spanish Louisiana or, for that matter, the broader Spanish America.[4] By contrast, significant levels of basic (signature) literacy have been documented in colonial St. Domingue (albeit a French colony); books, periodicals, and other printed materials were generally available within the Spanish empire; and Spanish universities in America may have issued as many as 150,000 degrees until 1810, with many of those degrees earned during the Bourbon period.[5]

In New Orleans itself, administrators, Catholic priests and nuns, and private teachers established a mixed education system, much as still exists in the city. Numerous men on the Spanish frontier bought, owned, and presumably read a wide variety of books, including some banned by the Inquisition, and its capital of New Orleans unsurprisingly had a middle class of literate professionals, merchants, shopkeepers, and sailors.[6]

The question of Spanish-era literacy in New Orleans, then, is useful in understanding not only the actual state of literacy within the late Spanish empire but also in understanding how French and American views shaped historical perceptions of Spain and its Louisiana colony. The question is also useful for understanding the challenges and opportunities literacy may have posed to Spanish rule, not only in New Orleans, but elsewhere in the empire. Given relatively high literacy among the city's white populace (and perhaps also among free people of color) and the great intellectual, scientific, and political ferment of the late eighteenth century, the challenges to a supposedly repressive Bourbon empire in busy ports like New Orleans, Havana, Veracruz, Cartagena, or Buenos Aires should seem evident.

LITERACY ANALYSIS: EMPIRICAL AND IMPERIAL DIFFERENCES

Unsurprisingly, at least some elites in New Orleans were literate and desired books: the French diplomat who governed Louisiana for three weeks in late 1803, Pierre Clément de Laussat, noted that, when he was forced to leave most of his "extensive library" in New Orleans, "A good number of books were easily given away, mostly the classics and some current works; the local people do not care for the sciences. One after another, I sold several of the dearest and most faithful companions of my life; it broke my heart to part with them."[7]

However, careful research indicates a much broader, daily literacy in Spanish New Orleans, to include simply signing one's name to notarial documents, the writing of receipts, the keeping of business ledgers, and the reading of newspapers. Focusing on three different aspects of New Orleans literacy during the Spanish era—basic, advanced, and scientific—will require varied sources and methods.[8]

By most historic standards, determining basic literacy within Spanish colonies is quite easy with existing colonial archives. F. W. Grubb reported in his classic article on colonial literacy, "Signature literacy is the only universal, standard, and direct measure available for the colonial period which provides a substantial quantity of evidence. Although a dichotomous measure, the ability to affix a signature is believed to correspond to a middle range of literacy skills or roughly the ability to read fluently."[9]

Within colonial structures, signatures on documents not only indicate who was writing his or her own name and how well, but also the *expectation* and *necessity* for various members within that structure, divided by class, racial, ethnic, or gender roles, to write their own names and write them well. Such signatures routinely appear in notarial, probate, and ecclesiastical records, civil petitions, and militia rosters. The Spanish-era New Orleans Notarial Archives, which comprise at least twenty thousand pages of handwritten documents, representing routine business transactions—sales, purchases, leases, powers of attorney, marriage contracts, wills, and manumissions—are an especially rich lode of such documents and are filled with thousands of signatures.

Beyond signature analysis, probate records of succession also provide a mundane but very reliable method to study basic, daily literacy: account books and bills. Most successions in the Spanish period include numerous detailed bills from creditors, and often entire pages, carefully composed and well written, removed from the ledgers of deceased or, much more often, from the merchants, small shopkeepers, hairdressers, chocolatiers, craftsmen, and even priests to whom the deceased owed money.

Additional data for measuring Spanish American literacy rates are currently very limited. Spanish-era primary and secondary education was mostly via Catholic schools, private schools, and contracted tutors; this was not public education, and student lists have not been published. Over thirty colleges and universities were notably active in Spanish America from the 1550s to 1810.[10] However, student lists of the Spanish-era universities have not been published, and to further complicate any study of the comparative academic level of these schools, the theses required for all Spanish-era degrees were written and presented in Latin. Lastly, the Spanish Crown and its governors only permitted the publication and dissemination of newspapers and journals in the late Bourbon era.[11]

Therefore, determining *advanced* literacy, that is, the ability not only to write one's signature, manage accounts, and read short newspaper articles, but to read and analyze sophisticated written works, including literature and theory, requires a lengthier, deeper study than basic literacy. New Orleans had only a tiny newspaper until early 1804, when American journalists arrived with a vengeance, and no list of newspaper subscribers for the Spanish-era paper is available. However, a small number of postmortem book inventories exist, as does a long panegyric on Governor Gálvez, written by local planter Julien Poydras. Book inventories in particular require translation and identification of individual works, but also permit analysis of how reading may have shaped public discourse in the city. Such book inventories, as well as bills of sale and Inquisition records, have been staples of Spanish American historical research for over a century.[12]

Finally, determining *scientific* literacy requires the study of scientific correspondence originating, in this case, from New Orleans. Such correspondence was not necessarily kept within the Spanish empire: at least twenty members of the American Philosophical Society in Philadelphia had connections with New Orleans, several before 1803. Those members actually resident or passing through Spanish-era New Orleans included an Eton-educated merchant, a planter who corresponded with Thomas Jefferson, two astronomers, an important Spanish painter, and a notorious American general. Their correspondence with the American Philosophical Society provides additional insight into the scientific interests and literacy of New Orleans elites.[13]

The archives of Spanish-era New Orleans greatly problematize, if not refute, the "black legend" of illiteracy in that Bourbon city. Indeed, most whites in the city and probably numerous free people of color were functionally literate; many kept detailed and accurate business records, and all worked via the often cumbersome, document-heavy Spanish legal and notarial processes. Some members of the elite read for pleasure; a few dabbled in amateur science or wrote poetry.

BASIC LITERACY

The simplest methodology for study of basic literacy is analysis of signatures in notarial, probate, and ecclesiastical records and in civil petitions. Fortunately, the New Orleans Notarial Archives provide a vast, signature-filled river of documents from which to take large samples. Take for example sections of two notarial books from Spanish New Orleans, one kept by Leonard/Leonardo Mazange in 1780 and the other kept by Rafael Perdomo in 1785. The selection from Mazange consists of 150 pages and contains at least 84 signatures; that from Perdomo, 106 pages and 92 signatures. Almost every notarial archival record in those books, if not all, was signed by distinctive hands and apparently preserved the genuine signature of the person attested to in the respective documents. Formulaic language in Spanish notarial archives did permit notaries to sign for illiterates, just as it would in the later American era, but no such language was noted in these Spanish-era documents, and certainly no "X" as an illiterate's signature mark was noted.

Of the 82 signatures in the 1780 sample, 62 (about 75 percent) had been written in a steady, refined manner, sometimes with great elaboration; of the 92 in the 1785 sample, 83 had the same attributes (about 90 percent). The decrease in mediocre and poor signatures, that is, marked by an unsteady or rough hand and even sometimes illegible, was easily noticeable between the sample volumes: the signatures in the 1785 Perdomo sample were merely mediocrely written at best; none were truly poor or illegible.[14]

The description of signatures, is, of course, subjective, but the merchant petition of August 1796 provides an excellent opportunity for comparison.[15] While it might be argued that such petition signatures are those of educated elites, the signatures themselves provide a benchmark for what may justifiably be considered a proper signature written by an educated man with a steady hand and in a refined manner, a mediocre signature, and a poor signature, written by an unsteady or rough hand and even sometimes illegible. For example, the signature on the top left corner of signature page 3 of this petition is that of the very prominent and well-educated Daniel Clark. His stylish, well-written signature, as well as that of Caisergues and Petit in the left corner, were clearly by educated men who prided themselves on their writing. Perhaps falling into the mediocre level would be that of Beltran Gravier, two signatures below that of Clark—Gravier, it may be remembered, was primarily a planter. By comparison, in the right-hand corner may be found the scrawled-print signature of Bartolome Bosque—certainly a poor signature.

Given that about 90 percent of the signatures in the notarial records in the 1785 sample were much more comparable to that of Clark, Caisergues, and Petit than a mediocre or poor signature, the ability to write at least a proper signature was reasonably high in Spanish New Orleans and actually increased within five short years. Beyond the city's elites, a large, literate middle-class did indeed exist in Bourbon New Orleans.

There is no indication that scribes, clerks, and paralegals were particularly important in Spanish New Orleans as writers for merchants, planters, or the common man in general—the latter wrote for themselves. Occasionally residents of the city advertised themselves or were labeled in city directories or notarial documents as translators, but not as scribes. The merchants of Spanish New Orleans often served as their own clerks; the probate court records richly demonstrate this, with dozens of carefully written bills and ledger pages in the same hands as the signatures in each of hundreds of files.

Such high rates for basic literacy in New Orleans were similar to those elsewhere in at least one other American colony. Based upon a close study of three parish registers from southern St. Domingue after 1760, perhaps 90 percent of the white males, 70 percent of the white females, 47 percent of the free men of color, and 34 percent of the free women color in southern St. Domingue (modern Haiti) after 1760 were able to write their own names on marriage registers—that is, had basic literacy. Clearly St. Domingue, albeit French, was the home of an increasingly cosmopolitan, literate populace.[16] St. Domingue was a colony very similar to southern Louisiana and was a trading, cultural, and demographic partner, and similarities between New Orleans and that colony should actually be expected.

By comparison within Spanish Louisiana, when seventy St. Louis heads of families signed an oath of allegiance to Spain in that then-small village in 1769, only thirty signed their names, and the others merely made marks; a similar ratio appeared in a 1775 contract for a new church. These years, of course, do not represent the village's literacy during the late Spanish era from 1780 to 1803, but they do indicate something of the village's remoteness from New Orleans. Finally, by comparison with the colonial United States, as early as the 1760s, both Baltimore and South Carolina already had signature literacy rates of 80 percent, and noted that "urban areas were systematically more literate" in both Europe and its colonies in the late eighteenth century and that the colonies were more uniformly literate than European homelands.[17]

Beyond the data, there are several potential reasons for a high level of basic literacy within New Orleans, including the city's role as a commercial entrepôt, its ethnic diversity, and the availability of printed materials from several cultural streams—not only Spanish, French, North American, and British, but also from the divisions thereof, for example, royalist, revolutionary, religious, secular,

Federalist, Jeffersonian. Each of these reasons, in turn, raise two new and exciting questions: what were the actual literacy rates within the various parts of the Spanish empire, and could the example of New Orleans indicate that other Spanish entrepôts with similar characteristics—Havana, Veracruz, Cartagena, Montevideo, Buenos Aires, Santiago—were more literate than is previously recognized?

An additional point of comparison between the New Orleans archives and the Spanish empire (and St. Domingue) can be found in the number of signatures in the notarial archives and probate records preceded and followed by a horizontal bar, consisting of two lines and containing a row of typically three dots. This bar marking has long been believed to be the distinctive signatures of Masonic lodge members in both France and St. Domingue, and can in fact be found on a surviving signature of Toussaint Louverture, who led the St. Dominguan/Haitian revolt. The first New Orleans Masonic lodge, the "Parfaite Union," founded in 1793, was ironically named after "a tumultuous Port-au-Prince lodge." The two New Orleans archival samples above contain signatures with similar, probably Masonic, markings for at least thirteen male individuals, all but one with French surnames. Of these, two appear as early as the 1780 volume, and the other eleven in the 1785 volume. Among these thirteen, the most prominent were Jean Baptiste Poeyfarre, a prominent merchant, and the clerk/city notary Pedro/Pierre Pedesclaux.[18] Given official Spanish disapproval of Masonry and its later connection with open revolution in the Western Hemisphere, these thirteen signatures not only indicate individuality—they may be considered dangerous and bold.

ADVANCED LITERACY

Determining advanced literacy in the Spanish empire may be expected to be somewhat difficult. This difficulty is multifaceted, stemming from the lack of early and extant newspapers, the lack of public education, and the effects of time and revolution. The Spanish empire imposed strict control over political discourse, and the very nature of mercantilism, including government and syndicate monopolies on both trading and shipping, theoretically ensured only a minimal need to publish ship arrivals or departures, commodity prices, and unfiltered news for the use by merchants in their own economic discourse. Similarly, the empire controlled religious discourse at some level, certainly via the ecclesiastical appointment process and the Inquisition. Even cultural discourse was somewhat controlled, because the centers and sponsors of such discourse were often the viceroys, governors, administrators, and clerics themselves. There was consequently no history of freedom of the press or religion in the Bourbon empire.

Consequently, throughout much of Spanish America, the first and only newspapers were small gazettes originating in the Bourbon establishment of a semi-free trade system, including the *Gazetas de Madrid.* For example, the earliest South American periodicals appeared in Lima in late 1790–early 1791, in Santa Fé de Bogotá in 1791, Buenos Aires in early 1801, regularly in Mexico City only in 1803, and in Veracruz in 1806.[19] Competing newspapers, as in the United States and France, were not necessary or financially viable for most Spanish colonies simply because there were no political parties within the Spanish imperial system.

By comparison with most of Spanish America, journalism came early to New Orleans via *Le Moniteur de la Louisiane,* a four-sheet paper founded in early 1794 by a French refugee from St. Domingue, Louis Duclot, evidently with the encouragement of then-Governor Carondelet. The earliest surviving edition of this newspaper, number 57, was filled by a somewhat inaccurate news article on negotiations with the Chickasaw, a gubernatorial proclamation on slave indemnities, and only three advertisements. The next two extant issues, from 1798, were preserved by American surveyor/commissioner Andrew Ellicott. These two issues, more typical of newspapers of the day than the *Gazetas de Madrid,* begin with lists of ship arrivals and departures, advertisements, personal notices, and some local news. However, the news reprinted in *Le Moniteur* was on political unrest in Europe, a British royal decree on food shipments from the Western Hemisphere, privateer activity in the Caribbean, free trade on the Mississippi River, the creation of the Cisalpine Republic, and French activity in Rome and Basel.[20] These articles were clearly chosen for their relevance to the literate residents of New Orleans and not merely by whim; even the news from the Cisalpine Republic, Rome, and Basel was relevant to the city, for many residents were not Spanish by birth, but rather Italian, and some French were actually from western Switzerland or nearby.

Most education in Spanish and Portuguese America was via the Catholic Church or private tutors, and Spanish New Orleans was no exception. The most notable church education program was famously that of the Ursuline Convent, which educated young girls across class and racial lines, but the actual list of students, although annotated in convent records from 1797 to 1812, have not been compiled for general historic use. However, a Spanish-era public school taught 25–150 students from 1772 until at least 1800, private schools taught another 400 a year, and a local military school also functioned during the period. Notarial archives also reveal at least nineteen contracts between residents (only some wealthy) and teachers during the Spanish era, all but one between 1782 and 1787. Notable among these contracts were those between free people of color and women: in the Spanish empire, it was legally acceptable to not only teach free people of color but also indigenous peoples and slaves, and education of women was not unusual.[21]

Records from the numerous colonial universities might provide names, educational levels, and specializations of tens of thousands of colonial students in Spanish America, presumably some residing subsequently in New Orleans. However, none of these sources, in their current state, provide sufficient data to conduct demographic analysis of education within Spanish-era New Orleans.

A final complication in determining advanced literacy in New Orleans and indeed throughout most of Spanish America lies in that, despite the vastness of the Spanish archives in Seville, many colonial archives and much correspondence remained within the Western Hemisphere and did not survive the vicissitudes of time and revolution—or have simply never been properly catalogued. This research problem is somewhat more difficult for New Orleans given its late arrival into the empire, the relatively sudden departure of many Spanish (and probably Italians, Greek, and Dutch) from New Orleans after 1803, and the generational loss of fluency in Spanish, presumably resulting in the eventual discarding of family correspondence and journals. The new American governor Claiborne's proclamations may be considered an indicator of the likely departure of many Spaniards and their language from New Orleans in 1804: only Claiborne's very first proclamation was published in English, French, and Spanish; the remainder were only printed in English and French.[22] It is not surprising, then, that the only journals and letters published to date on New Orleans were written in French and English.

A small window into advanced literacy in the city, however, can be seen in postmortem book inventories, a staple of Spanish American historical research. Among the first to utilize such sources was John Francis McDermott, who focused on book inventories not in New Orleans but in a small Spanish village far upriver, St. Louis. Given that both St. Louis and New Orleans were part of Spanish Louisiana and were bound by the same riverine commerce, McDermott's research provides both insight and questions regarding literacy in both locations.

When Pierre Laclede, the French-born New Orleanian who founded St. Louis, died in 1778, his personal library numbered more than 215 volumes, ranging from anatomy to Rousseau. Laclede was either a well-read man or an obsessive collector, but based upon his sophisticated choices of works, the first seems much more likely. More intriguingly, sixteen different men purchased portions of Laclede's library at a time when the now-Spanish village consisted of only about five hundred people. The book choices of these sixteen men provide much broader insight into advanced literacy within Spanish-era Louisiana than does Laclede's mere collection.

For example, Martin Duralde, the district surveyor, purchased thirty volumes and four maps, including works on commercial factories, the arts, sciences, mathematics, physics, and hydraulic engineering, which indicates that Duralde, of Spanish birth, probably read French very well. More surprising is his purchase of a French translation of John Locke's *An Essay Concerning Human Understanding*, a work banned by the Inquisition since 1734. Duralde, who first appeared in New Orleans records in 1785, returned to New Orleans shortly after he purchased his copy of Locke, and worked for both the Spanish and the US government.[23]

Francisco Vigo, Pierre Joseph Didier, and Auguste Chouteau were three more St. Louis residents purchasing and reading controversial, banned works. Vigo, a former Spanish soldier who provided direct financial support for the American rebellion and befriended some of its Western leaders, purchased many of Laclede's books, including both Mirabeau's *Théorie de l'impôt* (Theory of Taxation), which harshly criticized the tax farming then practiced in the Spanish empire, and Rousseau's *Du contrat social* (On the Social Contract), famously banned by the Inquisition in 1766. Didier was a prominent Benedictine who fled Paris for the American Midwest. His library of 264 works included a translation of Adam Ferguson's *Essay on the History of Civil Society* and Montesquieu's *De l'esprit des lois* (The Spirit of the Laws), another banned work. Auguste Chouteau, the most famous trader in the early American West, owned more than 600 books, and McDermott reported that a full one-fourth—an astonishing 150 books—were indexed by the Inquisition![24] Private libraries in St. Louis before 1804 may have contained 2,000 or 3,000 volumes, not including duplicates.[25]

Given the number of books available in somewhat remote St. Louis, many more works should appear in similar New Orleans successions, but such is not the case. Only two long book inventories have been previously reported; I have located only a third long inventory, although the vast records may hold more. At least three possibilities for the absence of books in archival New Orleans should be considered: (1) many of the literate populace from the Spanish era, of every nationality, moved from the city after 1803, (2) assessors in New Orleans did not value books in comparison to other more expensive property inside successions, or (3) the Spanish-era populace of New Orleans genuinely was illiterate.

Given the economic boom in sugar and eventually cotton, many residents were already relocating to plantations, and their successions are scattered throughout Louisiana. Many Americans who arrived during the Spanish era carved out significant fortunes and returned to the northern states; many Spanish residents, especially royal officials and troops, departed with the American annexation and spread throughout the hemisphere; many French residents eventually moved elsewhere, certainly to France but also to Cuba, where they founded the Spanish city of Cienfuegos. In all of these cases, some successions that might indicate Spanish-era literacy are too widespread for this project. However, most of the city's residents did remain there well into the American period, so the departure of its populace does not fully indicate why so few books appear in successions.

A second possibility is that New Orleans assessors, as they inventoried personal property, credits, and debts for successions, simply did not value books as compared to other property. After a thorough examination of almost all successions found in the Spanish probate court, it is striking how many of these successions did not include deeply personal items, such as personal clothing, jewelry, paintings, keepsakes, and books. This omission was true even among elite successions like those of Pierre/Pedro de Marigny. When clothing was mentioned, it was often in the inventory of a single room, for example a pair of pants, a coat, and a hat found in the stables. The assessors were clearly not shy about documenting everything they found in a storehouse, as can be attested by the succession for a deceased storekeeper of dry goods in which all of the individual sizes of nails, brackets, hinges, and other hardware were meticulously identified and counted. But the assessors in the Marigny case clearly and immediately fixed upon handwritten property (the account books and papers of the deceased) and next tangible property (land, buildings, machinery, vehicles, large supplies, and, perhaps most importantly, slaves). The only consistent variations seem to be when a member of the elite died and there was silver, furniture, art, and linen to be counted (again, not particularly personal in nature) or when a maritime or military officer died and his meager belongings in a trunk or small cabin were scrupulously inventoried.[26] It seems, then, that the assessors of New Orleans presumed that the personal goods of the deceased, including books, should be passed on within a circle of family and friends without royal interference, and this is why so few postmortem book lists have survived.

The third possibility is that the Spanish-era residents of New Orleans were not particularly literate, but this seems unlikely, based on a study of the book lists that have survived from the Spanish era and, more importantly, what happened to those books after their owner died.

The most significant book list from Spanish-era New Orleans found to date is that of Governor Manuel Gayoso de Lemos, who served twice in Portugal before serving in Louisiana for ten years until his death in 1799. Gayoso's library consisted of 165 works, divided into 411 volumes. Like Duralde, Vigo, Didier, and Chouteau in St. Louis, Gayoso owned a number of works banned by the Inquisition, especially Algernon Sidney's *Discourses Concerning Government,* seen as heretical because it argued that government was a compact between the ruler and the governed. Irving Leonard, the historian best known for his work on the books of conquistadors, also located this postmortem list of Gayoso's books. Leonard argued, "An examination of the book titles listed clearly suggests that this aggregation of volumes was no mere physical adornment of the former governor's home but, rather, the companions of their owner in his various needs and moods."[27]

Gayoso's library was filled with books on military topics, engineering, the practical sciences, and geography—reading especially useful to the governor of a frontier colony. The few works on medicine, especially a work on small-pox vaccination, indicate Gayoso was at least informed on the rudiments of public health. He had a few religious works, but many, many more on political science and history, including a copy of Grotius, the aforementioned French translation of Sidney, and histories of the American Revolution, the French Revolutions, and the founding of Kentucky. Gayoso's literary interests were especially wide-ranging, for his library included numerous English-language works, including those of Shakespeare, Swift, Sterne, Milton, Pope, Fielding, and even a collection of American tragedies. In his own Spanish language, he owned *Don Quixote,* pastoral novels, and a complete set of Quevedo's works. Surprisingly, for a man who read and spoke French, Gayoso's library showed little interest in French literature, although he did own a copy of Fenelon's famed *Les Aventures des Télémaque.* That work, while very popular, was also a scathing critique of imperial rule and mercantilism.[28]

Given the breadth of his interests and years of leadership, it can be presumed that Gayoso was an exemplar of literacy within the colony he governed. Indeed,

Irving Leonard opined of Gayoso, "His personal library stands as one more refutation of the accepted dogma of Spanish tyranny and intolerance toward literature and learning in the overseas colonies of the Americas."[29]

Beyond Gayoso, a closer analysis of his succession reveals that forty-six different residents from all walks of life purchased books when his library was auctioned. As in St. Louis, the list of purchasers and their choices indicate a level of advanced literacy within and noticeably beyond the city's elites. Many of Gayoso's works of practical use, especially military books and several on mathematics, were purchased, not by a well-known member of the elite, but by Vicente and Fernando de Texeyro, who do not appear in Spanish notarial archives from 1780 to 1800, and who also purchased a book of elegiac sonnets in English.[30] Similarly, most of Gayoso's religious books were purchased by a single man, Francisco Ramon Canes. Given the religious nature and number of the books, and that Canes represented the Ursuline convent in a business trans-action at least once in 1796, he presumably was purchasing the works on behalf of the convent.[31] While many of Gayoso's English works were purchased by American and British merchants, many of his other works went in more varied directions. Among the elite, Augustine Macarty, the very image of a successful planter, purchased works of science; Jean-Baptiste Labatut, a prominent Basque merchant, bought Gayoso's translation of Sidney; Gayoso's secretary, Andres Lopez de Armesto, purchased theatrical works including Shakespeare, a history of the Ottoman Empire, and a book of erotica. However, it was Antonio Boniquet, a small merchant, who bought works by Cervantes and Quevedo, a children's primer, and a work on smallpox vaccination; and Casteret, of whom nothing else is known, took home Thomas Jefferson's *Notes on the State of Virginia*.

In this multilingual city, many of the attendees at the sale of Gayoso's library purchased works not in their native tongue. For example, Juan de Dios Valdés bought a French grammar and a French translation of John Filson's *The History of Kentucky,* from which Dios Valdes may well have read aloud the tales of Daniel Boone; Bernardo Genoveva bought Portuguese and Castilian grammars and several books in English; Manuel Ximenez bought a Spanish-French-Latin dictionary, an English grammar, and an English dictionary; Alexander Mills acquired works in French, Spanish, and English. The American Richard Relf, who had just arrived in the city that year from Philadelphia, was there to buy Cervantes and a work on overseas colonies in the Spanish language.[32] Relf would later become an important American merchant in the city—and while he seems to have spoken Danish, how or where he learned Spanish is unclear.

The impression that one takes away from this great sale of the dead governor's books is that a large number of men, many of them then non-elite, were interested in procuring at least a few books to meet their own personal interests. Perhaps a few were traders who purchased books with future customers in mind, but the idiosyncratic, very personal nature of the purchases—Texeyro's of a dead man's book of elegies, Macarty's of science and English sermons, and Ximenez's language books—all give the impression of men who sought education, improvement, adventure, and solace in their book choices. Such men do not seem illiterate at all.

Two years later, in 1801, the prominent Spanish colonial officer Francisco Bouligny died, and his books, like those of Gayoso, were also sold. His library consisted of 48 separate works in 147 volumes. The books themselves were appraised for 96 pesos/6 reales and so were roughly comparable in value (but not number) to those of Gayoso, whose 165 works sold for 415 pesos/7 reales. By comparison, Bouligny's crockery was appraised at 81 pesos/4 reales, and his kitchenware at 147 pesos/7 reales, much more than his books—another indication of why the city's assessors may have not demonstrated interest in inventorying books that were in the end not very lucrative to sell.

Many of Bouligny's works focused on agriculture, but he was also clearly fond of history, or else very much liked it on his shelves. The history works included those of ancient Rome, France, America, the Russian Empire, Germany, Captain Cook's third voyage, and the conquest of Mexico. Some works were perhaps inevitable to be in his library, such as Buffon's *Historia Natural*, the much-beloved *Aventura de Thelemace*, and *Colon Juzgados Militares*, a Spanish military justice book also found in Gayoso's library. Bouligny, despite his birth in Spain and thirty-one years of Spanish service in Louisiana, preferred the French language for his private reading—only 5 of the 48 works in his library were in Spanish.[33]

A final library previously unnoted by historians is that of Juan Bautista Castillón, who had purchased 3 works (18 volumes) from Gayoso's library, including *Don Quixote*. Little is known of Castillón: he first appears in notarial archives in 1794, was never a member of the city's functional elite although he may have served as a French consul in the American era, was not even listed in the 1805 American-era directory, and died in 1809. Whatever his status, Castillón's succession included a library of 70 different works in 199 volumes. Many were reference works, legal works, encyclopedic dictionaries, and histories: his collection included a 30-volume French history, 6 works of Roman history by Rollin, and works on Denmark, Sweden's Gustavus Adolphus, and Russia. The entire library was valued at $371.50, a considerable sum of money. The most valuable by far were assessed to be two works in Spanish—the *Mine Regulations in New Spain* (Mexico) and *La Nueva Recopilación* (an updated compilation of Spanish colonial law) in 3 volumes, estimated to be worth 50 piastres/gourdes/ dollars, or almost one-seventh the value of the entire collection. The assessed value of these two Spanish works may indicate a continued importance of the Spanish imperial economy for New Orleans trade. The only similarly, albeit lower-valued, works were the multivolume *History of France*, several dictionaries, and a 24-volume set of the works of the popular writer Abbe de Mably.[34]

Each of these few book lists indicates that a wide range of the elite and middle class in Bourbon New Orleans were probably literate. Clearly, many of the city's elite and middle class were purchasing and reading a rather wide variety of works on every subject imaginable, including some that were banned and might well be politically controversial.

This evidence problematizes the argument that "There is little evidence of Anglo-American republicanism shaping Iberian Atlantic thinking."[35] Clearly the French and Americans were reading works on republicanism (whether Anglo-American or not); the book lists from both New Orleans and far upriver St. Louis indicate that *vecinos* in Louisiana, including the king's own governor and officials, were reading Locke, Ferguson, Sidney, Jefferson, Mirabeau, Rousseau, and Montesquieu.[36] Although New Orleans might have been an exceptional case among Spanish ports, one must also wonder whether book lists might similarly reveal republican works being read in other Bourbon ports.

However, in only one obscure case did a resident attempt to write his own work—and then it was in praise of a Spanish feat of arms, written in a European style, but with a decidedly independent cast of mind. "La prise du morne du Baton Rouge par Monseigneur de Galvez" is a forgotten remnant of Spanish-era elite literacy, written by Julien Poydras, a prominent planter and former brigadier general and governor general of Louisiana. Poydras wrote the poem within a few weeks of Gálvez's capture of Baton Rouge on 21 September 1779, given the work was printed late that same year by Antoine Boudousquie, the royal printer at New Orleans. The poem itself is of 182 lines of rhyming couplets without break, each line of roughly six feet, that is, in standard heptameter. "La prise" tells of a great noise of battle disturbing the god of the Mississippi River and his nymphs. The riverine god is impressed with the bravery of the invading Spanish Army and its brave and noble leader, Gálvez, and in the end celebrates the victory as bringing perpetual peace and prosperity to the river.[37]

The poem provided Poydras with the opportunity not only to rather conventionally praise Gálvez and his regular troops, but also to praise the local militia and even free soldiers of color:

> I have seen this hero who causes you alarms:
> He seemed a God, clothed in his weapons,
> Superbly flamboyant, heading into the wind,
> And his sparse hair served him as adornment.
>
> After them, marching without pretense
> Our fierce inhabitants, the intrepid militia
> And their skilled hands which plowed furrows
> With the same ardor, raised bastions,
> Made pits, parapets, and trenches,
> Machines and carriages invented for battle;
> For the art of conquest they seem to be born.
>
> The march ended with the men of color:
> Lively, ardent to give proofs of their courage.
> Intrepid Galvez encouraged them everywhere;
> His words, his face excite them to bravery.[38]

While the poetry is workmanlike, it tells a memorable enough tale of a significant Revolutionary Era siege, one that Julien Poydras certainly found worthy of formal celebration. While the work is based on classical models, it makes notable mention of perhaps less heroic characters in some European eyes—colonial militia working as combat engineers, supported by free men of color. Even the obligatory god is not Triton, Neptune, or Zeus, but instead is a powerful local deity, the god of the Mississippi.[39] Poydras's work may be derivative, but it also represents a colonial world literate and separate from the metropolitan. It is the praise of a Spanish governor-general written in French, yet there is no mention of either Spain or France in the poem; "La prise" indicates, in some small way, a colony that was already becoming independent of Europe, similarly to other colonies in the Americas.

In summary, a wide economic and social spectrum of whites, and perhaps free people of color, were reading and even writing in Bourbon New Orleans. Exactly what they were reading—including books banned by Spanish authorities—implies that literacy in this corner of the empire, if not others, provided challenges to Bourbon governors, but intellectual and perhaps political opportunities for the residents of New Orleans.

SCIENTIFIC LITERACY

US historians, when reviewing the scientific accomplishments of the Enlightenment, have generally focused on French, English, and American discoveries and have rarely discussed Spanish scientific accomplishments during this period. Spain's four great scientific expeditions of the late eighteenth century, including the botanical discoveries of José Celestino Mutis and his school in New Granada and the grand, five-year voyage of Pacific exploration led by Alejandro Malaspina, are largely forgotten even by scholars.[40] Consequently, US historians may be expected to be similarly incurious on the role of a single Spanish town, New Orleans, in science.

New Orleans was not a center of Spanish-era scientific discovery. The American Philosophical Society during the early American period corresponded with similar scientific organizations in England, the Netherlands, France, Spain (in Valencia), and St. Domingue (in Cap Français), but there was no such scientific organization in New Orleans.[41] Similarly, there is little indication that those interested in scientific endeavors were actually focused on natural history to benefit themselves economically, as elsewhere in the Spanish empire. Indeed, the most prominent scientist-planter in the colony wrote instead on astronomy.

However, New Orleans was not a frontier town bereft of any scientific interest, for several reasons. First, the city provided a logical stepping-stone for explorations and merchant ventures into the center of North America throughout the Spanish and early American eras. Such explorations during the late Bourbon era especially included that of the American Philip Nolan, who much to official consternation lived and traded with the Indians west of the Mississippi, explored and mapped modern-day Texas, spied on political machinations in the Mississippi Territory, was killed as a troublemaker by the Spanish in 1801, and was sadly metamorphosed for posterity into the central, traitorous character of Edward Everett Hale's wonderful tale "The Man without a Country."[42]

Second, some elite residents of New Orleans had both advanced literacy and an evident interest in science and broad networks of contacts within and beyond their own ethnicities; many of the books purchased from the libraries of Gayoso and Bouligny were works of science, often with a practical intent. At the highest levels of the elite, several governors and administrators, including Gálvez, Gayoso, and Carondelet (formerly the governor of El Salvador) had significant education; Gálvez's uncle had organized the first major Spanish scientific expeditions, and Carondelet, as the governor of Ecuador, would later provide invaluable assistance to famed scientist Alexander von Humboldt, botanist Aime Bonpland, and geographer/mathematician/astronomer Francisco José de Caldas.[43] A few residents corresponded with other amateurs interested in science, not only within the Spanish empire, but notably with members of the American Philosophical Society in Philadelphia, which was most famously led by Benjamin Franklin and Thomas Jefferson. The most notable of these correspondents from New Orleans must include Daniel Clark the elder, William Dunbar, José Francisco Xavier de Salazar y Mendoza, and James Wilkinson.

Of these, the most closely connected to New Orleans was certainly Daniel Clark the elder. He was elected to the American Philosophical Society as early as 1769;[44] he was then a British colonel serving in Pennsylvania before moving to New Orleans, but does not appear in the transactions of that society as a member in 1770.[45] What is especially surprising is that his better-known nephew and namesake Daniel was not later elected to the American Philosophical Society. It was the latter, reportedly Eton educated, who provided much of the firsthand data for the Jefferson administration report to Congress found in *An Account of Louisiana* following the Louisiana Purchase. Yet the younger Clark was not chosen to be a member; perhaps the sometimes sullen merchant was considered more of a politician than a scholar in Philadelphia.

Andrew Ellicott and José Joaquín de Ferrer y Cafranga, among the most important astronomers and surveyors of the day in their respective countries, separately visited New Orleans during the late Spanish era. Ellicott, who had previously assisted, then replaced, Pierre L'Enfant in the surveying of Washington, DC, visited New Orleans for two months in 1799. Ellicott visited the city to acquire supplies and a vessel suitable for his mission to survey the Spanish–US border in the Southeast; Ellicott's work still marks the border between Alabama and Florida. Ellicott was already a member of the American Philosophical Society; he borrowed the society's achromatic telescope for the assignment.[46]

Ellicott became acquainted with Ferrer in New York City; he referred to the Spanish astronomer as "my friend" and "an ingenious Spanish gentleman." Ferrer traveled up the US East Coast, down the Ohio and Mississippi to New Orleans in 1801, and throughout the Gulf of Mexico and the Caribbean, making scrupulous astronomical observations to fix precise latitude and longitudes of numerous cities, towns, and other geographic points; he also computed the height of several mountains in Mexico and the Canary Islands. Ferrer also made observations on a solar eclipse at Havana in 1803 and compared those with Ellicott, who had observed the same eclipse in Pennsylvania. Ferrer forwarded all of these calculations in Spanish to Ellicott and the members of the American Philosophical Society, where his data was translated, read aloud to the members, and printed in the society's journal. Ferrer was elected to membership in the society in 1801 and was an active participant, forwarding his observations on the comet of 1807–8 as taken from Havana, multiple astronomical and geographic calculations, and coining the term "corona" to describe the outer ring he observed during a solar eclipse in New York.[47]

Meanwhile, another American with ties to both New Orleans and Philadelphia was also observing the comet. William Dunbar, a Spanish-era planter and innovator, resided in Natchez but was a very familiar face in New Orleans, appearing in notarial records repeatedly from 1780 to 1796, often working through factors. Dunbar was also an amateur scientist who had studied astronomy and mathematics in Scotland and England; corresponded with the famed astronomer William Herschel and instrument maker Benjamin Rittenhouse; built a public observatory near his home in Natchez; served as Governor Gayoso's surveyor general for the District of Natchez; worked with Ferrer, Ellicott, and Philip Nolan in setting the boundary between Mississippi and Louisiana; and designed a cotton press. Daniel Clark introduced Dunbar to Thomas Jefferson thus: "for Science, Probity, and general information [he] is the first Character in this part of the World." Dunbar was elected to the American Philosophical Society in 1800. At the behest of Jefferson, Dunbar organized and helped lead an exploratory expedition up the Ouachita and Black rivers in 1804; he then provided organizational support and wise advice to the Freeman-Custis expedition up the Red River in 1806.[48]

Two other early members of the American Philosophical Society, José Francisco Xavier de Salazar y Mendoza and James Wilkinson, were also active in New Orleans. Salazar was a leading portrait painter of the era in the Western Hemisphere, born in Mexico, but he worked in New Orleans from 1782 until his death there in 1802. General James Wilkinson, the notoriously devious head of the US military during this period, was a frequent visitor to New Orleans (hardly surprising, given he was in the Spanish pay), led the American troops who formally annexed Louisiana in 1803, and was finally tarred by scandal for his role in the still-murky Aaron Burr conspiracy. Wilkinson was elected to the

American Philosophical Society in part for his meteorological reporting from the western interior and donation of unidentified animal bones and fragments.[49] He also eventually produced an 1804 map of the Spanish western possessions, evidently based upon work done by the unfortunate Philip Nolan.

Finally, at least two other correspondents with the American Philosophical Society should be mentioned. One, Dr. John Watkins, forwarded an article to the society in 1803 entitled, "Discovery of a Cantharides." A cantharide is a blister beetle, whose secretion was believed in the eighteenth century to be an aphrodisiac but in reality is a poison. More ambiguously, a "Mr. Ducald" submitted a paper on an unidentified topic in early 1803; his name was also spelled as "Durald," and his paper was submitted to the naturalist Barton for consideration,[50] and so "Durald" is probably Martin Duralde, the Spanish functionary who served in St. Louis but mostly resided in New Orleans and was reputed to be an amateur scientist.

However, despite these scientific contacts, Laussat may have been mostly correct about New Orleans when he wrote, "the local people do not care for the sciences."[51] New Orleans was not a vital node for scientific research within the Spanish empire; the city's elites do not seem to have actively participated in any imperial network of scientific knowledge associated with Mexico or New Granada, for example. But at least a few members of the city's elite *were* very interested in scientific affairs, and it is possible, given the city's later roles in agricultural, shipbuilding, and steam technology innovation and use of famed engineer and scientist Benjamin Latrobe, that there was always a bit of technological and scientific activity beneath the surface of the city, but the evidence is simply not there during the Spanish era.

CONCLUSION

Despite the "black legend" of Spanish-era illiteracy, most of the city's elite and middle-class population, and probably a significant percentage of the city's leading free people of color, had some level of literacy before the American annexation in late 1803. The majority of the white and free population signed their own names in the notarial records in a strong, often florid, hand; kept extensive business journals; supported a small newspaper long before many other notable Spanish cities would do the same; purchased, valued, and read a wide variety of books, some banned by the Inquisition; and often read (and so presumably conversed) in multiple languages. Beyond this advanced literacy, a few members of the elite dabbled in poetry and science, even corresponding with and eventually becoming members of the American Philosophical Society in distant Philadelphia.

This level of literacy may have set New Orleans somewhat apart from other Spanish American cities, but this is hardly surprising. New Orleans was not a Spanish city built upon a large indigenous workforce. Instead, New Orleans was a created city, an entrepÐt placed exactly in its geographic location for purposes of regional and trans-imperial trade, populated by a cosmopolitan workforce led by notable figures in the Bourbon imperial project. The colony's enlightened governors found themselves managing an urban populace connected by the written word—signatures on contracts, bills of obligation, books that spoke of Washington and Robespierre, and journals that told of Bonaparte, Toussaint Louverture, and Godoy.[52]

The populace was literate before the American annexation and remained so, supporting multiple newspapers (including two short-lived Spanish newspapers) throughout the early American era (1803–15). These newspapers all printed long, daily lists of letters waiting to be picked up at the post office, yet more evidence of basic literacy. That prior literacy amplified the immediate impact of American newspapers in early 1804 and accelerated the economic, political, and even scientific/technological assimilation of the city into the newest empire, the United States of America.

On 14 October 1808, the *Louisiana Gazette* printed Samuel Coleridge's grand poem "Hymn Before Sunrise, in the Vale of Chamouni": "Hast thou a charm to stay the morning star / In his steep course? So long he seems to pause / On thy bald awful head, O Sovran Blanc." The populace that found Coleridge in their newspaper in 1808 had not learned to read poetry only in the past five years under American tutelage and were not haltingly sounding out their words, even in English, like schoolboys and schoolgirls. Instead, the evidence argues that, on that long-ago October day, in the rough, booming town of New Orleans, men and women of every ethnic group and color, in the coffeehouses along the levee, the parlors of Bayou St. John, across the store counters and warehouse floors, not only read the words of Coleridge aloud to each other in clear, strong voices—they were moved.

6

The Judicial System in Spanish New Orleans

Crespo [to the king]: I see the justice of the King
As one undivided body.
One body, but with many hands.
   —Pedro Calderon de Barca, *The Mayor of Zalamea*

The Spanish empire was not democratic or republican. However, the concepts of self-rule, democracy, and republicanism, as well as their practical application, must not be dismissed as anachronistic, at least in the Spanish colony of Louisiana. The *vecinos* of Spanish New Orleans were literate, with access to newspapers and books that clearly referenced and sometimes openly espoused democratic and republican concepts. Even the Spanish authorities in New Orleans themselves read works that spoke of self-rule, democracy, and governance without kings. The city was uniquely positioned geographically within the Spanish empire to receive, trade, and disseminate those concepts, just as it disseminated cotton, wood, and corn. In addition, many *vecinos*, including prominent leaders like Clark, Marigny, and Fortier, had close foreign connections and were already quite familiar with the practicalities of self-rule. The joint power of proximity and trans-imperial trade, then, ensured that democracy and self-governance were certainly discussed in Spanish New Orleans— and perhaps not quietly.

Self-governance requires many skills of its citizens, including a strong sense of justice, developed by routine participation in an effective civil and criminal judicial system based upon law. Throughout the late eighteenth century, the *vecinos* of New Orleans lived and worked within a functional, rather typical Spanish colonial judicial system, frequent in its hearings and accessible to all regardless of ethnicity, race, or gender, despite the oversight of a military governor and a large military garrison. This was not a democratic system, but it was efficient and open, and this judicial system permitted Bourbon law and order to tame much of the "American" West, or at least to keep it systematic, long before the Americans and Jeffersonian democracy formally annexed the city. Indeed, the Bourbon judicial system was so effective that Spanish law and its administrative/notarial system survived beyond the American annexation and until the present day.

THE COURTS IN SPANISH NEW ORLEANS

The Bourbon judicial process is especially well documented in the New Orleans archives. Most of the Spanish probate records from 1766 to 1790 survive in the Louisiana Historical Center in the Old US Mint,[1] and close analysis of these records permits a deep understanding of how the judiciary system in New Orleans was structured, who actually heard cases, how those cases were directed to be resolved, and the process of the occasional appeals. The probate records, at both a statistical and a detailed level, reveal that the top level of Bourbon justice in New Orleans, at least, was conducted very conscientiously, was focused mostly on civil cases, especially debts, successions, and emancipations of free people of color, and permitted most criminal cases to be handled at a lower magistrate's level, more in tune with the needs of individual communities.

During this period, the governor routinely served as the sole judge of the probate court. However, several other officials also served on the court, sometimes alone and at other times with one to three other judges. These additional judges included the royal intendant; the *alcade mayor provincial* (chief provincial magistrate) and the *alguacil mayor* (city magistrate/jail warden), both appointed by the *regidores perpetuos* (*cabildo* members); and two other *alcades ordinaries,* elected annually by the other *cabildo* voting members.[2] Close analysis of the thirty-nine magistrates elected from 1770 to 1803 indicates that they were almost exclusively men of French (twenty) and Spanish (eighteen) origin. Among these thirty-nine, the Spanish elected no free men of color and only one man of northern European origin, Nicolas Forstall. Indeed, one is struck by how, after 1789, the city's *alcades ordinarios* were almost all of Spanish—not French—origin and often, despite Spanish law, active Spanish treasury officials. Of the twenty *alcades ordinarios* from 1789 to 1803, thirteen were of Spanish origin.[3]

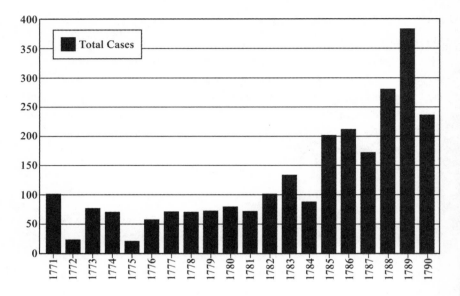

FIGURE 6.1. Court cases and files in Spanish New Orleans, 1771–90.

The judges in New Orleans faced a substantial workload. While criminal cases might involve an autopsy, a few witness statements, and limited findings of fact, civil cases could be quite burdensome. Complicated successions were probably the most onerous—the death of a planter/merchant with widespread commercial interests, loans extended, debts, and properties to inventory could occasion hundreds of pages of documents and testimonies from throughout the colony and beyond. If the probate cases preserved in the Louisiana Historical Center archives are reasonably comprehensive, the judicial system in New Orleans handled less than a hundred cases a year—about eight a month, or two a week—until 1783, as depicted in figure 6.1.

The number of court cases varied in 1772 and 1775, perhaps reflecting an absence of cases or the loss of cases from the archives due to the ravages of time. The number of cases notably jumped in the years 1782–90, probably a reflection of numerous challenges facing the Bourbon Spanish during this era: increased migration, an increasing number of free people of color and manumissions, the continued role of women in the New Orleans economy, the arrival of new merchants, increased trade, and skirtings and outright violations of Spanish trade regulations.[4]

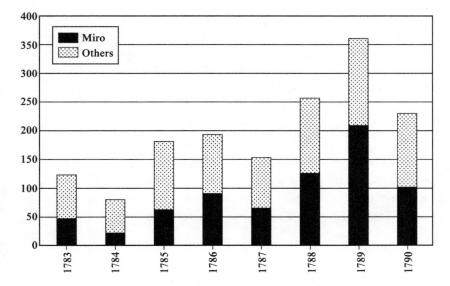

FIGURE 6.2. Court cases and files with assigned judges in Spanish New Orleans, 1783–90.

While Spanish governors might well be a focus of colonial justice, they were not the only judges who heard cases, as depicted in figure 6.2.[5] Analysis of the surviving cases and files from 1783 until the summer of 1790 indicate that, in New Orleans, Governor Miró typically heard 40–50 percent of the cases himself in any given year, but in each year he was assisted by one or two key judges, often Creoles, with other judges brought in as needed. He made sparing use of longtime Bourbon senior official Martin Navarro as a judge except in 1783, in his first full year as governor. Instead, he leaned upon the members of the *cabildo*: de Reggio in 1783–84, Forstall in 1785, Orue in 1786, Chabert in 1787, Argote and Postigo in 1788, and Ortega and, to a lesser extent Almonaster, in 1789 and 1790. Most of these served as the *alcade ordinario de primer voto* or *de segundo voto*. However, some of the *alcades ordinarios* did not handle many cases in the years it would have been expected. For example, Francisco LeBreton handled only a few in 1783, and de Reggio stepped in early. Joseph Foucher only heard a few more cases than Le Breton in 1788; his case load was handled by Argote (*de segundo voto*) and Juan del Postigo y Valderrama, the *auditor de guerra* and *asesor* (equivalent to both a judge advocate and a military inspector general) in garrison.[6]

Several of those who served as *alcades ordinarios*—Navarro, Morales, Orue, Foucher, and Serrano—were not in fact eligible for those positions because they were treasury officials and therefore prohibited by the legal procedures established by former colonial governor O'Reilly. However, this legal discrepancy was only broached in 1797, when one of the officials was elected and refused to serve.[7] The issue was not raised in any legal appeals and probably would have been ignored by the royal court, regardless, given the relative scarcity of colonial Spanish officials.

The Spanish probate courts not only handled civil cases; they also served as criminal courts and conducted many of the routine administrative functions we would associate with minor judges and notaries. For example, the probate court routinely investigated deaths and reported whether those were natural, accidents, and homicides.[8]

THE EQUAL RIGHT TO A FAIR TRIAL

Bourbon justice in New Orleans does not seem to have outwardly favored any particular economic class, ethnicity, race, or gender. Indeed, the Spanish probate records indicate that, as in so many Spanish colonies, the residents of the city were litigious no matter what their standing in the city's hierarchies and expected to be treated fairly by the court. They sued over items and issues that may seem minor to modern minds: coiffures swept away in a hurricane, the quality of silk handkerchiefs for sale, and a billiard table seized for a debt.[9]

Again, this litigiousness and expectation of legal rights by all *vecinos*, residents, and slaves was not unusual in Spanish America. Such a "law-oriented culture" was not, however, a creation of the savants of the eighteenth-century Enlightenment, filtered down through the Spanish royal administration. Rather, it was a bottom-up approach seized by colonial subjects throughout Spanish America, who pushed their legal system to make notable procedural changes to accommodate local colonial necessity. In fact, the judicial system in metropolitan Spain was slow to grant judicial review to the breadth of litigants and cases so common in its American empire, but eventually found itself following colonial precedents, for example revising alimony laws and legal fees to comport better with rulings in colonial Peru.[10] The residents and judges of Spanish New Orleans fit neatly into this paradigm of a colonial, "law-oriented culture."

Whites, mulattoes, and Africans, free and slave, sued each other routinely in New Orleans; indeed, slaves sued often for their own freedom. A free woman of color sued her former master in 1783, protesting that, after he emancipated her, he sold her. She presented an emancipation certificate, won her case, and was freed. Her former master was required to reimburse the new "owner" he had defrauded within six days, under the serious threat of the seizure of his properties. Similar cases followed over the years, some routine, others requiring more attention from the court. Francisca, a mulatto woman who Baptista Corce attempted to sell to his creditors, simply refused to be sold—she insisted that she had documentary proof, issued by Corce himself, that she was free. Corce later petitioned "to annul the letter of freedom that he had granted." Judge Josef de Orue refused to annul the letter, directed Corce that he must not attempt to "sell" Francisca, and directed that she be paid a salary of ten pesos a month until Corce no longer desired her services.

In another case, Linda, a free African American woman, had taken a servant's position in the house of Benjamin Davies in Jamaica in order to be near her enslaved daughter, also named Linda. When the elder Linda accompanied her daughter to her new master in New Orleans, she found that this master treated her as if she, too, was a slave. To substantiate her claim of already being a free woman, she presented the oral evidence of two white New Orleans merchants, Henry Alexander and the prominent David Hodge. The court, as so often when presented with any evidence, ruled in Linda's favor.[11]

These court cases of women proving that an employer was attempting to enslave them or re-enslave them were all brought before Spanish courts in New Orleans by the women themselves, and those plaintiffs won their cases. Clearly, the city's judges listened closely to the claims both of free people of color as well as of women when determining justice.

Similarly, the courts also focused on the details in cases involving the Spanish practice of *coartación*, by which an enslaved person or a friend might purchase his or her own freedom. Agustin, an enslaved man owned by Agata Lacroix, petitioned to be freed following the payment of his deceased master's debts. Lacroix had freed him in her will, but his freedom was held in abeyance until the debts were paid. Enslaved and free men alike also sued for proper cash-value appraisals of themselves or family members, so that freedom might be purchased. In one case, Valentin, a free African, questioned the validity of the slave price appraisal ($300) he was forced to use to purchase his enslaved brother Silvestre's freedom. When the court appraised Silvestre's worth at an even higher price of $800, Valentin paid the additional cost and bought Silvestre his freedom. Juan Santiago Mangloan purchased his own freedom for 1,050 pesos in 1788. Mangloan not only worked as a tailor, but provided financial assistance to a free man of color, Cristobal Francisco, who ran a successful mercantile business. Francisco, in turn, provided the additional sum required for Mangloan to purchase freedom.

The Spanish probate court expected to be obeyed by all parties when it established a purchase price for a slave. When the free woman of color Barbara worked through the court for a fair price to be established to purchase the freedom of her thirteen-year-old daughter, the master readily agreed. However, although Barbara paid the purchase price, the master's wife refused to accept the court's decision, and Barbara returned to the court for redress. The court directed the constable to enforce their decision against the recalcitrant wife.[12]

In at least one pair of cases, plaintiffs argued they could not be enslaved because they were actually Native Americans. Pedro "Morsu" (should be Morzu) and Baptista Bourguinon successfully argued in January 1790 that they were natural children of Catalina, a Native American woman of the "Chise" (perhaps the Chickasaw) tribe and thus half-brothers of Maria Paget, already recognized as a "Mestee" Indian, all originally from the Black Islands in the District of Illinois. Pedro Morzu was forced to again argue his case four months later, this time providing three witnesses. Governor Miró was no longer the judge, but Judge Postigo also granted Morzu's request for a letter certifying his freedom. By now, Morzu's assumed master was dead, and the estate curator had no objections to his freedom.[13]

Nor was marital status or being a woman an impediment to a lawsuit, as was true in general in Spanish America. Leonora Monsanto sought separation of her property from the community property—her husband Pedro Andre Feiser was in prison and his creditors were circling. Elizabeth de Villiers probably did not hesitate to sue her husband, Volsay, in 1781.[14]

Francisco Fontenelle sued his father in 1787 for the right to marry Francisca Barrios. The older Don Juan Bautista Fontenelle insisted that there was a disparity between his son's noble lineage and that of his proposed wife, the daughter of a tavern keeper. However, the younger Francisco instead that, "by virtue of the betrothal already performed he considers himself and his prospective wife obliged to marry, disregarding whatever slight disparity may exist . . . to be lawfully united in order to prevent the unpleasant consequences which will probably arise from the unfulfillment of their marriage," a likely implication that his betrothed was pregnant. Despite Francisco's protestations and the fact that he was already emancipated, the elder Fontenelle's refusal of consent was based upon a royal decree that marriage must be with the consent of both sets of parents. Accordingly, Miró judged this lengthy case, which occupied fifty-eight pages of text, in favor of the elder Fontenelle. However, the city's ecclesiastical records provide a charming epilogue. Juan Francisco Salomon Fontenelle and Francisca Barrios were married and baptized their daughter Maria in May 1792.[15]

In much of this litigiousness, the residents of Spanish New Orleans were typical *vecinos* of the Spanish empire. However, there was at least one notable difference: in Louisiana, there was no Republic of the Indians, because most if not all of the tribes in the vast colony of Louisiana were beyond actual Spanish control. Consequently, neither the colony nor its capital of New Orleans had a second judicial system and government protector/attorney for Native Americans. Nor was there an Inquisition, because Governor Miró had argued that such would discourage immigration and actually arrested Father Antonio de Sedella and deported him to Spain.[16] The only convent or monastery in the city was that of the progressive Ursuline nuns, who focused on education and medical assistance. Consequently, New Orleans legal cases were not typically muddied by any plaintiff's claimed recourse to Indian or ecclesiastical courts.

CRIMINAL CASES

Criminal cases were handled on at least three levels within the Spanish colony—at the local level, at the military level, and within the probate court. The local magistrates throughout the colony, in the case of New Orleans the *alguacil mayor* (city magistrate/jail warden), presumably handled routine criminal cases.

Separately, military officers would have presumably handled any criminal cases and violations of good military order and discipline committed by soldiers via military administrative hearings and trials, per the Spanish system of military jurisdiction known as *fuero*. Given the large number of royal and militia soldiers, many male *vecinos* in New Orleans would have fallen under military jurisdiction. The *fuero* was an especially invaluable protection for free men of color serving in the militia in several Spanish colonies, and presumably served the same purpose in New Orleans.[17] However, no military criminal or disciplinary records have been noted in the New Orleans or Spanish archives.

Finally, the probate court in New Orleans handled the most serious criminal cases, typically involving murder and theft. If a criminal case reached the probate court, it was likely to be harshly punished, despite the evident inconsequentiality of the alleged crime. For example, when Thomas Smith was accused in 1784 of stealing a few clothes from a Spanish resident named Molina, everything but a single sock and a white shirt was recovered, and consequently Molina reported that he "did not wish to be involved in any litigation." Nevertheless, Governor Miró convicted Smith and sentenced him to four years in prison and fined William Campbell 25 pesos "for having purchased stolen goods." It is possible that Smith was suspected of other robberies, or had been previously underfoot of Spanish authorities, but the four-year sentence imposed by Miró on Smith seems exceedingly harsh. By comparison, when Francisco Barba and Francisco Malos were convicted of numerous robberies, Barba was sentenced to six years in the *cabildo's* prison (only two more than Smith), and Malos was exiled from Louisiana.[18]

At least one case of alleged theft was more complicated: Miró found himself required to conduct a case because of a letter directly to him. Felipe Luis of Havana had written an official letter to Miró, requesting the arrest and return of his (Luis's) wife, Theresa de Flores, and her lover, Christoval Badia. Luis argued that the couple had run away with "various valuables and a sum of money belonging to the petitioner," were living in New Orleans as husband and wife, and already owned several properties there. Miró did indeed direct that Badia and de Flores be imprisoned and their properties confiscated and auctioned to pay their debts to Felipe Luis. However, once these properties were auctioned, Badia was permitted the remainder of the proceeds. Badia and de Flores remained active in the notarial record in the 1790s, and he was successful long after the imprisonment. The court record does not indicate if either Badia or de Flores were forced to return to trial in Havana, but it may be suspected otherwise.[19]

Many of the criminal cases handled by the probate court were assault cases, some involving men who had attacked women. One of the most notorious cases was that of Augustina Concha, whose husband, Juan Riquer, disguised himself and attacked her with a saber as she sat on her doorstep enjoying a night breeze. Astonishingly, her husband was only fined 96 pesos, the cost of proceeds and medical fees, and warned to avoid such behavior in the future! One wonders if there were other circumstances to this assault not discussed in the court documents that might explain such a light sentence. Other assaults were more prosaic, as when Pablo Collat was badly beaten by his former business partner Geronimo Roche.[20]

Other assaults were against slaves. Joseph Dugues, a master plasterer in the city, sued Pierre Malchoux for the "injury and loss of time caused by a severe beating given to Cezar," his African slave, a few days after Christmas

1789. Malchoux claimed that Cezar had been drunk and insulting pedestrians, and that Malchoux had prevented Cezar "from slapping a white boy." Another witness claimed that Malchoux had whipped Cezar and ordered him to return to his master's house, but Cezar refused and raised his hands to strike Malchoux, when another passerby (the witness's friend) struck Cezar. Governor Miró, as the judge, decided against Dugues, who was ordered to pay court costs. One may justifiably wonder if the case against Dugues (and more importantly, against Cezar) was a foregone conclusion, even in a more tolerant New Orleans.[21]

And some assaults were by enslaved men and women. The slave Julia was convicted of attempting to poison her master's wife by putting powdered glass in her breakfast. The convicted Julia was not executed, but instead was sentenced to two hundred lashes and publicly shamed "for eight days, two hours each day."

The slave Dominique was accused in the spring of 1790 of having murdered another runaway slave, Felipe. Dominique continued living in the woods, trapping and hunting ducks and squirrels, which other runaway slaves sold in the city. He was captured in August and brought to trial in October of the same year. His trial, however, was not a foregone conclusion—another runaway confessed to killing Felipe in self-defense under the influence of alcohol. Dominque was returned to his previous master, perhaps satisfied to have avoided execution. The guilty slave, Jacques, languished in the city's prison (or, perhaps, on a city work project) until 1793, when the new governor, Carondelet, sentenced Jacques to ten years at hard labor on the construction of fortifications in Havana and banishment from the colony. Surprisingly, the widow of Jacques's former master petitioned for his return in 1796 (she was elderly and needed the potential funds), but the court refused, reporting that Jacques still had seven more years to serve on his sentence. Obviously the three years he had spent in the *cabildo* prison (or elsewhere) had not been credited to his sentence.

At least two other cases in the Spanish probate records are intriguing not simply because they leave the reader curious about the fate of the accused but also because they illustrate that there were means to avoid the full brunt of Spanish justice in the colonial world. One such means, of course, was simply to escape from jail. Don Juan José Dorquiny attempted to kill his father-in-law in the winter of 1780; he was arrested but escaped a week later; he was recaptured a month later and, after a delay of two more years, was sentenced to six years in prison. Dorquiny escaped again in February 1784, evidently by scaling the wall, but was captured yet again.

Another means to escape a harsh sentence, even of death, was to appeal to authorities in Havana. Pedro Antonio Bidou, while sleeping at a plantation outside the city, was awakened at three in the morning by what he believed was a thief. He killed Juan De Fare, who was not a thief in fact, and Bidou admitted having done so. Governor Miró found Bidou guilty of murder and condemned him to be hanged. However, fortunately for Bidou, the appellate court in Havana commuted the sentence to two years of exile and imprisonment in Pensacola.[22]

Governor Miró, however, handled at least one other murder much more quickly. On 25 August 1785, a sailor, Juan Oliveros, was accused of the premeditated killing of another sailor; Miró was notified on the following day, and Oliveros was promptly hanged in modern-day Jackson Square without appeal. And, at other times, Miró seemed determined to use his court decisions for some other arbitrary, still harsh purpose of government. For example, four fugitive slaves attempted to free captured runaways in early 1783; they killed a Spanish government agent, but two of the four were captured in turn, and another was drowned. The two captured men each blamed someone else for the failed attack but were convicted of murder. In this case, Miró did not execute the two slaves; instead, he ordered they each be given three hundred lashes and exiled. On another occasion, two friends drank wine, argued, came to blows repeatedly, and one stabbed the other once, perhaps slightly. The victim was already suffering from liver and bladder problems and died two months later. After eleven more months of attempted litigation, de Reggio found the attacker guilty of murder, albeit indirect and unintentional, and sentenced him to six years in prison.

Criminal cases were not mere show trials: defendants had some choice of potential legal advisors, often prominent members of the community, and the government appointed a prominent prosecutor for each case as well. Nor did judges ignore evidence—indeed, they routinely ensured its proper collection. In the case immediately above, Governor Miró directed Morales to investigate the death. Morales interviewed the then-still-living victim, the accused, and two witnesses, and procured written testimony from the chief surgeon of the Royal Hospital, Dr. Montegut. After the victim died, the defendant appointed a prominent resident, Pedro Bertoniere, as his advocate.[23] The prominent Antonio Mendez also often appeared in court defending clients.

One criminal case, that of Pierre-Louis de St. Julien, actually was contested by not only the Spanish judicial system, but also by the French and American system. St. Julien claimed he was attacked on his plantation gallery and that a bullet meant for him had killed his wife. St. Julien was arrested, and the matter was much contested by French and Spanish officials alike. The incoming

French governor, Laussat, claimed that St. Julien had been framed—that Martin Duralde, "a Basque . . . a tool of Don Andres Armesto, secretary of the Spanish government . . . scheming, an insinuating meddler" had taken umbrage at St. Julien's use of the term *citoyen* in letters written at the behest of Laussat himself. If St. Julien had been tried by the Spanish governor, then he might have faced very harsh justice, indeed—but, immediately upon his official annexation of Louisiana, Laussat had St. Julien freed.[24]

However, C. C. Robin, a solid supporter of the French cause, was not convinced of St. Julien's innocence; in fact, Robin interviewed numerous people linked to the case. He decided that the St. Julien murder had not been the attempted assassination of a French supporter, and instead argued that that the case was simply one of murder: St. Julien had probably killed his own wife for her infidelity. Robin's thoughtful analysis indicates that, in at least this single case, the Spanish judicial system might have been more just than the incoming French governor, who criticized it so in his memoirs. The case continued into the American era, and Governor Claiborne traveled to the area to serve as a peacemaker and settled the case without a formal trial.[25]

The records of the lesser criminal court, the *alguacil mayor,* have not survived. However, these records do survive for the American era and provide insight into the work of the previous Spanish court. The American records reveal that free people of color in New Orleans had little to fear from legal oppression within the New Orleans court system in the early American era, and therefore presumably not in the early Spanish era. From 1805 to 1812, only 11 of 242 recorded criminal cases in the Orleans County Court and City Court were listed as being against free people of color, mostly for larceny, and only 2 for assault and battery. The courts seem to have been careful in their decisions—only 5 of those 11 accused were found guilty, and 1 of those confessed; a sixth suspect was ruled not liable as an "ignoramus."[26] If free men of color did fall afoul of the law in New Orleans, then they at least had the opportunity to testify and exert themselves within the legal system with some measure of success.

In summary, the Spanish courts in New Orleans could be harsh and swift in their handling of serious criminal cases—certainly Governor Miró seems to have leaned in that direction. However, overall, as in civil cases, those brought into the Bourbon court system in New Orleans seem to have been provided a genuine opportunity for justice. In fact, free people of color constituted a very small percentage of the lesser criminal cases heard in New Orleans (at least during the American era and so presumably in the Spanish era as well). However, some victims of crime, notably women like Augustine Concha (slashed by her husband) or Madame St. Julien (perhaps murdered by hers), received much less justice than they deserved.

SPANISH LAW'S SURVIVAL IN AMERICAN NEW ORLEANS

Many Americans assume that modern-day civil law in New Orleans is "Napoleonic law." Such could hardly be more removed from the truth, although the Spanish and French law had mutual roots in Roman law. Instead, it can be argued that French law was never operative in New Orleans, even during the twenty days of French rule in November–December 1803. One researcher emphasized that "there is not the slightest reference in Laussat's memoirs to a decision of any kind to revive the influence of French law in Louisiana."[27]

Certainly the first territorial legislators, most of French descent, did not believe the laws were "French" or "Napoleonic." On 22 May 1806, the bicameral Territorial Council of the Territory of Louisiana adopted a resolution calling for the previous colonial laws to remain in vigor, save the new laws on habeas corpus and trial by jury. Instead, they argued the state must return to

the laws and authorities following, to wit:

1. The roman Civil code, as being the foundation of Spanish law, by which this country was governed before its cession to France and to the United States, which is composed of the institutes, digest and code of the emperor Justinian, aided by the authority of the commentators of the civil law, and particularly of Domat in his treaty of the Civile laws; the whole so far as it has not been derogated from by the Spanish law; 2. The Spanish law, consisting of the books of the recompilation de Castille and autos acordados being nine books in the whole; the seven parts or *partidas* of the king Don Alphonse the learned, and the eight books of the royal statue (*fueroreal*) of Castille; the recompilation de indias, save what is therein relative to the enfranchisement of Slaves, the laws de Toro, and finally the ordinances and royal orders and decrees, which have been formally applied to the colony of Louisiana. . . .

Sect. 2. And be it further declared, that in matters of commerce the ordinance of Bilbao is that which has full authority in this Territory, to decide all contestations relative thereto.

Thus the laws in New Orleans were considered to be founded strictly upon Spanish law, as represented by several specific works, in turn founded upon Roman law, again represented by several more works. However, many American lawyers and merchants were clearly upset by this legislation because it required them to learn the intricacies of both Spanish and Roman law from works with which they had no familiarity. Given that some American lawyers might have had dubious education and legal training, the prospect of learning law in at least two foreign languages and then attempting to sway a judge on the fine points of that law must have seemed truly daunting.[28] Only two weeks later, on 10 June, the *Louisiana Gazette* published a wag's call to the legislators:

To the honorable Isaac Hebert, M. Prudhome and J. Etienne Bore!

AUGUST LEGISLATORS!
   A citizen anxious for information . . . begs you to explain to
him the merits of the law which the council . . . approved, and for
the rejection of which our governor is esteemed so censurable. I
am particularly desirous to know in which century the code of the
emperor Justinian was written? Of how many volumes it is composed?
And whether the seven parts or partidas of the king Don Alphonso the
learned can be purchased in this City?
   If the Recopilaction de Castille, and autos acordados, the laws of
Toro, and the ordinance of Bilboa [*sic*] are in either of your libraries?
   I beg you gentlemen, to furnish your constituents with a short
commentary.

A MERCHANT[29]

This early American controversy reveals that all territorial residents, of whatever ethnic origin, understood the colonial law to be Spanish law and nothing else. While at least one American merchant and the new American governor might mock them or vent frustration, the territorial legislators were expressing a wish to continue that Spanish law—with some notable exceptions.

The legislators were pleased with the American concepts of habeas corpus and trial by jury—they recalled that Spanish governors occasionally imprisoned and even banished political and social dissidents, like Pedro Bailly. But the same legislators who applauded American criminal justice also smelled an opportunity to tighten their own control over Louisiana society, while offering an equally attractive proposition to the Americans in return. This proposition was encapsulated in a single phrase within the resolution: "the recompilation [sic] de indias, save what is therein relative to the enfranchisement of Slaves."

It was by this phrase, this legal mechanism, that the planter/merchants of Louisiana would quickly remove the right of enslaved men and women to testify against their masters, sue their masters, and purchase their own freedom as they had under Spanish law. Such a phrase was not only readily understandable to the incoming American merchants and lawyers—it met their shared understanding of how the United States of America should be structured in regard to race.

Such a phrase would have been unacceptable under Bourbon Spanish rule, and this vital phrase alone represented the end of Spanish racial law in the United States. The deadly phrase "save what is therein relative to the enfranchisement of Slaves" instead meant a turn in the road, a continuation and significant geographic expansion of North American racial law, and a detour that would lead to war decades later.[30] The first shot of that war, not ironically, would be fired by General Pierre Gustave Toutant-Beauregard, the descendant by birth and marriage of so many of the "French" planter/merchants who had turned from and closed off the road to peaceful emancipation so many years before.

CONCLUSION

It was the *vecinos* of Bourbon New Orleans who truly established law and order—a well-functioning civil and criminal judicial system—in not only that city, but also in the vast portion of the "American" West encompassed by the Louisiana colony. The Spanish civil system could be cumbersome, with its pages and pages of probate documents, but it was inclusive of all *vecinos* and even non-*vecinos*. Everyone in the colony had the right to file suit, no matter their ethnicity, race, or gender—just as in every other Spanish colony. The Bourbon criminal system in New Orleans could be more harsh and perhaps more arbitrary, but, especially as administered at the lower levels by Creole judges, the system seems to have left the bulk of the population unmolested. Being generally left alone, of course, and having an expectation of justice when one must appear in court, is a major step toward true political discourse.

Political Discourse and Practices in Spanish New Orleans

> *Don Lope:* Socially speaking, you accept
> All sorts of impositions—no?
> *Pedro Crespo:* Upon my house and money—yes—
> Upon my reputation—no.
> I'll give up life and property
> At the King's word. But honor is
> The offspring of the soul of man
> And the soul, God tells us, is his.
> —Pedro Calderón de Barca, *The Mayor of Zalamea*

In the 1790s and early 1800s, the merchants of Spanish New Orleans retrenched economically, built new trans-imperial connections, saved their capital or invested it in land, and, based on the sudden surge in trade in 1803, waited for a more permanent political change in their colony. During this same period, the city's literate population, including the merchants, continued to diversify ethnically, racially, and linguistically and increasingly used the Spanish court system. It should be unsurprising, then, that it was also during this very period that the merchants of New Orleans acquired an increasing role in their own government via the city's *cabildo*, organized themselves socially, and used the imperial petition system to sometimes publicly and strongly disagree with their governor, their ministers, and even their king.

These merchants and planter/merchants were still working within the Spanish imperial rules, but they no longer needed to see themselves as Spanish. Many hailed from several nations and spoke several languages; most built their wealth via trans-imperial trade. As the merchants exercised more political power via their *cabildo*, they expanded the number of participants, sometimes via small elections, in what might be labeled limited self-rule. They organized themselves not into the religious brotherhoods or guilds so typical of the Spanish empire, but rather into Masonic lodges, like their French, British, and American contemporaries. And they dared challenge the king's economic policy—and signed their names to that impolite challenge.

These small steps brought the merchants and the populace further in political discourse from the Spanish king and closer to that of *los Americanos*. Such small steps would therefore bring them from being colonial to becoming, in the broadest sense, American.

CIVIC DISCOURSE IN THE SPANISH EMPIRE

Spanish history and literature are replete with tropes that indicate there were always limits to authority in Spanish society. Even Columbus returned in chains to Spain for alleged tyranny. Pedro Crespo, Calderón's fictional mayor of Zalamea (apparently based on a real historical character), expressed some of those limits when he implemented justice against a military officer for a heinous crime. He defended his rights based upon popular concepts of both justice and honor that transcended Spanish law. His rights were argued to and accepted, at least in Calderón's drama and clearly in popular thought, by even the king himself. A 2016 analysis wrote of Crespo and his justice: "The outcome brings a poetic justice which does not conform with formal legal procedures, but which underlines a desire for democratization within an absolutist monarchial concept."[1]

Within Bourbon society and rule, too, there were limits on repression and rapacity, based not only upon justice and honor, but also upon concepts of Catholic faith, civil society, the right to petition and seek redress even from the king himself (Philip II in Calderón's play), the rule of premodern law, and a Bourbon sense of practicality and decorum. Consequently, although the Bourbon governors in New Orleans did hold significant military, judicial, administrative, and economic powers, they were limited both ethically and practically in the application of those powers.

Unsurprisingly, then, the enlightened governors of Spanish New Orleans accepted substantive civic discourse. The Spanish concept of *vecindad* permitted quick assimilation for the city's and colony's foreigners; the city's *cabildo* provided a forum for limited self-government; residents assembled at least

within the Masons and limited ethnic celebrations; and residents availed themselves of the right to petition Spanish authorities. These residents then brought
their Bourbon-era perceptions of civic rights and responsibilities with them
when they were annexed by the United States.

Of course, political or civic discourse anywhere in the Bourbon empire was
not as unguarded, organized, and channeled through elective positions as in
the American, British, Dutch, and French systems. Nonetheless, hierarchical
political systems like the Spanish empire could permit guarded, informally organized political discourse, channeled through acceptable elites and procedures.
A modern comparison may be found in the manner in which many hierarchical
governments not only tolerate discourse from government employees and even
military officials, but also entrench or reshape policies based on the intensity
and nature of that discourse. Such was the discourse within Bourbon New Orleans: the city's *vecinos* may not have found democratic representation, but they
could often find a representative, and they had clear expectations about their
own rights within the government and empire.[2]

Some prominent textual critiques will provide context on how Spanish
governance in New Orleans has been seen by historians. In particular, two
letters in English from the Spanish archives, which have evidently never been
used before by historians of Spanish America or the United States, will document a positive Anglophone/American view of the Spanish colonial government, or certainly at least the Bourbon governor.

Four crucial aspects of political discourse may be discerned within Spanish
New Orleans: citizenship (as represented by the Spanish concept of *vecindad*),
the right to assemble peacefully, the right to petition the government, and the
rule of law. Crucially, these aspects of Spanish governance were translated,
almost immediately upon cession, into two important but barely studied documents of US history—the citizenship petition of free men of color, detailed
here for the first time; and the remonstrance to the US Congress, both written
in 1804.

These documents challenge conventional perceptions that the people of
New Orleans were taught democracy and earned citizenship during the Jeffersonian period.[3] Instead, the people of New Orleans already held strong views
on citizenship, natural rights, and law long before the US Army marched into
the Plaza de Armas. Accordingly, the "black legend" of Spanish tyranny must be
revisited—at least as it might apply to New Orleans and the Louisiana colony—
to clarify what several key historical sources reported.

THE BLACK LEGEND, ONCE AGAIN

As might be expected, the French-born Pitot, Robin, and Laussat were biting in their disparagement of Spanish government in New Orleans. Pitot moaned:

> isolated like a gangrenous growth from the body of the state, but useful for the preservation of one of its members [Mexico], the Louisianans were always Spanish in name, French at heart, and often ran the risk of contraband trade with foreigners.
>
> If . . . the intention of Spain by such an administration was to allow a colony to vegetate . . . dangerous by its population (because it was French), then she could not have adopted a better plan. At the time of my arrival, the indifference in the colony, I could say its hatred for the government, was at its peak.[4]

And again, "Why, if everything prospers under the control of an Englishman, does it all disintegrate under that of the Spaniards? Pensacola is now nothing but a hovel."[5] And finally, in praising Governor Carondelet, implying that a Spanish governor would have been more prone to use excessive force, "a man of French origin who, in fulfilling his duties as a Spaniard, committed few errors where another might have resorted to violence."[6]

Laussat, although a newly appointed diplomat, could be much less diplomatic than Pitot; he praised the intendant, Morales, as difficult but incorruptible and talented, but trashed other Spanish officials as dishonest, manipulative, and corrupt. His most famous and oft-repeated quote, "All Louisianans are Frenchmen at heart!" may have been merely a repetition of Pitot's earlier words that "the Louisianans were always Spanish in name, French at heart."[7]

It was also apparently Pitot (labeled by Laussat as "Picot," or was this an editor's error?) who brought Berquin-Duvallon's harsh *Vue de la Colonie Espagnole du Mississippi* to New Orleans in the spring of 1803. Laussat seconded the book's description of the Spanish intendant, Vidal, labeling him "a diseased heart, a more twisted mind . . . the personification of the Spanish spirit in this country." Daniel Clark, however, reported that Laussat had quite a strong hatred for the Spanish authorities in New Orleans, "augmented tenfold" when Spanish officers and their families refused to assist at a dinner hosted by Madame Laussat. The latter, according to Clark, publicly and loudly labeled the Spanish officers "souls of filth" and "mean slaves."[8]

Robin also roundly complained of Spanish corruption, especially accusing

Andre Almonaster and Vidal, the latter of whom he referred to as the *Auditeur* who "would have been better named the *Preneur* (taker)," accusing him of official thievery. Somewhat oddly, he also claimed that, in Louisiana, "justice has resulted from injustice, for the inhabitants have lost their taste for litigation and have adopted the habit of accepting the decisions of arbiters. I have often heard the colonists lament these depredations of justice and blame themselves for not having deputized some of their number to carry their complaints to the court at Madrid." Robin reported that outlying magistrates administered summary justice and could "hardly sign their names."[9]

Pitot also dismissed the utility of formal social and political discourse within Spanish New Orleans; he reported that the city's *cabildo* was "absolutely useless . . . because of the domineering influence that the governor general takes toward them." He felt similarly about the *syndics,* a sort of Spanish chamber of commerce, considering them ineffective, underutilized and unfunded by the government, although he himself served as an appointed *síndico* his first four years in the city, from 1796 to 1799.[10]

These four most quoted sources on the Spanish governance of Louisiana, it is evident, were all French and very prejudiced indeed. Only one of these, Pitot, remained in Louisiana afterwards. Historians, therefore, would be wise to carefully consider these sources.

Laussat was hardly interested in republican democracy. Like the Spanish before him, Laussat chose to appoint municipal officials rather than hold elections for his own short-lived French government. Of the fifteen officials he appointed, all but three were of French ancestry. One of the appointees, Jacques Villere, was the son of the French rebel who had died during his arrest or incarceration, perhaps violently, after the failed planters' revolt of 1768–69. Laussat was probably making, at least in his own mind, a political point that France had justifiably returned and supplanted a Spanish government that had brutally quashed a revolt of Frenchmen.[11] He was not attempting to make a point about democracy.

Despite his appointment of three Anglophones to his municipal council, Laussat certainly did not trust them to support his own colonial project. It was in this very period, in November 1803, that Daniel Clark assembled a militia unit of US citizens (and probably other Anglophones) for use if necessary to ensure an eventual cession to the United States. Laussat in turn distrusted Clark and believed that he had provoked the French versus American disturbances known as "the Battle of the Ballrooms" in January 1804, after the American annexation.[12]

However, despite the anti-Spanish opinions of French loyalists like Laussat, many *Americanos* in Spanish Louisiana and its capital of New Orleans seemed to genuinely like and respect their own Spanish administrators. For example, in 1796, a large group of Anglophones in modern-day Mississippi, most if not all US citizens, wrote Governor Gayoso in Natchez, thanking him for Carondelet's assurances that their real property rights would be protected on lands that would be later conceded to the United States. They wrote in English, confiding themselves to "his Majesty's Paternal Protection: But now we are satisfied that this happened thro' a diplomatick oversight, and not through a Contemptuous abandonment of us."

The landowners were of course grateful for the property rights "now secured to us by his Majesty's Royal Bounty," but they went on to emphasize their great respect and perhaps fondness for Gayoso, although the line between affection and diplomatic flattery can be difficult to determine:

We are extremely flattered by your Excellency in imputing to our Dispositions, the good order that has prevailed in this Country under your administration: But *we* beg leave to attribute it to your Excellency's great Talent for Governing; for Harmonizing discord and Spirits, and to the Conciliating powers, which you possess in so great a Degree. We confess Sir that we have improved by your vigilance and mild admonitions, and profited by your Examples. One Merit we claim, which we hope your Excellency will acknowledge to be our due, that is, that we always paid the Strictest Obedience to the Laws, and testified on all occasions, an unequivocal fidelity to our Sovereign.

Subject as you are in your Military Capacity to be removed from us, by the orders of your great Master, we only can say, that whenever, that Event shall take place, Our prayers shall be most fervently addressed to the Lord of Hosts, to take you under his Holy Protection, and to Crown your Enterprizes with glorious success. Whether our Lot shall place us, on this, or t'other side of the Line, these good wishes for your Excellency, we shall always cherish and retain.

December 23, 1796

This kind letter indicates that the twenty-seven men who signed it recognized themselves, at least temporarily, as still faithful and obedient subjects of the Spanish empire. They publicly complemented the governor for ensuring "good order" and his "mild admonitions," with evident affection for Gayoso.

All twenty-seven had English names, and the signatures were grouped by families, which speaks much of how Americans settled the southern United States. Daniel Clark the elder—whom historians always consider a permanent resident of New Orleans, was the first signer and quite possibly the organizer and drafter of this letter. He was followed by John Wall, three Joneses, seven Lovelaces, three Roaches, five Smiths, a Collins, four Ogdens, and two Percys—names that would reappear in Mississippi and Louisiana history.[13] In a word, the letter above indicates that the future Americans near Natchez saw the Spanish governor as a genuine friend.

A slightly smaller group of eighteen "inhabitants of the District of Buffalo" in modern-day Mississippi again wrote to Governor Gayoso two years later, on 13 July 1797. Many were the same men who had signed the December 1796 letter only eight months before, including five members of the Lovelace family, Daniel Ogden, and Daniel Clark. On this occasion, they thanked Gayoso for "your cooperation with Commissioner Elicot [sic] and Lieutenant Pope in the Service of the United States, and with a Committee of the notables of your Government in suppressing the disposition manifested lately by a number of inhabitants of Natchez to destroy all order and regular government, and to introduce confusion . . . [preventing] mischief to the sober and industrious subjects and citizens."

Although Daniel Clark's signature was not the first, the letter was addressed from his home at "Clark's Ville," the modern-day ghost town of Clarksville, Mississippi, two miles south of Fort Adams, 40 miles south of Natchez, and yet still 150 miles from New Orleans, quite a distance by boat or horse.[14] The distance between Clark's homes—and similarly those of men like Santiago Mather and David Ross, who lived in both Natchez and New Orleans—makes it clear that Spanish concepts of domicile, residency, vecino, and citizenship were rather fluid in Louisiana. In this frontier colony—and perhaps in other Spanish colonies as well—the Clarks, Mather, and Ross could maintain valid residency and thus be recognized as genuine vecinos, with all due rights and responsibilities, in two distant and different locations, albeit within the same colony. Simultaneously, all four men could also consider themselves to be members of another empire, that is, truly dual-citizens.

In summary, historical French biases about the justice and efficiency of Spanish Bourbon government in Louisiana and its capital, New Orleans, must be compared to the views of Anglophones living and working in the same colony and city. The fond and respectful letters written by the Natchez merchants to the Spanish governor in 1796 and 1797 clearly demonstrate that there is another historical view that must be considered—the view of the incoming Anglophones, most of whom were American.

VECINDAD (OR CITIZENSHIP?) IN SPANISH NEW ORLEANS

New Orleans merchant Enrique Darcantel penned a long letter to the very powerful minister of the Indies, José de Gálvez, in 1789. Darcantel's very first concern in that letter was who should be permitted to consider themselves colonists in Louisiana and therefore who should have the right to conduct business in the Spanish empire. He wrote,

> 1st. The newly arrived, or known to be transient, should not be considered as a colonist nor participate in the *gracias* conceded to those of this class, and there should be no doubt that this latter class includes those who recognize Your Majesty; that they have been settled in the province or married with a woman born in the province or established in it or have remained continuously two years in the country with an occupied house, owing above all to profess the Catholic Religion, make the oath of fidelity and vassalage to the King to permit them to live in it, and obligate themselves to the contributions and responsibilities to which vassals elsewhere are subject.[15]

Darcantel's view was that genuine Spanish *vecinos* must formally recognize the Spanish king, have lived in the colony for two years, profess the Catholic faith, and obligate themselves to "contributions and responsibilities," including militia duty. These views on who should be considered genuine colonists, and therefore permitted to participate in the colony's commerce, were similar to those in much of the Spanish empire. The Spanish and their colonials considered themselves *vecinos* (roughly "good neighbors," but also implying responsibilities, thus often translated as "citizens"), but not necessarily subjects in the British sense. In the Spanish empire, for example, a Frenchman by birth could simply reside, work hard, and be accepted in Mexico or Peru as a *vecino*, with the right to conduct business, marry, hold high positions, and so forth. This was considered a natural right, and no royal recognition was required.[16]

Therefore many Spanish officials in Louisiana were not Iberian or Hispanic at all: they were instead often Irish, French, Italian, and Greek by birth. Such were Governor-Generals O'Reilly and Carondelet, Geromo La Chiapella, and Miguel Dragon. Correspondents and petitioners in the Spanish empire, including Darcantel, would identify themselves first as *vecinos* even in letters to the king and his governors, rather than as *sujetos*, although they would inevitably refer to their fidelity to the king.

The British differed from the Spanish in identifying subjects by their birthplaces: British courts, administrators, and famously naval officers before the War of 1812 believed that a person born in Great Britain or a British colony was forever a British subject (with some natural rights), no matter where that person might be. To become a British citizen, however, required naturalization. Herzog argued that some of this difference between Spanish and British concepts of citizenship arose from Spain's loose confederation of sometimes autonomous kingdoms/provinces, which encouraged a looser concept of being a "subject" and a more inclusive concept of being a member of a larger entity.[17]

The Spanish concept of being a *vecino* was therefore more open than even modern concepts of citizenship. Within Louisiana, and perhaps in other Spanish colonies, an individual could be a *vecino* of more than one location simultaneously. Anglophones, including Mather, the Clarks, and Ross, were often simultaneously documented as *vecinos* in Spanish notarial, church, and census records in two different places—Natchez and New Orleans.

It may be for this reason that one recent historian assumed that Clark in 1798 "had traded both his British identity and his Spanish allegiance to become an American citizen" and later serve as American consul in New Orleans. In fact, Clark could not have, in British jurisprudence, "traded" his identity; the British king still considered him a subject, however unrealistically, and Clark could have even been impressed into the British Navy, as was done to other Americans in the early 1800s. Nor would he have needed American citizenship to serve as a consul. Governor Someruelos in Cuba had not been as much concerned about the potential double-allegiance of John Morton as consul as he was about Morton's simultaneous command of Spanish soldiers. Indeed, after the annexation, Clark's close associate Richard Relf served as the Danish consul in New Orleans despite his own US citizenship.[18]

There were exceptions to this inclusive view of citizenship within the Spanish empire itself. Socolow, citing a prominent case in colonial Buenos Aires, claimed that "All merchants born outside of the Spanish realm had to obtain *cartas de ciudadania* from the Crown. Petitions for naturalization were granted only when a man had spent many years in the colony, had married a native or

Spanish-born woman, and was well established in commerce." However, such was clearly not the case for the merchants of New Orleans—no similar *cartas* or requirements have been noted in the Spanish archives for Louisiana or its capital city. The Spanish probate records hold many formal requests for recognition as a resident *vecino,* but these seem to have been associated only with specific voyages or vessels and were mostly made by merchants of French ancestry or their factors.[19]

A final point should be made about *vecindad* in the Spanish empire—it might have included numerous foreigners and free people of color, but it was also hierarchical, based upon social status, wealth, and race. Therefore, to actually hold an appointed or purchased position in the Bourbon government, or for women to marry a Bourbon official, one had to be able to demonstrate *sangre pura* (pure blood)—"of pure race without any mixture of Moorish, Jewish, Mulatto or Indian." It is not surprising, then, that Spanish probate courts in New Orleans occasionally issued documents certifying purity of blood for various *vecinos* of both sexes. Such certificates were issued typically for colonial administrators, their widows, or their intended wives; such was the case for Antonio Mendes as he sought to be named city attorney, Juana de Grand Pre, the widow of the former colonial assessor, and even Colonel Gilbert St. Maxent, one of whose daughters was the widow of Governor Gálvez.[20]

In summary, it was not difficult to claim *vecindad* in Bourbon New Orleans, and that claim might even be rather fluid, encompassing two locations and even two simultaneous citizenships. This inclusiveness of *vecindad* was not as common elsewhere in the Spanish empire. However, as elsewhere in the empire, that *vecindad* was bounded both in rights and in responsibilities by a hierarchy of race.

THE RIGHT TO ASSEMBLE: THE *CABILDO*

Vecinos in the Spanish empire always assumed the natural right to assemble— they certainly did so for a multitude of religious and social occasions, and sometimes did so for economic and political reasons. The central place for legitimately sanctioned political discussions was the *cabildo*—the city hall. Most if not all Spanish cities had a *cabildo*: some of these have been documented by the Consejo Superior de Investigaciones Científicas in a series of compilation works published in the 1990s. Among these, the scholar Javier Ortiz de la Tabla Ducasse notably compiled and edited letters and summaries of the work of the *cabildos* in the *audiencias* of Guatemala City, Quito, Santa Fe de Bogota, and Lima.[21]

The *cabildo* fulfilled multiple roles in urban society, within the judiciary, finances, slave control, public health, medicine, markets, public works, building regulations, land grants, and liaison and ceremonial functions. Numerous *vecinos* participated in the routine activities of the *cabildo* and enjoyed relationships with the governor and intendant.[22] It was through their assembly and participation in the *cabildo* that many residents of Spanish New Orleans demonstrated their fulfillment of the responsibilities inherent in genuine *vecindad*—and this participation was therefore an important element in the overall political discourse of the city.

It would be easy to assume that the *cabildo* was a mere arm of the Spanish governor filled with collaborators; Laussat and Pitot portrayed it in that manner. However, the truth was quite the opposite. The number of *cabildo* members, the many collateral roles of its members, the size of its required staff, and the demographic and elite position of those members and staff all resulted in a *cabildo* very much aware of the issues and challenges acting within the Louisiana colony, and certainly within the relatively small city of New Orleans. To a certain extent, this awareness meant that the *cabildo* very much represented the city's interests to the Spanish Crown—admittedly often the interests of elites, but such elite interests were nonetheless important to the efficient management of the colony and city.[23] It is therefore important to understand just how many government posts and responsibilities were encompassed within the *cabildo*, at least in Bourbon New Orleans.

The *cabildo* was presided over by the governor or his agent, but consisted of six voting members until 1797 and twelve voting members from 1797 until 1803. Most of the voting members were known as *regidores perpetuos* (permanent aldermen), with five of those also holding collateral offices and the other one (and later seven) filling positions without collateral requirements (*regidores perpetuos sencillos*/basic permanent aldermen). The five collateral offices included an *alferez real* (royal standard-bearer), *alcade mayor provincial* (chief provincial magistrate), *alguacil mayor* (city magistrate/jail warden), *depositario general* (property/funds custodian), and *receptor de penas de camara* (court fines manager). All of these positions could be either assigned by the Spanish Crown or, more often, sold to those willing and able to purchase the position.

Two other *alcades ordinarios* also served as voting members (*de primer* and *de segundo voto*); both of these were judges elected annually by the other *cabildo* voting members. The *cabildo* was also supported by numerous nonvoting members, including the *sindico procurador general*, the *mayordomo de propios* (both elected annually), the *escribano* (permanent clerk, appointed or sold), *alcades de barrio* (ward captains, elected), and syndics within New Orleans (*sindicos de distritos,* also elected), and numerous employees.[24]

The above composition of the *cabildo* may seem all rather banal and typical of other cities within the Bourbon Spanish empire, and that is exactly the point. The New Orleans Cabildo was structured very much like other *cabildos,* and this structure marks the city, at least in the minds of the Bourbon governors, as just another Spanish imperial city, albeit challenging. This similarity in structure also marked the officials who filled the necessary municipal positions as functionaries of the Bourbon government—in other words, it provided them with an identity within the larger Spanish empire. This self-designation as Spanish officials is yet another element layered onto *vecindad*/citizenship that formed the basis of political discourse within the city and colony.

The twelve voting positions on the *cabildo* were assigned or sold to a total of twenty-nine *vecinos* during the thirty-four years between 1769 and 1803—a turnover of about one member every year. Of these twenty-nine appointments, only five were relinquishments from a father to a family member, usually a son, upon a *regidor's* death; such were those by de Reggio, Almonaster y Roxas, to de la Ronde (his brother-in-law), Olivier, Beauregard, and Ducros. Sometime, the post was simply sold by the current *regidor* (Olivier, de La Garciniere, and Glapion) to an aspirant. At other times the post was simply vacated, sometimes for a successor (as with de la Barre), sometimes by death (as with Arnoul and Bienvenu), sometimes abandoned (as by Braud), and sometimes simply renounced (by Fleurian, Andry, and Danycan).

However they reached the *cabildo,* the voting members were roughly representative of the interests of the colony. The *regidores perpetuos* represented the old generation of French planters, but they were typically led by one or two *regidores* of verifiable Spanish loyalty, including Almonaster y Roxas (1790–98) and the Beauregards (1779, 1783–92), and two more of likely Spanish trust, the de Reggios (1769–90, and of Italian/French origin) and Forstall (1772–78, 1795–1803, of English origin). However, by 1797, two of the "French" positions had been in litigation for several years, two more were constantly ill, and the *cabildo* often lacked adequate members for a quorum or decisive vote. In addition, the Spanish authorities had probably determined they required new *regidores* more in tune with the city's commercial economy. Consequently, the Spanish appointed six new *regidores perpetuos sencillos.* Of these six, three were Spanish in origin (de Riano, Jorda, and de Castanedo), Danycan was Irish, and Andry was likely Italian. Of the original six, Leblanc was of French origin (although Bouligny, a long-time Spanish senior officer, would replace Andry, and Fonvergne would replace Danycan).[25]

The composition of the voting *cabildo* members, then, evolved in line roughly with the changing demographics in the city. This was certainly not representative government from an American or French perspective, but it was still not removed from the composition of the actual populace.

In addition, it will be recalled, the city council voted for two *alcades ordinarios* (local magistrates), a *sindico procurador general*, and a *mayordomo de propios*. Close analysis of the thirty-nine magistrates elected from 1770 to 1803 indicates that their composition was a logical mixture of men of French (twenty) and Spanish (eighteen) origin; unsurprisingly, the Spanish elected no free men of color as judges, but very surprisingly, they also only elected one man of northern European origin, Nicolas Forstall, among these thirty-nine judges. Indeed, one is struck by how, after 1789, the city's *alcades ordinarios* were almost all of Spanish origin and often, despite Spanish law, active Spanish treasury officials. Of the twenty *alcades ordinarios* from 1789 to 1803, thirteen were of Spanish origin.[26] The city's magistrates, then, were decidedly unrepresentative of the populace, especially when compared to the voting members of the *cabildo*.

The *sindico procurador general* was a position something like a municipal inspector, meant to safeguard the public, propose solutions, and fight in court for public rights. The position was held by numerous *vecinos*, many of whom would serve later in the other municipal posts, but it required great activity and was an unpaid position. The *mayordomo de propios*, something akin to the city treasurer but also responsible for city lighting and night watchmen, was generally held for several years, although it, too, was elective. Only nine men held the position from 1770 to 1803; the most notable of these was probably Juan de Castanedo, who served in that role from 1793 until the end of Spanish rule.[27]

Whether they purchased their position, were assigned it, or elected to it by others, the *cabildo* was meant to "assemble every Friday." This is not to presume that the New Orleans Cabildo was an example of representative democracy, for it was not. Din and Harkins reported, "There is no evidence that any of the governors ever interfered in the *Cabildo's* annual elections. In fact, the elections were often decided beforehand, and the election day balloting was a formality. Only occasionally were elections contested."[28] However, this is to presume that the *cabildo* was a vehicle by which at least the elite of New Orleans, planters, planter/merchants, merchants, and craftsmen alike, might assemble and express their concerns publicly to Spanish officials, with an expectation of being heard with some respect.

The *cabildo* maintained generally cordial relations with the several Spanish governors of Louisiana. Among these governors, the first, Ulloa, did not establish a *cabildo* because he did not wish to ruffle the very French planters who would depose him. His successor, Alejandro O'Reilly, famously dealt with the recalcitrant planters by shooting five of them; he established the *cabildo* on the same day he installed Unzaga as governor. Unzaga, in turn, was conciliatory to the planters and married the daughter of Spanish supporter (or Spanish collaborator) Gilbert Antoine de St. Maxent. The next governor, Gálvez, married another daughter of St. Maxent; his successor, Miró, married the daughter of prominent planter/merchant de Macarty; Carondelet was already married when he arrived, but Gayoso married two daughters of an English officer,[29] perhaps an indication of which way the colony was already turning demographically.

Marriage connections within the elite notwithstanding, the *cabildo* doubtless saw the value in cooperating with the Spanish governors, most of whom exercised military power and had their own political base. Unzaga was supported by the specter of O'Reilly's executions; Gálvez was a war hero, and his uncle was the minister of the Indies, to whom all the *cabildo's* appeals would have been forwarded (via the captain general of Cuba). Miró had been a trusted administrator for Gálvez; his replacement, Carondelet, was an experienced governor and the brother-in-law of the captain general of Cuba, Luis de Las Casas, to whom, again, all appeals would have been forwarded. The next governor, Gayoso, expanded the *cabildo* with six new *regidores,* mostly Spaniards, but the "French" elite were already being Hispanicized and even replaced within their own social circles by Spaniards and northern Europeans.

It was only in 1799 that the *cabildo* began to quarrel with Spanish governors—in this case, not the military governors Bouligny and Casa-Calvo, but rather with the acting civil governor, Vidal, who exerted his authority in a legalistic, moralistic, and decidedly uncordial manner. His replacement, Salcedo, a former military commander in the Canary Islands, worsened relationships, and Vidal exacerbated these by continuing to serve as the governor's legal advisor. Some of the arguments were over protocol; others focused on more substantial issues like vaccination and slave importation.[30]

The issue of slave imports by sea arose in August 1800, following the petition of a group of likely French planters to the *cabildo.* The *cabildo,* Din and Harkins reported, "debated the issue heatedly," and the *cabildo* members voted six to five to oppose a reopening of the maritime slave trade. However, Vidal, Casa-Calvo, and the intendant Lopez, who all favored reopening that trade, argued that the *cabildo's* vote was merely advisory, and Lopez directed the importation of slaves from Africa. The *cabildo* refused to recognize Lopez's authority on this matter and appealed to the Crown; Lopez departed for another government assignment, and the new intendant, Morales, rescinded his predecessor's decree. The *cabildo* had beaten the Spanish governor at least once, if only until the French annexation.[31]

Clearly, the *cabildo* was the logical place for political assembly, participation, and discourse within Spanish New Orleans, as it was in the Spanish empire elsewhere. The painting of the famed *cabildo abierto* (open *cabildo* meeting, admittedly only used in emergencies) held in Buenos Aires on 22 May 1810 is a stark reminder that the Bourbon Spanish, in their respect for the right of assembly—if not representative government—were not so very different from their rivals in Great Britain, the United States, and eventually France. The *cabildo* can be positioned in a natural evolution or chain of political discourse—from *vecindad* to municipal participation and, next, to discourse outside the walls of the *cabildo*.

THE RIGHT TO ASSEMBLE:
THE FREEMASONS AND ETHNIC CELEBRATIONS

Beyond the *cabildo,* there were always other opportunities for the *vecinos* of New Orleans to assemble for open discourse. The market, the levee, promenades, social events, plays, hunts, militia drills, Catholic mass, religious functions and festivals, and trials all provided numerous opportunities for social, economic, and political discourse.

Unlike perhaps every other city in the Spanish empire, there was no prominent *confradia,* that is, religious fraternity focused on a particular saint, in Spanish New Orleans. There were surely small cells of men and women who supported the cathedral, the convent, or religious processions—but these were hardly if ever noted in historical accounts. Instead, surprisingly, the most active social groups in Spanish New Orleans were perhaps the Freemasons and the free militia of color.

The Freemasonry movement was one of the most potent symbols of free assembly and political discourse in the eighteenth and nineteenth centuries. Consequently this secret society, which rose to prominence in the late 1700s throughout Europe, North America, and the Caribbean, was viewed with great suspicion by Spanish Bourbon authorities. However, the Freemasonry movement was not clandestine in Spanish New Orleans; indeed, it was established there during Carondelet's governorship. The original organizers, reportedly refugees from St. Domingue, formed a lodge in 1793, received a charter from the Grand Lodge of South Carolina as Parfaite Union No. 29, and installed their officers in the York Rite in the following spring, on 30 March 1794. That same year, another group of Brethren of the French, who practiced the "Modern Rite," organized another lodge in New Orleans, the Étoile Polaire (Polar Star), and applied for a charter from the Grand Orient in France. Given that the Grand Lodge had suspended activity because of the French Revolution, they obtained a provisional charter from the Provincial Lodge La Parfaite Sincérité at Marseilles in 1796. Dominique Mayronne, the prominent planter/merchant, then established the new lodge under the French Rite on 27 December 1798.[32]

Albert Gallatin Mackey, a late-nineteenth-century historian of Freemasonry, wrote that it was believed "that the Brethren who formed these two lodges were from the Island of Guadeloupe"—not St. Domingue—had fled after the slave insurrection on Guadeloupe of 1791, but had split into two lodges once in New Orleans because of differences over the French Revolution. At least one and perhaps two other lodges were established in New Orleans before the American annexation: Candor Lodge No. 90, from the remnants of Candor Lodge No. 12 in Charleston, South Carolina, and chartered by the Grand Lodge of Pennsylvania in May 1801, and Charity Lodge No. 93, also chartered in Pennsylvania in March 1802. Given that both of these lodges were led by N. Definieto, they might have been the same lodge after all.[33]

The growth of the Masonic movement in Spanish New Orleans and Louisiana may be best demonstrated by a simple but intriguing symbol found within numerous signatures in letters and documents. The symbol is a double-lined bar with three, sometimes four, dots inside the bar, on each side of a signature. The symbol associated with membership in Freemasonry. It is especially remarkable that so many merchant petitions, letters to royal officials, and even letters *from* royal officials contain signatures that *likely* indicate open membership in the Masonic movement. Within the Spanish archives in Seville, the 1796 merchant petition from New Orleans included five such signatures, including prominent merchant J. B. Labatut; the 1797 petition included two; most of these seven signatures were of French surnames.[34]

But it is not merely the signatures of merchants that appear in Spanish archives with these marks. Rather, many letters to and *from* royal officials contain signatures that likely indicate open membership in the Masonic movement. Among signatures from Spanish officials may be included those of

Antoine St. Amant from the German Coast to the Spanish auditor, M. Andry, and Louis Blanc to Carondelet himself, Elias Beauregard from Nogales, and Filhiol from Ouachita, all entrusted with important duties within the colony.[35] Dozens of such signatures appear in New Orleans Notarial Archives, as well, with doubtless more to be identified.

The Freemasonry movement in New Orleans, then, was not hidden at all, and provided an opportunity for civic discourse and service permitted by Spanish authorities. Indeed, one of the most famous portraits from New Orleans, that of Dr. Joseph Montegut and his family, depicts the doctor holding a triangle—a mark of Masonry. Based upon surviving records from the American era, several Masons can be positively identified who were present in Spanish New Orleans. These include J. B. Labatut in La Parfaite Union, Domingue Mayronne and Lefebvre in L'Étoile Polaire, and Michel Fortier in La Charité.[36]

How the Bourbon authorities really viewed the Masonic movement is a question, but they also proved to be equanimous about honoring the leaders of foreign rivals, at least if those leaders were potential or deceased. When three of the Bourbon French princes visited the city in 1798, the Spanish Bourbons were very hospitable. Louis Philippe d'Orléans (who would rule France from 1830 to 1848) and his two brothers were famously entertained by the de Marigny family and Julien Poydras.[37]

A somewhat similar, if more somber, assembly occurred on 5 February 1800, with a commemoration of the recent death of George Washington. Prominent Americans Evan Jones and William Hulings received Casa-Calvo's permission for a small gathering and a procession to the levee to witness a gun salute from an American warship.[38] For Casa-Calvo, the concession may have seemed not only magnanimous but decidedly appropriate, for Washington had been the leader in war and peace of Spain's sometime forgotten ally—the United States of America. For a military man, it might have simply seemed the honorable thing to do.

In summary, the Bourbon governors in New Orleans seem to have permitted their ethnically diverse population some ability to demonstrate their "otherness" within the confines of the Spanish colony. Carondelet's recognition of a Masonic lodge (and therefore secret meetings of mostly French residents), Gayoso's reception of the poor French princes, and Casa-Calvo's permission for a simple ceremony to recognize the passing of the US president all indicate a willingness to accept that the residents of New Orleans were, after all, still not quite Spanish.

THE RIGHT TO PETITION

In fact, Spanish *vecinos* of whatever nationality and color did have a very useful means to participate in political discourse within their communities and the larger empire: the right of petition. This right was quite similar to the limited political rights enjoyed by British and French imperial subjects as well, at this time, and was precisely one of those natural rights for which the North Americans had declared their right to independence.

Although Enrique Darcantel's long letter to José de Gálvez was reviewed, edited, and reissued by the provincial intendant, Juan Ventura Morales, the merchant felt comfortable in providing his views and seeking the assistance and clarification to the royal court. He immediately stated, "I offer some concerns on the fulfillment of the Royal *Cédula* of 22 January 1782 on the commerce of this province." Darcantel's very first concern was for *vecindad*. He then addressed eight economic concerns in his letter; their content here matters less than the fact that he felt he could address these concerns forthrightly with the powerful minister who managed all of Spain's overseas empire. Darcantel boldly expressed concerns that might have all angered one group of Spanish mercantilists or another. However, in the end, he wrote that he would give the king of Spain "the most exact obedience, and I inform your Majesty of this for your knowledge. Let Our God grant your Majesty many years."[39]

Admittedly, Darcantel was only a single bold man, trusted by the Spanish regime. However, he was not the only man in New Orleans to believe himself entitled to speak to the king's ministers, even to the king himself. Four petitions are especially revealing of the opportunities for political discourse within Bourbon New Orleans and, by extension, of the potential for stretched political boundaries elsewhere in the Bourbon empire. The first two petitions are on economic issues and date from 1796 and 1797. The third petition, from free militia of color, was on a social issue, and the fourth, again from the free militia of color, on a political issue with very longstanding ramifications for the history of both Latin and North America.

THE ECONOMIC PETITIONS OF 1796 AND 1797

Two petitions in the Spanish archives demonstrate the confidence with which the New Orleans merchants directly addressed their king. The first petition, written in 1796 and signed by at least fifty-nine New Orleans merchants, was in fact quite long and surprisingly insistent.[40] The petitioners declared themselves to represent the city's merchants: "Señor, The commercial sector of New Orleans, to Your Serene Royal Majesty with the deepest respect with which it can convey. . . ."

They immediately appealed to the king's financial concerns, yet they left no doubt they considered themselves just as much beset by the King's wars and foreign policies: ". . . as by the well-known, disastrous calamities of three violent hurricanes and a raging fire suffered in the city during the last epoch, which nearly entirely ruined the fortunes of laborers and merchants."

Similarly, the merchants immediately informed the king that his treaty was causing his merchants in New Orleans to be treated unequally and that they were facing an economic choice between "final extermination" or "the sad necessity of emigrating elsewhere," unless the king should make "a judgement transcendental to the State," that is, rescind or rewrite his own treaty or grant them additional economic privileges. These proposed privileges included free, untaxed trade for Spanish merchants with American producers and merchants, permission to export silver (with a minor tax), sail ships directly from Europe without detours into Spanish ports, and the establishment of an elected *consulado* to handle mercantile business, navigation, and other incidental issues, supported by a small excise tax.

Finally, the merchants appealed to the financial focus of the Bourbon king, assuring him that "said *gracias* will consolidate the security and prosperity of these your dominions, so necessary for the conservation of the Kingdom of Mexico, which serve as a barrier and without which it [Mexico] will remain very exposed to the greed of our ambitious neighbors."

Most of the signatories to this petition were French merchants, including the two final signatures of the *deputados*, Francisco Caisergues and Pedro Petit. However, notable Spaniards like La Chiapella, Armas, Riano, Dragon, Bosque, and Poeyfarre also signed the petition, as did leading northern Europeans like Wikoff and Garland, William Stephen, and Daniel Clark (presumably the younger). Only one, Labatut (but perhaps two, Petit or Cavelier) of the signatories would be later included in Laussat's short-lived municipal government in December 1803.[41]

The second petition, from 1797, is difficult to read, but it partly focused, as had Darcantel's letter, on preventing hard currency from being shipped out of the colony and, in this case, also on the use of paper money. This petition was signed by at least twenty-two merchants, mostly French surnames including M. Fortier, Francisco Mayronne, and Labatut, but also including two prominent Spanish names, Geromo LaChiapella and Domingo de Lemos, as well as the

Anglo James Kennedy.[42] The omission of several Anglo-American and Spanish merchants, however, may indicate that *los Americanos*, and even some well-placed Spanish, accepted the flow of hard currency out of the colony, perhaps believing it was safer beyond the reach of their king's taxation, or perhaps not requiring as much currency because of their intensive use of letters of exchange.

It might be argued that Darcantel's letter, these merchant petitions from New Orleans, and the Anglophone merchant letters from near Natchez can all be considered merely economic discourse, and not political discourse at all. In each case, the writers were admittedly deferential to the king and his court, assuring His Majesty of their loyalty. This petition, however, greatly problematizes such historic views, at least on the Spanish colony of Louisiana. The New Orleans merchant petition of 1796 was an important political document precisely because it was about economic issues—the very issues about which the Bourbon court often cared the most. The merchants of New Orleans felt it proper and justified to bluntly challenge their king on his own economic policies and an international treaty—certainly a political request, if not a demand. It was not necessary to accuse Charles IV of being corrupt—they were instead accusing him of being misled by presumably corrupt and foolish ministers, as American colonists had spoken so often of George III.[43]

However, the merchants had not pulled any punches: their implication that Mexico (and the king's Mexican silver) would be endangered without Louisiana bluntly implied that Charles IV might lose the colony, by either its collapse or turning to a foreign power, a barely veiled but very real threat. Again, the petition sounds very much like a demand—and a political threat at that—however it was couched.

THE SOCIAL BALL PETITION OF 1800

The third petition to consider is not on economic issues, at all—it was focused on dancing. It will be recalled that, when Casa-Calvo arrived in New Orleans in mid-September 1799, he immediately focused on military issues. Meanwhile, however, the acting civilian governor, Don Nicolas Maria Vidal, focused upon those domestic issues he considered most important—and one of those was the conduct of public dances and plays. The city's small theater had struggled since its construction in 1792 during Carondelet's regime, but had also seen the performance of the city's first opera in 1796 and, only two weeks earlier, a play entitled *Renaud d'Ast*. The *cabildo* itself rented a theater box, but as its membership grew so did its demands upon the theater, sparking a feud between Vidal, *cabildo* members, and the acting military governor, Bouligny. Vidal issued an ordnance on 26 October that year, closing the theater and threatening "to beat [attendees] with batons, because it is a crude thing, besides being incompatible with public decency. . . . It only helps to perturb good order and tranquility, so that the public amusement is nothing but confusion."

A month later, on 21 November, the *alcades ordinarios* Francisco de Riano and Gabriel Fonvergne wrote Casa-Calvo to warn that the city's public was manifesting some annoyance over the suspension of the customary theater performance, which Vidal kept closed. Casa-Calvo was puzzled and concerned enough to seek guidance from Someruelos in Havana. He wrote on 27 December that the public was pressuring public officials on opening the theater. He wrote that theater attendance was "a custom of this town" since Carondelet himself had opened the theater. Casa-Calvo in turn worried that the public believed itself insulted, and he questioned, if there was nothing to signify the royal approval or disapproval for theater in Europe, why the operation of a theater should be a police matter in New Orleans.[44]

Fonvergne and other *cabildo* members may have worried about theater, but public dances were another matter entirely. Din and Harkins outline how a city-owned dance hall was built in 1792; white-only dances began then, but Santiago Bernardo Coquet and José Antonio Boniquet, both white businessmen, received a concession for dances for free people of color on Saturday nights. In return, Coquet and Boniquet also subsidized *El Coliseo*, the city theater. However, white men and slaves began to attend the Saturday dances, and it was Fonvergne, as *sindico procurador*, who petitioned in 1796 for the dances allotted to the free people of color be ended by prohibiting slaves from attending. The *cabildo* agreed with Fonvergne, but Carondelet did not. He instead forbade whites from attending and allowed slaves to attend the dances, with the written permission of their masters, to which the *cabildo* again agreed.[45]

However, during Vidal's term as acting civil governor, accusations of racial mixing, gambling, and criminal activity at the dances for free people of color had again surfaced within the *cabildo*. Given his opposition to the theater, Vidal surprisingly refused to prohibit the dances, at least until after the carnival season. Coquet purchased his own dance hall on Conti Street and then refused entry to at least one of the *alcades*, Francisco Caisergues. Like Carondelet and Vidal, Governor General Salcedo also considered a new petition to end the dances in 1801, but permitted the dances to continue.[46]

It was on 24 October 1800 that four free military officers of color offered their own petition, requesting that the governor and the *cabildo* grant them permission to hold a weekly public dance from 4 November 1800 until the following Mardi Gras, at the end of the winter. At least three of the officers had served since the early 1790s; three were captains, typically the highest rank held by free men of color in the Louisiana militia, and the fourth, Galafate/Calpha, was the nephew of a previous captain/commander of the city's mulatto militia. The four were clearly notable within both the free community of color and, just as importantly for the governor, within the Spanish military. They were proud of their military service to the Crown, and therefore justifiably proud to ask consideration of their petition. A partial but lengthy translation is useful:

October 24, 1800

MOST ILLUSTRIOUS CABILDO

Captain Juan Bautista Saraza and Ensign Pedro Galafate of the Battal-ion of Octoroons, and Captain Pedro Tomas and Captain Juan Bautista Bacusa of the Battalion of Quadroons of the Disciplined Militia of the Province of Louisiana, with the greatest reverence and due respect to Your Lordships, come before you and expound: That various indi-viduals came in our company from the recent expedition . . . [to] Fort San Marcos de Apalache where the men experienced bad times such as irregularity of weather and nourishment, blistering heat due to the harsh season . . . , mosquitoes, night air, humidity, and other nuisances . . . and, finally, shelling from the cannons which they expected to receive at any moment.

The men give infinite thanks to the Most High for granting them their wish to come back to their homeland. To recompense them in some manner, to cheer up their spirit, so that they can forget the hard-ships of the expedition which they undertook . . . we jointly solicit the permission of the President of the Cabildo [the governor] and Your Lordships to give weekly a public dance on Saturdays until the end of the next Carnival, beginning on the day of our most august Sovereign Charles IV. . . . The dance will not interfere with the one the white people regularly have, for they have their dance on Sundays.

Through the kindness of Don Bernardo Coquet, we have his permission to use his house for the dances. We ask that you be kind enough to the petitioners to provide them with the guards of the city. . . . When we were on the expedition, we were informed that some people came to the dances . . . determined to disrupt the peaceful diversions. . . .

Therefore, we humbly plead that Your Lordships be kind enough to concede this solicitation which has nothing to do with violence and consequently will not cause any harm. This is the season for such diversion, both in America and in Europe. We shall always keep in our hearts your renowned benevolence and kindness.

> New Orleans
> Cpt. Jean Baptiste Scarasse
> Pierre Tomas
> Pierre Calpha
> Jean Baptiste Bacuse[47]

The petition was respectful, reminded the governor and *cabildo* of the services recently performed by free soldiers of color despite the disparagement of some *vecinos,* praised the king's upcoming birthday, was practical in its proposed arrangements, requested assistance from the governor to ensure order, and noted a shared culture: "This is the season for such diversion, both in America and in Europe." The petition was well considered and well crafted, with a minimum of fuss.

What is most notable here, however, is that these free men of color—admittedly, free military men of color—considered themselves perfectly entitled to petition their governor and *cabildo,* based upon their fulfilled responsibilities as *vecinos* proud to serve under the "most august Sovereign Charles IV" and to celebrate his day with a dance—and of course, to hold a day every future Saturday for the next few months, at least.[48] The *cabildo* clearly approved of the petition, and the dances continued.

THE PETITION OF FREE MEN OF COLOR OF 1804

It can be little wonder, as the Spanish military departed, that the leaders of the free people of color in New Orleans considered themselves as *vecinos* of the Spanish empire and were determined to establish their *vecindad*—in this case, clearly seen as an equivalent to full citizenship—for the incoming American government as well. Accordingly, fifty-five of the male leaders of the free community addressed a petition to the territorial governor within days of his arrival in New Orleans. This petition was far more important than a request for winter dances—it was a request to be recognized as full citizens of the territory and their new nation. It was a request that the United States, however, would repress and forget. However, given that this request has never been used in any historical article or analytical text, to my knowledge, it bears full quotation:

ADDRESS FROM THE FREE PEOPLE OF COLOR

To His Excellency William C. C. Claiborne: Governor General and Intendant of Louisiana

We the Subscribers, free Citizens of Louisiana beg leave to approach your Excellency with Sentiments of respect & Esteem and sincere attachment to the Government of the United States.

We are Natives of this Province and our dearest Interests are connected with its welfare. We therefore feel a lively Joy that the Sovereignty of the Country is at length united with that of the American Republic. We are duly sensible that our personal and political freedom is thereby assured to us for ever, and we are also impressed with the fullest confidence in the Justice and Liberality of the Government towards every Class of Citizens which they have here taken under their Protection.

We were employed in the military service of the late Government, and we hope we may be permitted to say, that our Conduct in that Service has ever been distinguished by a ready attention to the duties required of us. Should we be in like manner honored by the American Government, to which every principle of Interest as well as affection attaches us, permit us to assure your Excellency that we shall serve with fidelity and Zeal. We therefore respectfully offer our Services to the Government as a Corps of Volunteers agreeable to any arrangement which may be thought expedient.

We request your Excellency to accept our congratulations on the happy event which has placed you at the Head of this Government, and promises so much real prosperity to the Country.

NEW ORLEANS January 1804[49]

The petition of January 1804 was a well-written document, and given its evident appearance in English, one must wonder who drafted it: only a handful of the signatories (the Hardy family) bore English surnames. Instead, it is logical to believe that a British- or American-born resident of New Orleans drafted the petition, presumably at the request of the free militia officers. Given the letter's use of the term "your Excellency," it might even be suspected that Daniel Clark or another longtime resident drafted the letter.[50]

Whoever drafted the letter does not diminish its initiation and intent. The letter is short and to the point, in an eighteenth-century sort of way. The signatories immediately defined themselves as citizens, entitled to petition their government, joyful about that new government, and eager to serve in its military. They did not ask for anything at all—they simply presumed they were citizens and they offered support and congratulations.

The 1804 petition of the free men of color of New Orleans letter is a sharp reminder of how every *vecino* claimed the right to petition his *cabildo,* his governor, and his king. To that extent, New Orleans and the Louisiana colony seem like most other places in the vast Bourbon empire.

CONCLUSION

New Orleans was not completely different from the other cities of the Bourbon empire. Indeed, in providing *vecindad,* limited representative government (at least for elites), opportunities for social assembly and limited ethnic celebrations, and the right to petition, it can well be argued that Bourbon New Orleans and the colony of Louisiana were very much like most other Spanish colonies.

However, New Orleans does problematize previous histories of the Bourbon empire. Louisiana was clearly not like other Spanish colonies, because the *vecindad,* governmental roles, limited ethnic claims, and even the right to petition were not being assumed by indigenous peoples, as in Peru, or by mestizos and native-born whites in Mexico City, Cartagena, or Buenos Aires. No, in New Orleans, these roles and rights were being assumed and assiduously exercised by non-Hispanic whites and free people of color, with their own concepts of *vecindad*/citizenship, democracy, ethnic and national identity, and civic rights. These non-Hispanic concepts had not only been shaped by their very "otherness"; they had been shaped by their very real economic power—if not domination of the colony's economy, despite Bourbon restrictions—along with their literacy and access to information outside Spanish control and their expectation to be treated at least as well as any other Spanish colonist. These were the concepts that shaped public and political discourse in Bourbon New Orleans.

Conclusion

The Transition between Two Empires

This work began by stating that the Bourbon family ruled a vast global empire in the eighteenth century, an empire where, although the sun set, it was not dark long. However, such a vast empire was not to last.

Although historians generally focus on the abdication of Charles IV and Ferdinand VII in 1808 and Napoleon's seizure of Spain as the catalysts that broke apart the Bourbon empire, the empire actually began to disintegrate much earlier. Certainly that official disintegration began in early 1803, when Charles IV ceded his largest and newest colony, Louisiana, and its strategically placed capital, New Orleans. But the real disintegration began even earlier, during the rule at least of Charles IV—in part, based upon the choice of Charles III.

Charles III acquired the dismal French colony as a defensive march to protect Mexico from the British. It was then a wise move—the colony was immense, mostly unexplored, mostly populated by indigenous peoples, and separated even more by the vast Appalachian Mountains. Charles and his officers could have ejected the French residents of New Orleans and some of the communities upriver—it was militarily feasible, although some residents would have eluded his forces for a time. However, he decided instead to attempt to accept, suborn, and dominate the existing residents of his new colony.

And his decision seemed to have been wise, indeed: his officers used a British colonial rebellion as an opportunity to seize British West Florida, and the now expanded colony generally prospered. However, there were significant challenges to the colony—after recruiting Acadian refugees from Canada, Charles III's governors in New Orleans were never able to encourage significant external migration, nor did they turn to other imperial colonies, such as Mexico, for mestizo or indigenous migrants. The city and colony grew, but that growth was mostly not of Spanish-speaking workers, farmers, and merchants, but instead people of many ethnicities and free people of color, each granted the rights of a Spanish *vecino*. More troubling, the former British rebels had formed a robust nation, the United States of America, and they were already acting like an empire, expanding demographically, economically, and even, haltingly, militarily. Much of that expansion was toward the Spanish borders of Louisiana.

Charles IV succeeded to the throne in 1788, but he paid little attention to New Orleans, the colony of Louisiana, or perhaps any colonies at all—he was a weak and passive king. Meanwhile, the trade in the Bourbon imperial city of New Orleans expanded in a dangerous manner, for it became dominated by US goods, handled by mostly US and French merchants, and moved by US vessels to US ports. Charles IV and his ministers shrugged off such a challenge— trans-imperial trade was becoming a norm in the Rio Plata in roughly the same era, and perhaps they believed it was the same with both colonies. The ministers themselves seem to have paid attention to New Orleans only when they required additional funding, as when they imposed devastating restrictions on the city's tobacco exports or attempted to enforce warehousing/taxation on US goods coming downriver. But the city's merchants retrenched, building new trans-imperial connections, saving their capital, and waiting for another day.

And while they waited, the people of New Orleans, of every ethnicity and color, worked within the Bourbon Spanish system. They began a newspaper and they read; they used the notarial and court systems and acted as *vecinos/citizens*—for what else could they do? They strengthened and modernized their own *cabildo*, formed a Masonic lodge, and aggressively petitioned their governor and king. They did not have long to wait.

New Orleans was a genuine, fully functioning colony of the Bourbon empire, in many ways like any other Spanish colony. White and free troops of color alike marched in the plaza before the *cabildo* and the cathedral; women shopped for the produce and spices for a new, syncretic colonial cuisine; merchants traded, officials filled reams of paper, judges heard cases, and everyone probably sued someone else at least once in their lives.

But it was not the same as every other Spanish colony at all. There was hardly an indigenous face to be seen, and, save for the Mexican military garrison, not many *mestizos* either. The *vecinos* of New Orleans walked about and argued and joked in several European languages and spent their money on British tableware, French wine, and American goods and produce. The whites and the growing free populace of color could read, and probably read whatever they wished, albeit discreetly. They heard the unfiltered news from France where the king had been executed, from St. Domingue where free men of color and slaves had risen in turn against the French, Spanish, and British, and from the new United States, full of political controversy and economic dreams. They worked constantly with American flatboats, American cargoes, and American ships, and they schemed to acquire American (and British and Dutch) capital funding. They read their newspapers, met in their lodge, wrote their petitions, and perhaps unlike anywhere else in the Bourbon colonies, they waited.

What made Louisiana and its capital New Orleans truly different from the other colonies was that the people—of every ethnicity, race, social position, and economic status—could see a radical change coming. They saw it arrive floating down the river every day, and they saw it sail farther down the river and to sea on the cool evenings, underneath the flag of the United States. That change, their change, was in becoming American, at least in the larger sense, independent of Spain and European empires—but many, including the Spanish governors, probably already suspected that the colony would soon have a US flag flying over the *cabildo*.

This change, this disintegration of one edge of the Spanish empire, happened long before the American annexation of late 1803. This disintegration began with demography, was driven by trade, and was shaped by a mature political practice and discourse. When the US troops marched into the city in December 1803, they found a fully developed city on their new frontier, a Bourbon creation on the banks of a great and busy river. As the new governor, W. C. C. Claiborne, wrote upon arrival to his mentor and president, Thomas Jefferson, "New Orleans is *already* a great commercial City."[1]

APPENDIX 1

The Foundational Merchants of Spanish New Orleans

Name	Conducted notarial activity for at least 18 of 20 years within 1780–99	Conducted seven or more transac- tions for three years within 1780–99	Held major governmen- tal positions in Louisiana 1780–1803	Conducted ten or more notarial transac- tions for three years within 1780–99	Ethnicity
Almonaster y Roxas, Andres	Yes		*regidor,* son-in-law de La Ronde also *regidor*	Yes	Spanish
Andry, Gilberto			*regidor sencillo*		French
Armas y Arsila, Christoval de	Yes				Spanish
Arnoul, Juan			*regidor*		French
Badia, Christoval		Yes			Spanish
Baudin, Alexandro		Yes			French
Baure, Alexandro	Yes				French
Beauregard, Luis Toutant		Yes	*regidor*	Yes	French
Beauregard, Santiago			*regidor*	Yes	French
Bertoniere, Pedro	Yes				French
Bouligny, Domingo			*regidor sencillo*		French
Bouligny, Francisco de	Yes				French
Boutte, Hilario	Yes				French

Broutin, Francisco	Yes				French
Castanedo, Juan de			*regidor sencillo*		Spanish
Clark, Daniel Jr.		Yes		Yes	North European
Conand, Joseph	Yes				North European
Cornu, Luis	Yes				French
Danycan, Luis Darby			*regidor sencillo*		Northern European
Daunoy, Nicolas	Yes				French
De La Chaise, Carlos			*regidor*		French
De La Roche, Pedro			*regidor*		French
De La Ronde, Pedro Denis			*regidor*		French
Despres/z, Enrique		Yes			French
Ducros, Joseph			*regidor*		French
Ducros, Rudolfo José (son of Joseph)			*regidor*		French
Duplessis, Francisco	Yes				French
Farge, Filiberto	Yes				French
Fonvergne, Gabriel			*regidor sencillo*		French
Forstall, Nicolas			*regidor*		North European
Fortier, Miguel, Sr.	Yes				French
Gravier, Beltran		Yes			French
Gravier, Nicolas		Yes		Yes	French
Jones, Evan	Yes				North European
Jorda, Jaime		Yes	*regidor sencillo*	Yes	Spanish
Jourdan, Pedro/Pierre	Yes				French
La Barre, Francisco Pascalis de, Sr.	Yes		*regidor*	Yes	French

La Barre, Francisco Pascalis de, Jr.	Yes				French
La Chiapella, Geromo	Yes	Yes		Yes	Spanish
Leblanc, Joseph			regidor sencillo		French
Lauve, Nicolas	Yes				French
Macarty, Juan Bautista	Yes				North European
Macarty, Luis	Yes				North European
Magnon, Arnaldo	Yes				French
Marigny de Mandeville, Pedro de		Yes		Yes	French
Marre, Guillermo	Yes				French
Mather, James/Santiago	Yes	Yes		Yes	North European
Mayronne, Francisco		Yes		Yes	French
Mazange, Leonardo		Yes		Yes	French
Mendez, Antonio		Yes			Spanish
Merieult, Juan Francisco		Yes			French
Miró, Estevan		Yes	governor	Yes	Spanish
Montegut, Joseph	Yes				North European
Morales, Juan Ventura	Yes				Spanish
Navarro, Martin		Yes	intendant	Yes	Spanish
Olivier, Carlos Honorato (son of Pedro)			regidor		French
Olivier, Pedro Francisco			regidor		French
Pedesclaux, Estevan		Yes			Spanish

Perdomo, Rafael	Yes				Spanish
Poeyfarre, Juan Bautista	Yes				Spanish
Pollock, Oliver/ Olivero		Yes			North European
Pontalba, Joseph Xavier de		Yes		Yes	French
Ramis, Antonio	Yes	Yes			Spanish
Reggio, Carlos de (son of Francisco)			*regidor*		Spanish
Reggio, Francisco Maria de			*regidor*		Spanish
Riano, Francisco de	Yes		*regidor sencillo*	Yes	Spanish
Ross, David	Yes				North European
Saizan, Juan Bautista	Yes				French
Sarpy, Juan Bautista		Yes			French
Sauve, Pedro		Yes			French
Segond, Pablo/Paul		Yes			Spanish
Wiltz, Joseph	Yes				North European
Wiltz, Lorenzo	Yes				North European

If we consider only the longevity of their commercial activity, the foundational merchant group in New Orleans consisted of thirty-four individuals who conducted commercial transactions for at least eighteen of the twenty years between 1780 and 1799. On the other hand, only ten individuals conducted ten or more transactions in three or more years. Finally, considering political position, we must recall that the *cabildo* normally consisted of the governor (never from Louisiana), five permanent *regidores,* who held collateral offices based upon their ranking; one permanent *regidor sencillo,* who held no collateral offices; two annually elected judges (*alcades*); and numerous nonvoting members and lesser employees. From 1783 until 1803, fifteen men served as *regidores.* These positions were normally purchased and were often transferred from father to son or son-in-law, but in 1797 they were expanded to include six new purchased/appointed *regidores sencillos* (Din and Harkins, *New Orleans Cabildo,* 56–61). Note that the plural of *regidor* is *regidores.* The *cabildo's* membership mostly consisted of planter/merchants and mid-level merchants, and was clearly not structured to represent strictly mercantile interests. Instead, that membership permitted Spanish governors to exert political control over the city and nearby parishes and reward the loyalty of ethnically French planters such as the de La Barres, Beauregards, Bouligny, and de La Ronde.

In total, the three paths provide a total of seventy-two different candidates which, when further winnowed to require a place on at least two of the three lists, becomes much more manageable. The shorter list consists of only fourteen names: Andres Almonaster y Roxas, Francisco Pascalis de La Barre Sr., Luis Toutant Beauregard, Daniel Clark Jr., Nicolas Gravier, Jaime Jorda, Geromo La Chiapella, Pedro de Marigny de Mandeville, Santiago/James Mather, Francisco Mayronne, Estevan Miró, Martin Navarro, Joseph Xavier de Pontalba, and Francisco de Riano.

APPENDIX 2

The Foundational Merchants of American New Orleans

Name	Held at least five corporate board positions	Were corporate directors concurrent with city-council positions	Ethnicity
Blanque, Jean	Yes	Yes	French
Callender, Thomas	Yes		North European
Cavalier, Antonio, Jr.	Yes		French
Chew, Beverly	Yes		North European
DuBourg, P. F.	Yes	Yes	French
Duplessis, Francis	Yes	Yes	French
Fortier, Michel	Yes		French
Girod, Nicolas	Yes	Yes	French
Kenner, William	Yes		North European
Labatut, J. B.	Yes		French
Lanusse, Paul	Yes	Yes	French
Livaudais, J. F.	Yes		French
McNeil, Joseph	Yes	Yes	North European
Morgan, Benjamin	Yes	Yes	North European
Nott, William	Yes		North European
Pitot, James	Yes	Yes	French
Relf, Richard	Yes	Yes	North European
Shepherd, Rezin D.	Yes		North European
Soule, Joseph	Yes	Yes	French
Tricou, Joseph	Yes		French
Urquhart, Thomas	Yes		North European
Winter, Samuel	Yes	Yes	North European

APPENDIX 3

Petition from the Merchants of New Orleans, August 1796,
to King Charles IV of Spain

Señor,

The commercial sector of New Orleans, to Your Serene Royal Majesty with the deepest respect with which it can convey when it insists on coveting the vigor and growth in the beneficial soul of Your Majesty regarding the exemptions which were worthily granted via Your cédula of January 22, 1782, which at the same time enlivened the fallen agriculture of this province. Only do they now sadly see such priceless advantages arrive wasted, as much because of the considerable burdens in gold currency to assist and subsidize the war expenses which Your Majesty imposed on 10 June 1793, increasing import fees from 6 percent before payment up to 15 percent after payment, and which decrease was expected with the peace, according to what was hinted on the part of Your Majesty, as by the well-known, disastrous calamities of three violent hurricanes and a raging fire suffered in the city during the last epoch, which nearly entirely ruined the fortunes of laborers and merchants. But the anxiety of finding their total destruction threatened especially appears to them today, if Your Majesty's kind munificence does not relieve them from such misfortune, as they hope.

The treaty, Señor, established by Your Majesty with the United States of America and which was published, concedes them [the Americans] a considerable portion of our establishments on this river, its free navigation, and likewise the free import and export of goods and agricultural products. This will prevent the National family from any real success in its mercantile operations, as long as the enjoyment of equal prerogatives do not facilitate the means of rivaling it, providing residents throughout Louisiana the same convenience or modest prices with which those who will secure exemptions and thus supplant our mercantile sales commerce, as well as the purchase of agricultural products and hides.

There is, Senor, no other means to impel this achievement upon which the ambitious looks of such harmful rivals are fixed, and to avoid the final extermination of the supplicants, but a judgment transcendental to the State. This [treaty] will render useless the many precautions taken to guard against clandestine American commerce; the open expanse of 20 leagues of river from the sea to the environs of Natchez limits their new possessions, which allows its lengthened riverbank to supply all the province without the least obstacle, and to take in payment all that the province produces.

To this inevitable reef, from which [illegible] can save an exemption so complete as that which those infrutan in its commerce; consequently the contingency is no less disastrous to the proponents, who will lose everything they owe to the upriver cultivators and traders, who can no longer expect appropriate prices from them which would not permit them your restrictions rights aspecto [or respecto?] of the Americans; they [upriver farmers and merchants] will prefer trading with them [American merchants], taking advantage of your jurisdiction and mocking their former creditors, thus completing the unhappiness of the Spanish merchants, and inciting them in such cases to the sad necessity of emigrating elsewhere to procure their subsistence.

To avoid such imminent damages and those by which the Americans little by little lord over all Louisiana, they [the merchants of New Orleans] flee to Your Majesty's paternal goodness, imploring for the indicated remedy, which they entrust to your innate mercy. We do not only act, Señor, to obtain from Our Señor's mildness the appropriate exemptions to be able to make our commerce comparable to or balanced with the American, but also so that this balance may be advantageous to the State. They [the merchants] completely promise the benefits with which Your Majesty's kind-hearted soul has always inclined to the prosperity of these domains; it would be worthwhile to grant the *gracia* solicited by these leaders and this body of commerce, to be permitted to export, based upon a modest contribution, the silver money so necessary to invigorate mercantile speculations, particularly in a country whose products barely succeed in covering half of the goods which it consumes, and is overall abandoned with nearly the entire cultivation destroyed by crop failure—three consecutive harvests. At the same time, Señor, to energize navigation and accumulate new export items to supplement the mentioned main branch which today it is lacking, it would be very opportune if Your Majesty should permit that, in this capital and outpost of your jurisdiction, your vassals can buy from the Americans the agricultural products which originate from your districts with the same liberty that they are permitted to extract them, and that those not necessary to the Province's use, on departure in Spanish ships, be granted an exemption equal to that which the proponents do not doubt Your Majesty will grant to the products of this country. Without this *gracia,* it will not be possible for your commerce to bear the American agreement, which undoubtedly absorbs everything, as long as our own trade earns more value than 4 percent for the importation of merchandise and 2 percent for the export of agricultural products: for a larger excise tax would give it the advantage and preponderance to make itself exclusive. This would be inconvenient beyond what is the only preservation from said diminution of our wealth, and the now-sought abolition of the article in your incorrect order which requires ships coming from Europe to this colony to detour into the ports of Corcubion or Alicante, a serious circumstance for this commerce because of the higher cost, delay, and risks caused without producing any utility to your funds, for which the proponents promise this *gracia* of Your Majesty.

Finally, Senor, so that our national commerce remain in turn well-organized, and sheltered from the prejudices which it suffers in the judicial process, which after serious delays and costs come to be terminated by arbitrators, [we] pray humbly to Your Majesty to deign to authorize this body to establish a *consulado,* which especially knows your reasoning on mercantile business, navigation, and other incidental issues, authorizing it to name, via a plurality of votes among its members, those considered most suitable by the Administration of Justice and Economic Direction for the interests of the body, and to permit it to impose and receive the small contribution judged necessary to meet the expenses of said *consulado,* as in the example of those in Vera-Cruz, Lima, Cartagena, and la Havana, but proportionate to the poverty of this province as compared to the mentioned wealthy lands.

The said *gracias* will consolidate the security and prosperity of these your dominions, so necessary for the conservation of the Kingdom of Mexico, which serve as a barrier and without which it [Mexico] will remain very exposed to the greed of our ambitious neighbors: in whose attention [illegible].

Your Majesty, we humbly implore that you grant attainment of these prayers by way of your innate goodness and worth. Thus they [we] promise to the benign, munificent soul of Your Majesty, whose precious life may God lengthen as many years as he can.

New Orleans, 31 August, 1796

Source: AGI, Papeles de Cuba, 212B, microfilm E-106, roll 68, pp. 28–33, dated 31 August 1796. Translation is mine, with more modern punctuation and occasional clarifying words inserted in parentheses for clarity. I have left most of the misspellings, mindful that the petition was written in a time when the Spanish language was evolving and that the petition was written by bilingual petitioners. Some words are also illegible in the original, but may well be supposed. In other cases, dashes have been substituted for illegible words.

APPENDIX 4

Petition from the Free Military Officers of Color, 24 October 1800,
to the Cabildo of New Orleans

MOST ILLUSTRIOUS CABILDO

Captain Juan Bautista Saraza and Ensign Pedro Galafate of the Battalion of Octo-roons, and Captain Pedro Tomas and Captain Juan Bautista Bacusa of the Battalion of Quadroons of the Disciplined Militia of the Province of Louisiana, with the greatest reverence and due respect to Your Lordships, come before you and expound: That various individuals came in our company from the recent expedition executed in accepting Fort San Marcos de Apalache where the men experienced bad times such as irregularity of weather and nourishment, blistering heat due to the harsh season in which the expedition was undertaken, mosquitoes, night air, humidity, and other nuisances harmful to human nature, and, finally, shelling from the cannons which they expected to receive at any moment.

The men give infinite thanks to the Most High for granting them their wish to come back to their homeland. To recompense them in some manner, to cheer up their spirit, so that they can forget the hardships of the expedition which they under-took—for which some people compared them to irrational animals which are only led and take shelter under the hot sun which bakes their brains—we jointly solicit the permission of the President of the Cabildo (the governor) and Your Lordships to give weekly a public dance on Saturdays until the end of the next Carnival, beginning on the day of our most august Sovereign Charles IV, which falls on the fourth of the coming month. The dance will not interfere with the one the white people regularly have, for they have their dance on Sundays.

Through the kindness of Don Bernardo Coquet, we have his permission to use his house for the dances. We ask that you be kind enough to the petitioners to provide them with the guards of the city who previously guarded the house when dances were given to prevent disorders. When we were on the expedition, we were informed that some people came to the dances that were given there, determined to disrupt the peaceful diversions—some by provoking fights, others by chewing vanilla and spitting it out for the purpose of producing an intolerable stench, others by putting chewed tobacco on the seats so that the women would stain their garments—in short, doing and causing as much havoc as they could. This example of maliciousness was never experienced in the innumerable dances that were given in the chosen house while the guards were present. The guards, once you give them orders to attend, will be anxious to come, owing to the special privileges we shall offer them on the nights the dance is given.

Therefore, we humbly plead that Your Lordships be kind enough to concede this solicitation which has nothing to do with violence and consequently will not cause any harm. This is the season for such diversion, both in America and in Europe. We shall always keep in our hearts your renowned benevolence and kindness.

New Orleans
Cpt. Jean Baptiste Scarasse
Pierre Tomas
Pierre Calpha
Jean Baptiste Bacuse

Source: "Letters, Petitions, and Decrees of the Cabildo," 204–10, document 367, dated 24 October 1800, trans. Morazan.

NOTES

INTRODUCTION

1. Charles II, the last Spanish Hapsburg, died in 1700, and named Philip, Duke of Anjou, as his successor in his will. Philip ascended the Spanish throne as Philip V in November that year, renouncing any claim to the French throne. The subsequent War of the Spanish Succession (1702–1713), initiated by Louis XIV of France, merely resulted in the political status quo in Spain. Long before the war ended, Philip V began Bourbon centralization in 1707 with the *Nueva Planta* decrees, ending the independence of Aragon. The Spanish colonies and settlements ruled by the Bourbons from 1700 to 1808 included, among the most obscure and often short-lived, Fort Nunez Gaona in modern-day Washington state, Fort San Miguel in modern-day British Columbia, Amat (modern-day Tahiti), Santa Cruz (in the Solomon Islands), Spanish Guinea, and various North African ports.

2. Among works on the Bourbon empire in Spanish America, see Brading, *Miners and Merchants in Bourbon Mexico, 1763–1810*; Caneque, *The King's Living Image*; Fisher, *Commercial Relations between Spain and Spanish America in the Era of Free Trade, 1778–1796*; Glasco, *Constructing Mexico City*; Paquette, *Enlightenment, Governance, and Reform in Spain and Its Empire, 1759–1808*; and Prado, *Edge of Empire*. Works on the colonial transitions to independence include Adelman, *Sovereignty and Revolution in the Iberian Atlantic*; Anderson, *Imagined Communities*; Rama, *The Lettered City*; Mahoney, *Colonialism and Postcolonial Development*; and Marotti, *Heaven's Soldiers*. For examples on post-1808 Spanish America, see Jensen, *Children of Colonial Despotism*.

3. For Charles III's reluctant acceptance of the colony, see Mapp, *The Elusive West and the Contest for Empire, 1713–1763*, 404–11. Although it bordered New Spain (Mexico and the American southwest), Louisiana and the Floridas were de facto managed/supported via Cuba, based on the proximity of Havana. New Spain contributed only funds (occasionally) and a regiment.

4. AGI, Audiencia de Santo Domingo, 2595, doc. 1, Colonie de la Louisianne, 1763, *Récapitulation generale des recensements ci-joints faits a la Nouvelle Orléans et dans tous les quartiers qui en dépendent depuis le bas du fleuve jusqu'a la jurisdiction de la Pointe Coupée, inclusivement, en l'année mil sept cent soixante trois.*

5. Surprisingly, as a young naval officer captured by the British, Ulloa became a fellow of the Royal Society of London! He was a metallurgist who managed mercury mines in Peru and the first person to describe the element platinum; he was also an astronomer, collector of natural science, and author. The revolt had probably been abetted by British merchants, then establishing themselves in British-controlled West Florida. See John G. Clark, *New Orleans, 1718–1812,* 162–69, on the British influence during this period.

6. Gayarré, *History of Louisiana* 2: 272–359, 342–43.

7. The Frenchmen most active against cession to Spain were "Lafrenierre the Attorney-General, Doucet, St. Lette, Pin, Villere, D'Arensbourg, Jean Milhet, the wealthiest merchant of the colony, Joseph Milhet, his brother, St. Maxent, De La Chaise, Marquis, Garic, Masan, Massange, Poupet, Noyan, Boisblanc, Grand-Maison, Lalande, Lesassier, Braud, the King's printer, Kernion, Carrere, Dessales, etc." (Gayarré, *History of Louisiana* 2: 127). Of these, O'Reilly arrested Lafreniere, Doucet, Villere, Jean Milhet, Joseph Milhet, Marquis, Masan, Poupet, Noyan, Boisblanc, as well as de Caresse, and Petit; he executed Lafreniere, Joseph Milhet, Marquis, Noyan, and Caresse and sentenced the others to prison in Havana in the Morro Castle (337–38). The king pardoned Doucet, Jean Milhet, Masan, Poupet, Boisblanc, and Petit, but none returned to Louisiana and instead moved to Cap Français in St. Domingue (343). Unsurprisingly, most of these surnames were inconsequential in Spanish New Orleans; the notable exception was St. Maxent, who served as a Spanish officer and married two daughters to senior Spanish officials—one to Governor Gálvez.

8. Throughout this work, the word "demography" is understood to mean "the composition of a particular human population" rather than "the study of statistics such as births, deaths, income, or the incidence of disease, which illustrate the changing structure of human populations" (both definitions in the *Oxford English Living Dictionary,* en.oxforddictionaries.com [accessed 22 November 2018]). Similarly, the word "discourse" is understood to mean "written or spoken communication or debate," as defined in the same dictionary. Academic debate on the nature, depth, and expanse of that discourse will inevitably vary, based upon the period of discussion and often retroactive concepts of what should be included within that discourse and whether, if that discourse is limited, whether it qualifies as actual discourse at all.

1. A CITY OF CHAMELEONS

1. The concept that demography shapes culture is the basis upon which both political science and advertising are based, and is widely used in archaeology. Demography, of course, is not determinative of culture, but neither is it merely suggestive—instead, demography is often predictive and even probabilistic. A simple consideration of American elections makes this obvious.

2. Curtis and Scarano, "Puerto Rico's Population *Padrones,* 1779–1802," 200, University of Wisconsin Data and Information Services Center (DISC) and Inter-University Consortium for Political and Social Research (ICPSR). The first may be found at disc.wisc.edu/archive/index.html,

under the title *Puerto Rico's Padrones, 1779–1802*. Among other Bourbon-era *censos*, for example, Cuenca, in modern-day Ecuador, compiled a *censo* in 1778 (Jamieson 41).

3. AGI, Audiencia de Santo Domingo, 2595, #1, Colonie de la Louisianne, 1763, *Récapitulation generale des recensements ci-joints faits a la Nouvelle Orléans . . . en l'année mil sept cent soixante trois*; AGI, Audiencia de Santo Domingo, 2595, #3, *Primer Padron y lista de los vecinos habitants de la Lusiana y Milicianos de ella*. Martin (*History of New Orleans from the Earliest Period*) also reported that the 1766 census counted the New Orleans population to be 3,190, consisting of 1,902 whites, including 31 black and 68 of mixed blood, 1225 slaves, and 60 "domiciliated" Indians, living in 468 houses, mostly on "the third and fourth streets from the river, and principally in the latter." (Gayarré, *History of Louisiana* 2: 354–55); AGI, Papeles de Cuba, 2351, *Padron general de todos los individuos de la provincial de Luisiana, 12 May 1777*; AGI, PC, 1425, *Resumen general del padron hecho en la provincial de la Luisiana, distrito de la Movila y plaza de Panzacola, 1788*; Acosta Rodriguez, *Población de Luisiana Española (1763–1803)*, 485–88, also summarized in Holmes, "A New Look at Spanish Louisiana Census Accounts: The Recent Historiography of Antonio Acosta," 77–86. Holmes noted that Acosta was not able to use the 1791 census of New Orleans, which remains in that city's library. The padron data for 1788 appears in Gayarré, *History of Louisiana* 2: 215.

4. Cindy Ermus, "Reduced to Ashes: The Good Friday Fire of 1788 in Spanish Colonial New Orleans," 292–331.

5. Ingersoll, *Mammon and Manon in Early New Orleans*, 149–50. An earlier example is Clark's statement that "the French Creole, the Anglo-Saxon, and the Negro jostled for living space" (Clark, *New Orleans, 1718–1812*, 254).

6. See Borah, "Trends in Recent Studies of Colonial Latin American Cities," 535–54. Borah noted that some Latin American historians were "drawing inspiration directly from France and England, focused on parish registry data (547). He also noted prosopography as another European inspiration for Latin studies. He labeled prosopography as the "perhaps specialized . . . study of families and occupations in cities," a rather limiting label, given the methodology may be applied in rural, trans-imperial, and now transnational research (550). There are also many prosopographical sources for the residents of Bourbon New Orleans from the early American era, including lists of letters awaiting retrieval, hundreds of silhouettes, and notarial, judicial, and military archives.

7. New Orleans Census, 1791; *U.S. Census, 1790*, Charleston, South Carolina; Baltimore City, Maryland. Although Savannah, Georgia, is more proximate to New Orleans than Charleston, the census records for Georgia from 1790 to 1820 have been lost; however, statistics elsewhere indicate that Savannah had a population of 5,146 in 1800 and 5,215 in 1810. Prado indicated that the total population of Montevideo in 1807 was 11,379, given that he reported that 165 foreigners constituted "1.45 percent of the estimated population" that year (*Edge of Empire*, 50–53).

8. These were then-Governor Esteban Miró, the Asesor (undetermined), the Auditor de Guerra Dr. Nicolas Maria Vidal, and Bishop (then actually auxiliary bishop) Cirilo de Barcelona. The Asesor was the intendant's legal advisor who also supported the *cabildo* courts (Din and Harkins, *New Orleans Cabildo*, 95); the Auditor was the *auditor de guerra*, who served as both a military judge advocate and the lieutenant governor. For Vidal's role as *auditor de guerra*, see Holmes, "Vidal and Zoning in Spanish New Orleans, 1797," 270–82. Bishop de Barcelona (1787–1793) and later, more famously, Bishop Luis Peñalver y Cárdenas (1795–1801) led the Diocese of Louisiana and the Two Floridas, then part of the Archdiocese of San Cristobal de la Habana. The priest, identified as Fran-

cisco, was presumably Padre Francisco Ildefonso Mareno, better known to history as Antonio de Sedella. He assumed the name "Antonio" when he entered the Capuchin order. Father de Sedella was originally sent to New Orleans to represent the Inquisition, but the priest and the project were both rejected by the governor and sent back to Cuba. De Sedella later returned as the parish priest for New Orleans and remained long after the American annexation. He also served after 1803 as the Spanish governor in Havana's spymaster within New Orleans. Three extra entries represent the Ursuline Convent, the patients, and perhaps the staff of Charity Hospital, and the city church (mistakenly listed as "La Villa Ingles," although the entry might refer to a British official instead).

9. The percentage of the entire free population was 11 percent, but we must subtract the 241 female heads of family from the 830 names to consider what percentage of the population the census taker labeled a *don*. The results are 44 of the 90 names, minus a few whose surname nationality is problematic. Another 35 carried French surnames; 7 were of North European ancestry.

10. Within my data, the French category includes a wide range of actual ethnicities, including Bretons, Normans, Provençals, Canadians (including Acadians), and St. Dominguans. Spanish includes not only Castilians, but also Catalans, some Basque, Majorcans and Minorcans, Canary Islanders, Italians (many under Spanish control in the eighteenth century), and even a few Greeks. The northern Europeans included British, Irish, Scottish, and German surnames, most therefore probably from the British Empire or the new United States. The free people of color are only those clearly identified as such in notarial records.

11. De Ville, *The 1795 Chimney Tax of New Orleans*, v–vii.

12. See Prado, *Edge of Empire*, 18–20: ecclesiastical records in Colonia also divided the populace as white, free *pardo*, free African, and slave.

13. Most free families of color chose to live on Rues Bourgogne (modern-day Burgundy), North Dauphine, Orleans, St. Ann, and Bienville. Rue Bourgogne, in fact, was the spatial heart of the free community of color in New Orleans, with the highest percentage of free people of color in the city, although it was also the home of many white and enslaved residents. Of 412 residents on Rue Bourgogne, almost half were free people of color. There were also 126 white residents on the street, but these whites were relatively poor, including a few whites living with women of color. There were also enslaved people of color living on the Rue Bourgogne; of these 85 slaves residing on the street, half were owned by 3 whites, but at least 30 more were owned by free people of color. Other black households sprinkled themselves elsewhere along several streets, including St. Peter, Toulouse, Douane (Customs), Hopital, and north Bourbon (author's analysis of *New Orleans Directory and Census, 1805*). The residents of Rue Bourgogne with the most slaves were Juan Morales (15 slaves), Madame Peyroux (16), Pierre Bertoniere (11), and Valentine Deblen (6), all white residents, and Marie Defere (7) and Madame Victorine (6), both free women of color.

14. Hanger, *Bounded Lives*, 22–23.

15. Author's analysis of *New Orleans Directory and Census, 1805*.

16. The Vieux Carré (Old Quarter) of 1795 at first glance seems a relatively young place—of the 1,480 residents, only 97 (8 percent) were over the age of fifty. The age ratio for the three age groupings was 9:18:2. The group numbers were 462/921/97. Comparison with Spanish *censos* and *padrones* is difficult without readily available and complete publication of such statistics (Goldberg, "La Población Negra y Mulata de la Ciudad de Buenos Aires, 1810–1840," 76). However, the age ratios for free *pardos* and *morenos* in Buenos Aires in 1822 (three decades after our period) were

9:15:2, a notably younger ratio than in 1795 New Orleans (based upon Goldberg, "La Población Negra y Mulata de la Ciudad de Buenos Aires," 86n and 87, cuadro 3). On the other hand, comparison with the 1790 US Census indicates that New Orleans males were, on average, much older than those in the United States. The 1790 US Census used only two age groups, and then only among free white males (under sixteen years of age and of sixteen years and upward)—the resultant age ratio was roughly 1:1. If the same age division is applied to the 1795 New Orleans census, the city's male population age ratio was roughly 1:2 (*1790 Census of the U.S.*, 4). None of the individual US states and counties came close to an age ratio significantly more than 1:1.

17. For the earlier role of indigenous tribes in the French-era economy, see Usner, "American Indians in Colonial New Orleans," 164–86. See also Usner, *Indians, Settlers, & Slaves in a Frontier Exchange Economy*. For comparison to Buenos Aires, see Goldberg, "La Población Negra y Mulata de la Ciudad de Buenos Aires, 1810–1840," 75–99.

18. Din and Harkins, *New Orleans Cabildo*, 138–48. Despite its depth of data, the 1795 census was inferior to that of 1791. The 1795 census taker generally used French but spelled many names wrong in every language, especially in English. He did count widowed, married, and single women, but not consistently or, presumably, comprehensively. Furthermore, he was willing to accept any name for a resident—often only a first name for free people of color—whereas the census taker in 1791 had insisted that every resident provide a first and last name. He double-counted people who owned more than one property, and even then misspelled the same names elsewhere.

19. For comparison, the 1791 residents on both Rampart and Esplanade were deleted from this chart. The 1791 census did not list any residents on modern-day Iberville, Burgundy, or Barracks (which was then literally the location of military barracks) Streets.

20. Within the small group named by position, 15 were Spanish; the remainder were French (only 1), and northern European (2), and, as might be expected within eighteenth-century imperial positions, included no free people of color. Those identified as such were Mr. Docr. (Doctor) Morand within the French, Don Andre Almonaster, Don Marie Argott, Don Andrés Armestro, Don Jean Calla, D. M. V. Auditeur, Rev. Father Diego, Don André Fernande, Don Manual Lausaus, Don Jean Morales, Don J. de O (presumably de Orue), Don Juan Prieto, Don Fque. Rendon, Don Ml. Serzane, Don Fque. Vidal, and Don Pedro Villamil among the Spanish, Doctor Daw (Dow) and Rev. Father Wals(h) among the northern Europeans, and none among free people of color. Within the 1795 census, 148 entries for *Monsieur* appear: 86 French, 41 Spanish, 17 northern European, and 3 free people of color.

21. The definition of *vecino* is arguable: Herzog, *Defining Nations*, 164–200, makes a strong case that a *vecino* must not be confused with the British concept of a subject (in Spanish, *sujeto*) but instead is closer in meaning to the then French/Italian/Dutch concept of citizen. The concept of citizen versus subject was familiar enough to the residents of Spanish New Orleans—their colony abutted and traded with a large democracy. The term *vecino* is used throughout Spanish records, but the term *sujeto,* which the bilingual and trilingual residents of New Orleans surely understood as being more restrictive in its political meaning, was used much less often, perhaps only in formal requests to the governor, ministers, and king himself. I favor Herzog's argument.

22. Ingersoll, *Mammon and Manon in Early New Orleans,* 149–51; Din and Harkins, *New Orleans Cabildo,* 6.

23. Din and Harkins, *New Orleans Cabildo,* 5–7, esp. notes.

24. The reasons why notarial records generally captured a wider swath of the city's population than sacramental records are numerous. High infant-mortality rates discouraged baptisms, and the expense and access to priests discouraged formal marriage; burial in family plots outside the city meant that many deaths were unrecorded in the city's ecclesiastical records. The large number of transients in the city rarely appeared in city church records. Quietly ignored Protestants, deists, and Jews were also not documented in church records. See also Hanger, *Bounded Lives, Bounded Places*, 91–92. A printed register of all confirmations (another Catholic sacrament) in New Orleans and other Louisiana parishes for this period is held in the Daughters of the American Revolution Library in Washington, DC.

25. The estimation of nationalities is an admittedly rough and somewhat subjective process, based upon the determination of individuals to be of one or another national descent based upon their surnames. For this project, Italian surnames were grouped with Spanish names, based upon the centuries-old and prominent role of the Genoese in the Spanish colonial project, long before Columbus. In counterpoint to the author's calculations on immigration, see Ingersoll, "The Slave Trade and the Ethnic Diversity of Louisiana's Slave Community," 149–50.

26. The numbers were ten were from France, two from former French colonies (Canada and Acadia), six from eastern Spain (at least three from Catalonia), six from Spanish colonies (especially the Canaries), and one from Genoa. Eight were native-born (most, but not all, of French ancestry); several of the Spanish and Spanish colonials were military men. Twelve died by 1799, perhaps within seven years of their immigration to New Orleans. Two other names could be identified, but had no clearly identified birthplace.

27. DuVal, *Independence Lost*, 238–45, 256–69, 309–12.

28. AGI, Papeles de Cuba, 597, microfilm E-87, roll 116, pp. 45–48 (draft), pp. 49–51 (final version, with minor changes in spelling, abbreviations, etc.), letter of Enrique Darcantel, countersigned by Juan Ventura Morales, dated 19 March 1789.

29. Hodson, *The Acadian Diaspora*; Winzerling, *Acadian Odyssey*; Jobb, *The Cajuns*, 180–86. Hodson's and Winzerling's works both indicate how the Acadians were generally abandoned by their own empire. According to Winzerling, about 1,100 Acadians arrived in Louisiana in 1764–65; about 400 more came in 1766–67 under Spanish governor Ulloa, but perhaps 200 emigrated to St. Domingue in 1771–72. Finally, another 1,600 arrived in 1785 under Miró's auspices. Hodson does not estimate the Acadians who arrived in Louisiana before 1785, only noting, "Dozens—hundreds, perhaps—crossed the Gulf of Mexico to Spanish Louisiana" (116). More research on early Acadian migration to Louisiana is clearly required.

30. Din, "The Immigration Policy of Governor Esteban Miró in Spanish Louisiana," 155–56. On the Acadians, see Hodson, *The Acadian Diaspora*, esp. 194–95, for a brief account of Spanish negotiations for Acadian migrants.

31. The cathedral records from 1791–94 reveal only six natives or residents of that island, including Lieutenant Colonel de Montault, a captain of dragoons, and a prominent Capuchin priest who promptly died. Similarly, the records for 1795–99 only reveal eight natives or residents of the island in the city, half of them women marrying or having their children baptized.

Nathalie Dessens also reported a scarcity of St. Dominguan immigrants to New Orleans: "Very low figures of direct arrivals to Louisiana during the colonial period are generally given," perhaps "fewer than 100 refugees . . . between 1792 and 1794" (*From Saint-Domingue to New Orleans,* 15). A further complication is that many white St. Dominguans were born in France and had only lived in that island colony *after 1782.* Consequently, these immigrants did not appear in sacramental records as natives of St. Domingue, but instead of France.

The city's notarial records do indicate an increase in French business activity in the years 1792 and 1793, and based upon surnames, some of the new transactors probably came from St. Domingue, but these increases match those of other ethnic/racial groups during the same years, implying that St. Dominguan migration may not have notably increased, but that more St. Dominguans simply appeared in the record as the economy improved. Comparing the names of new business transactors with the lists of St. Dominguan refugees who subsequently sought and received reparations: of the 76 new business transactors of probable French origin in 1792, at least 44 had surnames that also appear on the St. Dominguan reparations lists. While some were common French surnames, other names like Chaix, Escoffie, Mahy, and Masicot were more distinctive. Additional research is therefore possible on these potential St. Dominguan immigrants. The research above is the first historical comparative analysis of New Orleans demographic records or data with that available on St. Domingue, to the author's knowledge.

32. Gayarré, *History of Louisiana* 3: 170–71, for 1785; 215 for 1788. Gayarré asserted that the population of New Orleans in 1785 was only 4,980; the entire colony numbered 31,433 persons; three years later, in 1788, the city's population was listed as 5,338, with the colony numbering 42,346. Gayarré's sourcing is unclear; he was probably referring to the general colonial *padrones* of those years. For comparison, see the *U.S. Census,* 1790, South Carolina.

33. Gayarré, *Spanish Domination,* 2nd ed., 170.

34. Din, "Immigration Policy of Governor Esteban Miró," 159–75. Others who proposed immigration were Agustin Macarty, William Fitzgerald, Mauricio Nowland, James Kennedy, William Butler, and Peter Paulus.

35. *U.S. Census,* 1790, Kentucky; Din, "Empires Too Far," 280.

36. Din, "Empires Too Far," 282–85; AGI, Papeles de Cuba, 212A, microfilm E-106, roll 67, pp. 293–300, esp. 298–300, dated 10 November 1796.

37. AGI, Secretaria del Despacho de Guerra, legajo 6929.7, sur Baron de Carondelet, letter dated 20 August 1795, pp. 9–12.

38. AGI, Papeles de Cuba, 1550, Casa-Calvo letter #10 with spreadsheet, dated 22 October 1799. The colony's military was divided into three groupings—regular infantry (which included artillery), cavalry, and militia (infantry and artillery). In late 1799, the regular infantry numbered almost 1,200 men, with another nearly 800 militia. However, over 700 mostly regular troops were deployed in nineteen posts throughout the colony, especially Pensacola. The regular infantry included a small artillery company (92 men), the Regiment of Louisiana (851 men), and most importantly, for the purposes of our discussion, the Second Battalion of Mexico (244 men).

39. Archdiocesan archives indicate that at least 59 natives of Mexico remained in New Orleans under more undesirable circumstances. They died there in the years 1791–99. Of these, roughly 40 percent were soldiers, 44 percent were convicts or former convicts, and the remainder civilians, including one female, a widow. The convicts were from central Mexico; none were from the north or the Yucatan, and only three from the southwestern coast. The average age of the dead soldiers

was 27 years, that of the convicts 33 years, and the others 27.6 years; together they averaged 29.6 years of age. The convicts were notably older than the regular soldiers, but they were still young men (author's analysis of ADNO, 1791–99).

Some of the convicts in New Orleans were not from Mexico itself. Several were listed as convicts "of this plaza," that is, convicted in Louisiana itself, and at least two were convicts from Havana. One may not have been Mexican at all: Juan Chino was from Las Amipas, in Oaxaca province, but his surname means "Chinese" in Spanish, and perhaps he was the descendant of an East Asian or Filipino in Spanish service or slavery, far away from his ethnic home.

Mehl reported that, among 4,000 Mexican troops and convicts sent to the Philippines in the late Bourbon era, almost one-third were convicted vagrants, convicted criminals, or military deserters. If we consider that the ratio of soldiers and convicts who died in New Orleans was roughly equal, but that the percentage of convicts dying may have been higher based upon their age, physical health, and assigned tasks, the ratio of convicts sent to New Orleans was probably similar to that sent to the Philippines. However, the Mexico Regiment was the only unit sent to New Orleans, and it never numbered much more than 1,000 men. The number of soldiers—and therefore the number of convicts—sent to Spanish New Orleans was always far less than those being sent to far-away Manila (*Forced Migration in the Spanish Pacific World*, 2–3).

40. A few other natives of Mexico do appear in the ecclesiastical records, some notable for their positions and others for their enigmatic tales. Manuel Serrano, the colonial assessor and a native of Havana, was actually from a Mexican family in Cordoba, near Veracruz, an indication of some mobility for Creole officials in the Bourbon world. Francisco Bermudez, a regimental sergeant and later city notary, was also a native of Mexico. José Albino/Alvino Herrera, a native of Puebla, was discharged from the regiment, in New Orleans, and married and raised several children with Rafaela Montoya, who had been "born, according to her, in Santo Thome in New Mexico, rescued from the savage Indians." One suspects that Rafaela Montoya Herrera's odyssey from a once bustling town in central New Mexico (present-day Tome) through captivity to the port city of New Orleans would be a most interesting tale (ADNO, vol. 5, "Serrano, Manuel Maria Ignazio"; on Bermudez, baptism for "Carreras, Miguel"; "Herrera, Joseph Albino" and "Montoya, Rafaela").

One limitation of any such plan, however, was the relative immensity of the Spanish empire and the number of positions that needed to be fortified and held by troops. Another was the need for troops and forced labor, including convicts, to work on civil projects in the various colonies (Mehl, *Forced Migration in the Spanish Pacific World*, 85–90).

41. Farriss, *Maya Society Under Colonial Rule*; Humboldt, *Ensayo político* 2, esp. chapter 4 and p. 373, full statistics on the population of Mexico City, and 131.

42. Wortman, *Government and Society in Central America, 1680–1840*, 154. These locations are in modern-day Honduras; none of the Spanish efforts were successful. Roatan is an island 65 kilometers from the coast; Rio Tinto is now known as Rio Sico. See the online *DLB*, "Carondelet, Luis Francisco Héctor de," https://www.lahistory.org/resources/dictionary-louisiana-biography/.

43. Guatemalan or Spanish imperial archives may shed light on how much Guatemalan efforts to attract white migrants, including those of Carondelet, were actually shaped by racism.

44. Casa-Calvo worried greatly about North American "unwarranted ambitions that they constantly try to impress upon their youth from their most tender years." See Archivo Histórico

Nacional, Madrid, Estado, legajo 3888m, Casa-Calvo to de Urquijo, 8 October 1800, cited in Din, *Casa-Calvo*, 184, and Hilton, "Movilídad y expansión en la construcción política de los Estados Unidos: 'estos errantes colonos' en las fronteras espanolas del Misisipi (1776–1803)," 63–96. He inherited and approved a proposal by Philippe Enrique Nering, the self-styled Baron de Bastrop, to introduce five hundred families, but Intendant Ramon Lopez y Angulo not only halted Nering's sale of land to an American officer, but also stopped all further land grants. Casa-Calvo protested that he should have been allowed to build settlements as he desired, in West Florida (Din, *Casa-Calvo*, 184–85). In West Florida itself, Governor Arturo O'Neill had previously but unsuccessfully proposed missionary work and intermarriage between his troops (many mestizo) with indigenous tribes. O'Neill departed West Florida in 1792 and became the governor/captain-general of the Yucatan until 1800.

45. While the use of indigenous migrants to expand Spanish rule was implemented in California, New Mexico, and Texas, an intellectual rationale for the practice could have easily been based upon the work of José del Campillo y Cossío, who argued in 1743 that indigenous peoples should be used as a free peasantry and treated as "Spanish of the same social class." Campillo y Cossío's work was an important influence upon later Bourbon thinkers/colonial leaders including Pedro de Campomanes and José de Gálvez. See Wortman, *Government and Society in Central America, 1680–1840*, 130, and Campillo y Cossío, *Nuevo Sistema de gobierno económico para la America*.

46. St. Louis Cemetery #1 Records, two different cemetery stones; ADNO, vol. 5: 43 and vol. 6: 32; García Carraffa, *El Soler Catalán, Valenciana y Balear* 1: 287–90, San Sebastian, 1918; Joaquim Llovet, *Cartas a Vera Cruz, Comerce América*, 13, 23, 71, 146–47, 154; Natchez Court Records Abstracts, 66–67; ADNO, vol. 5: 43, "Bosch," 156, "Fanguy"; NONA, Pedesclaux vol. 8, Perdomo vols. 13 and 15; Ximenes vols. 1, 3, and 5; Flannery, comp., *New Orleans in 1805; Ship Registers, New Orleans* 1: 176, "Comet"; De Grummond, "Cayetana Susana Bosque y Fangui, 'A Notable Woman,'" 277–94, 282–86; *Jornal Económico Mercantil de Vera Cruz*, 108; NONA, Pedesclaux, #35, will of 3 September 1799; *Ship Lists, New Orleans* 2: 7, 11, 47; *Louisiana Courier*, 3 February 1817, French letters list; Claiborne, *Letter Book* 6: 115; *National Intelligencer*, 10 October 1812; *New Orleans Democrat*, 7 August, 1871, 294.

At least two recent historians have referenced Cayetana Bosque. Faber wrote of her marriage and that of Celestine Laveau Trudeau to James Wilkinson: "These marriages argue strongly against any assumption that Louisiana ever was, or ever could have been, fully 'Americanized.' American leaders were assimilating to Louisiana ways and adopting the culture and mores of the New Orleans elite, not the other way around. In the vacuum left by the evaporation of the republican idealism, the sense of superiority, and the aspirations to dominance that many Americans brought to New Orleans in 1804, stood the figures of Cayetana Bosque and Celestine Trudeau. For Claiborne and Wilkinson it was probably a happy exchange" (*Building the Land of Dreams*, 310–11).

Kastor, on the other hand, wrote less about Bosque's wedding (it was Claiborne's third, and she was apparently pregnant) and more about her subsequent lawsuit as a widow, in 1819. However, he noted, "The wedding and the lawsuit each connected numerous facets of incorporation," in this case the marriage of the American Claiborne (then thirty-seven years of age) to a sixteen-year old Creole by a Spanish priest (Father Sedella) (*The Nation's Crucible*, 221–23). It may be argued that the progress of Claiborne's marital choices indicates something more about the interaction of Spanish and American culture in New Orleans. Claiborne's first wife was the American Eliza

Lewis, who died in Claiborne's first few months in New Orleans; the second was Clarissa Duralde, the daughter of an important Spanish official. Claiborne's third wife, even if accidental, so to speak, was also the daughter of a prominent Spaniard in New Orleans (223).

Similarly, Bernard de Marigny's choices of wives are instructive—his first wife was Mary Anne Jones, the daughter of US consul Evan Jones, but his second was Anne Mathilde Morales, a daughter of the former Spanish intendant (Arthur, *Old New Orleans*, 318). Coincidentally, Bosque's daughter by Claiborne, also named Sophronie, married Marigny's son, Antoine Jacques (319). If any of their three children had lived (they did not), that child would have been the descendant of a Mallorcan merchant, a Spanish intendant, a French planter/merchant, and an American governor—truly a chameleon.

47. Given the movement of many Irish and Scots in western Europe and Spanish America, it is difficult to determine exactly how they might have labeled themselves. Even their surnames were subject to change; for example, the Irish name Berrigan was transmuted into the Spanish word *barragan*, a type of Arabic textile. The author's surname, Rodriguez, was similarly transmuted into Roderick in early American censuses; clearly, Ellis Island was not the first place where names were changed. However, Spanish notarial and probate archives indicate most Irish and Scots in Spanish New Orleans used English routinely.

48. James Carrick, from Sterling, Scotland, first appeared in the notarial archives in 1791, but was listed as a "resident merchant" only in 1797, the year he married the daughter of Pablo Segond, whose own mother, Maria Francisca Conand, was Irish. Carrick was later a founding member of *La Charité* Masonic Lodge and commandant of St. Bernard Parish, south of New Orleans; he worked into the early American era but died early in 1808 (NONA, Ximenes, vol. 1; Pedesclaux, vol. 12; Ximenes, vols. 2, 3, and 4; ADNO, entries in vol. 6, Carrick and Segond; *Claiborne Letter Book*, 575–77.

49. Jairus Wilcox, a Connecticut native who served in the Revolutionary War as an officer (or his son), did somehow remain in New Orleans until he died in 1807 (NONA, Ximenes, vols. 3, 4, and 5; *Lineage Book of the Daughters of the American Revolution* 28, entry for "Mrs. Ethel Julia Grant Quarles," #27983, also #10854). But in 1831, a Reverend Jairus Wilcox was the "initial propagandizer of 'western emigration fever'" in Bergen County, New York, and convinced numerous neighbors to move west and found Geneseo, Illinois, near the Mississippi River (Meyer, *Making the Heartland Quilt*, 177).

50. Hanger, *Bounded Lives, Bounded Places*, esp. 17–54. For more on *coartación*, see Borucki, *From Shipmates to Soldiers*; Carroll, *Blacks in Colonial Veracruz; Territorial Papers*, 174–75.

51. In counterpoint, see Ingersoll, "The Slave Trade and the Ethnic Diversity of Louisiana's Slave Community," 149–51; Stewart, "Fashioning Frenchness," 526–28.

52. Rodriguez, "City of Chameleons," chap. 3, "Women in Spanish New Orleans," 158–84, emphasizes that most women in Spanish New Orleans were native-born women who frequently intermarried with incoming migrants. The city's limited archaeology indicates that, during and after the Spanish era, the city's residents—almost certainly the women—replaced their French colonial/Native American diet with more continental Spanish tastes, supplemented with African culinary choices, and their cookware and tableware with American and British goods—neither French nor Spanish.

53. Braudel, *The Identity of France* 1: 91–103.

54. Winzerling, *Acadian Odyssey*; Jobb, *The Cajuns*, 180–86.

55. Much the same might be said of other "French" immigrants to New Orleans, both before and after the US annexation. Given that the 1808 migration was *not* from France or St. Domingue, but rather from the eastern end of Spanish Cuba, it could be argued that these "French" immigrants, albeit born in France or St. Domingue, were no longer French at all by 1812, and were not necessarily Francophone. They had been in the Americas for at least two decades, living under alternating French, Spanish, and British rule in St. Domingue, and living in Spanish territory for at least six years (and often much longer) before arriving in New Orleans (*DLB*, "Beauregard, Bartolomé," and "Beauregard, Elias Toutant"). It is unclear how the Beauregards perceived themselves culturally during the Spanish era, although research in surviving family correspondence and archaeology at one of their plantations might provide some evidence. The famous US Civil War officer P. G. T. Beauregard was born at a plantation named "Contreras"—not a French name.

56. *DLB*, "Andry, Louis Antoine"; NONA, Pedesclaux, vol. 7; NONA, Ximenes, vols. 2 and 3; Laussat, *Memoirs of My Life*, 77–79. Andry did eventually muster his militia unit for Laussat's use, and entrusted them to Laussat's orders following the formal ceremony of cession. See also *1841 Orleans Parish Death Index*, Louisiana Archives, vol. 8: 670, indexed on Louisiana Genealogical Web Archives, www.usgwarchives.net/copyright.htm: entry for Gilbert Sosthene Andry, died 10 January 1841, age seventy-seven years. How Andry saw himself—as French, Spanish, or American—is unclear.

57. Ingersoll's own statistics indicate similar findings: if most French immigrants are factored out of his death statistics for 1810–12 because they did not arrive until 1808–10, the demography of free people in New Orleans was about 3/6 native-born (many Spanish or free people of color), 2/6 French, and 1/6 Spanish in 1803 (Ingersoll, 258–59 and 165, table 12). Ingersoll's statistics on the marriage records for 1772–1803 also indicate that about 40 percent of the locally born white brides in New Orleans married local men—mostly men born and raised in Louisiana during Spanish rule. Another 19 percent married Spaniards or men from Spanish colonies.

58. Author's compilation of statistics from NONA: Perdomo, Ximenes, Pedesclaux, and Broutin, 1788–92.

59. Korn, *Early Jews of New Orleans*, 29–40, 47–54; *DLB*, "Urquhart, Thomas." The Monsanto family moved to Puerto Rico and eventually cofounded the eponymous multinational firm. Robin makes a reference, at the very end of his work, to a leper identified as "the Jew Carick in New Orleans" (*Voyage to Louisiana, 1803–1805*, 270). This reference would seem to indicate prominent merchant James/Santiago Carrick was Jewish of origin. However, Carrick was Scottish by birth, married in the Catholic Church in New Orleans, and had his namesake son baptized and buried (young) by the Catholic Church (ADNO, vol. 6, "Carrick," 47). Perhaps this reference was meant to be a hateful slur, rather than accurate, or Robin was confusing names.

60. Hanger, *Bounded Lives, Bounded Places*, 22, census records. The increase in males among free people of color was from 233 to 324, while the number of females actually decreased from 587 to 538. The decrease of slaves was from 2,131 to 1,789.

61. Le Glaunec, "Slave Migrations and Slave Control in Spanish and Early American New Orleans," in *Empires of the Imagination*, 204–33, esp. 209.

62. More exact research on the ethnicity of the slaves arriving in New Orleans would be complicated by the frequent lack of specificity in Spanish notarial records on the slaves' actual

African heritage, given most slaves arrived in Louisiana from French or British colonies or from the United States via the river.

63. *National Intelligencer,* 27 January 1804, from the *Moniteur de la Louisiane,* undated article; *Louisiana Union,* 16 January 1804.

64. *Oxford Desk Dictionary and Thesaurus,* ed. Jewell, "Cosmopolitan," 171.

65. Laussat wrote that the onrushing Americans tended almost instinctively, "to exclude . . . any generation but their own" (*Memoirs of My Life,* 103).

2. THE MERCHANTS OF SPANISH NEW ORLEANS

1. Socolow, *The Merchants of Buenos Aires, 1778–1810,* 18–25.

2. James Mahoney roughly categorized these colonies as colonial centers "that especially concentrated Spanish people and institutions, and that served as a heartland of the overall colonial project" (for example, modern-day Mexico/Mexico City, Peru/Lima, and Bolivia/Potosi), intermediate semi-peripheries (Guatemala, Colombia, and Ecuador), and colonial peripheries (all the rest of the Spanish colonies) (*Colonialism and Postcolonial Development,* 50–51). Note that Mahoney did not include Cuba, Puerto Rico, Louisiana, or Florida on his list of Spanish colonies.

3. For a broader discussion of the role of merchant communities in the Spanish empire, see Lamikiz, *Trade and Trust in Eighteenth-Century Atlantic World,* esp. 185–86.

4. By comparison, see Clark, "The Business Elite of New Orleans before 1815," 94–103, esp. 96nn. Clark counted in these groups seven pre-1801 Americans (Evan Jones, Oliver Pollock, James Mather, George Morgan, William Hulings, Daniel Clark Jr., and Joseph McNeil), four Frenchmen (Francis Duplessis, Michel Fortier, Nicholas Girod, and Paul Lanusse), and six 1801–3 American immigrants (Thomas and David Urquhart, Beverly Chew, Richard Relf, William Kenner, and Samuel Winter). My own full lists of the merchants in each category may be found in appendix 1.

5. These officeholders were Almonaster y Roxas, de La Barre, Beauregard, Jorda, La Chiapella, Miró, Navarro, and Riano in the Spanish era and Clark and Mather in the American era. Pedro de Marigny's father was a French nobleman, and his father-in-law was the royal treasurer of Louisiana, J. B. Destrehan. Pedro entertained the future king of France, Louis-Philippe, Duke of Orleans, and his two brothers at his New Orleans plantation in 1798. De Marigny's famed son Bernard would be a spirited city councilman, president of the Louisiana Senate, and twice gubernatorial candidate during the early American period. Joseph Xavier Delfau de Pontalba was already a retired French and Spanish officer and would eventually return to France in 1797, where he would write a memoir on Louisiana for Napoleon Bonaparte; two weeks after the submission of that memoir, Napoleon coerced Spain to retrocede Louisiana via the Treaty of San Idelfonzo. Pontalba served in 1803–4 as the mayor of Colombes, in the Hauts-de-Seine department of the Île-de-France region, and was named baron for his services. An ardent Bonapartist, Pontalba reportedly proposed to assist Marshal Ney to flee to Louisiana and was involved in a conspiracy to rescue Napoleon from St. Helena (*Liste de maires de Colombes,* www.wikiwand.com/fr/Liste_des_maires_de_Colombes [accessed 9 August 2017]). Oddly enough, Pontalba is listed not with the title "Baron de Pontalba" as he appears in other French works of the time, but as the "Baron de Carondelet"—the title of the Spanish governor of Louisiana, who had only died in 1807. Years later, Pontalba would shoot his daughter-in-law several times—Almonaster y Roxas's daughter Micaela—and then himself. Micaela

lived and became the famed baroness de Pontalba, who built the building flanking modern-day Jackson Square, as well as the modern-day residence of the US ambassador to France in Paris. For the entire sordid story, which intrigued Stendahl, see Vella, *Intimate Enemies*. Also see *Stewart–de Jahan Genealogy Pages*, "Joseph Xavier Delfau de Pontalba," www.raymondjohnson.net/genealogy/getperson.php?personID=I3579&tree=stewart (accessed 9 August 2017).

6. Arthur, *Old New Orleans*, entry for "de Kernion," 400.

7. Seven were Spanish and naturally spoke that language; numerous records and correspondence indicate that Clark and Mather spoke and wrote both Spanish and French, and Beauregard served as an officer in the Spanish military and was thus required to speak that language. Similarly, six of the group were French, Clark and Mather both spoke and wrote French, and among the Spanish, at least Riano certainly spoke French, while Almonaster y Roxas, Jorda, La Chiapella, and Miró were all married to French women (to de La Ronde, de Reggio, Lemelle, and Macarty, respectively). Only the older Navarro may have struggled with the French language. On their religion, see ADNO, vol. 6, multiple entries. In counterpoint, see Faber, *Building the Land of Dreams*, 78–79.

In the same vein, Faber also implied that the city's merchants were unnecessarily proud and impractical in their clothing: "wrapping themselves in dark velvet suits in the tropical heat, with high collars and triple cravats, sweat flooding the folds of their collars. . . . The old-fashioned still wore powdered wigs. . . . others preferred military uniforms. . . . Such gaudy militarism was anathema to most American newcomers" (76). However, the portraits by the most famous Spanish American portraitist of the early nineteenth century, José Francisco Xavier de Salazar y Mendoza (in New Orleans 1782–1802), indicate that even English-speaking merchants like Mather presented themselves in uniform for Salazar. The uniform jackets ranged in color, depending upon the military units assigned, not a preference for dark colors. Boys wore white linen shirts and cravats; the women wore light fabrics of mostly white and lighter colors. All were well-dressed, as would be expected for such an expensive and permanent undertaking, but they were not dressed impracticably for the weather in Louisiana. (For the best collection of original Salazar work, see Louisiana State Museum Collections, "José Francisco Xavier de Salazar y Mendoza," www.crt.state.la.us/louisiana-state-museum/collections/visual-art/artists/jos-francisco-xavier-de-salazar-y-mendoza [accessed 27 January 2018].) While dark velvet suits may seem illogical "in the tropical heat," they are actually quite logical there in the cool months—New Orleans is decidedly not tropical.

8. Arthur, *Old Families of Louisiana*, 27–31.

9. Many of Beauregard's transactions were in 1783, 1785, 1786, 1792, and 1794–96.

10. Author's database of notarial activity, 1780–99. La Chiapella was characterized by Evan Jones as "A beast in grain; without the smallest education talents or Respectability tho one of the Richest men in the Country," and by a second source as "Merchant—Born in Genoa rich but deeply ignorant much devoted to the Spanish Govt, from which he Receivd many favours; however incapable of holding any Office—dubious morals" (*Terr Papers* 9, 250, 253). La Chiapella died in Bordeaux on 22 August 1822 (NONA, Legacy by testament, 23 November 1818, addendum). Neither Jorda nor Mayronne appears in the *Territorial Papers*; neither was considered significant by the incoming Americans.

11. On Navarro, see Coutts, "Martin Navarro." Navarro returned to Spain in 1788 and was appointed a special commissioner, visiting European factories. He was able to enrich himself

considerably during his years in Louisiana; when he died in Spain in 1793, his estate was valued at 3,711,330 *reales de vellón*, or 463,917 pesos. John Kukla reported that Navarro actually never married, but did legally recognize his daughter. See Kukla, *A Wilderness So Immense*. On de Riano, see University of Notre Dame Archives, Correspondence of 18 and 24 November 1797, between Bishop Peñalver y Cárdenas and cathedral pastor Father Sedella, regarding baptismal record of Gilberto Manuel Riano, son of Juan Antonio Riano and Victoria Maxent y Roca, and of their daughter Rosa Victoria. Sedella certified an entry for Gilberto's baptism on 21 September 1783 (for which Francisco stood for Governor de Riano in Sicily), and for Rosa Victoria's baptism on 27 August 1784. The certificate noted that Juan Antonio de Riano was "a native of Lierganes," next to the diocese of Santander, and his wife was Victoria Maxent, native of New Orleans; the godfather in the latter was Colonel Gilberto Antonio Maxent. Juan Antonio was very close to Gálvez, requested to follow him to Mexico, and walked beside Gálvez's funeral bier. Juan Antonio would rise to the rank of *capitan de fragata*, colonel of royal troops, and the intendant of Guanajuato, Mexico, from 1792 until 1810. It was he who would build the great granary in Guanajuato, the *Alhóndiga de Granaditas*, and he and his son Gilberto would die there defending it on 28 September 1810 from Father Miguel Hidalgo. See also Beerman, "'Yo Solo' not 'Solo': Juan Antonio de Riano," 174–84.

12. Wohlip, *A Man in Shadow*. On Mather, see NONA, multiple entries.

13. NONA, multiple entries; see also NOPR, doc. #611, "Case of Daniel Clarck vs. Juan Bautista Desilet," file #3547, 1780, pp. 1–28; in NOPR, Black Books 123: 88–89, this case focused on Clark's sale of fifteen slaves to Desilet and suit to seize Desilet's properties for nonpayment of that sale debt (Wohlip, "A Man in the Shadow"). One of Clark's proceedings against his creditors, Simon Ducourneau, indicates a likely source of Clark's slaves: it reports that Ducourneau owed for three unnamed African slaves, "brought here from Jamaica in his (Clark's) schooner named *New Orleans*." See NOPR, doc. #2462, box 58, "Incidental Proceedings Instituted by Don Daniel Clark," file #53, 16 April 1790, pp. 1–6; in NOPR, Black Books 146: 15–16. Another New Orleans resident but not a Spanish *vecino*, Oliver Pollock, had conducted forty-five transactions in 1778. However, additional research is required to determine how many of these transactions might have involved slaves.

14. NOPR, doc. #1826, box 51, "Proceedings Instituted by Don Francisco Bouligny," file #68, 16 July 1788, pp. 1–3; in NOPR, Black Books 136: 113. The authorization was required because Bouligny's original land deeds were destroyed in the great fire of 21 March 1788. The land encompassed twenty-six arpents (about twenty-six acres). See NONA, numerous entries for "Daniel Clark" and "Ebenezer Rees" (their longtime partner until 1791). Clark Senior was still alive in mid-1790, when he appointed his nephew with an alternate power of attorney. See NOPR, doc. #2526, box 59, "Clark vs. Blair (Agent)," file #1765, 12 June 1790, pp. 1–18; in NOPR, Black Books 147: 88–94. This case pitted Clark against Peter Whiteside of London via their powers of attorney, assigned by Whiteside to Samuel Chollet of Santo Domingo and Santiago Blair of New Orleans. The process naturally required the services of the public interpreter, Juan Joseph DuForest. The successful suit, for the surrender or nullification of a bill of exchange worth 24,063 pesos held in London, indicates how transatlantic and trans-imperial the world of a New Orleans merchant might be. On the younger Clark's relationship with Coxe, see Arena, "Philadelphia-Spanish New Orleans Trade in the 1790s," 436–38. When the elder Coxe was appointed to his Treasury position in 1790, he transferred his business property to his younger brother, Daniel. On the tough times for the Clarks in the 1790s, see NONA, multiple entries for "Daniel Clark." In 1798, Clark registered

nineteen transactions—the most in the city—but they were protests (legal requests for payment by debtors), not sales or purchases.

15. NONA entries for Mather in Perdomo, vols. 1, 2, 3, 4, 5, 7, 9, 11, 13, and 15; Pedesclaux, vols. 4, 11, and 12; Ximenes, vols. 1, 4, 6, 7, 9, 10, and 15; and Broutin, vols. 15 and 25.

16. *Louisiana Gazette,* 22 March 1808; but also see the unkind description, "deficient in dignity of character & sterling veracity . . . liked by few of the Americans here," by another prominent American, albeit a Jeffersonian (*Terr Papers 9,* 9). Although he professed the Catholic faith as a Spanish *vecino,* he would serve as a vestryman for the city's first Protestant church (*Louisiana Gazette,* 22 April 1808). Considering Clark's shooting of Claiborne, it is small wonder, then, than an American newspaper later claimed that "in his manners many complain that there is something forbidding; something that keeps at a distance even those who esteem him most" (Wohlip, "A Man in the Shadow," 172, 200; *Louisiana Gazette,* 22 March 1808). Although Clark provided vital intelligence and support to the US annexation of Louisiana, the Jeffersonians seem to have disliked him immediately. The list of characterizations used by Thomas Jefferson said of Clark that he "possesses capicities [*sic*] to do more good or harm than any other individual in the province—He pants for power, and is mortified by disappointment," and elsewhere, "from further investigation it seems Mr. Clarke is rather an Englishman at heart, that he is unpopular & too assuming here. Therefore it might be unwise to countenance at present his cunning & overbearing pretensions" (*Terr Papers 9,* 255, 253).

17. *Terr Papers 9,* 251. The characterization of Mather and over a hundred other residents was drafted by Evan Jones, a longtime resident of the city, supplemented by a Franco-American "Labigarre . . . who only visited the country for 6 or 9 months. . . . he married a Livingston" (258). The characterizations were marked "Confidential" and forwarded to Thomas Jefferson, who annotated them in his own hand (*Terr Papers 9,* letter of Joseph Briggs to the President, 17 August 1804, 276–78, esp. 277).

18. The painting of Mather, ca. 1800, is in the Louisiana State Exhibit Museum in New Orleans.

19. Schavelzon, *Historical Archaeology of Buenos Aires,* 54–55, 144. These numbers would change only after independence, but how much and how quickly are for further research. Even between 1821 and 1842, about 35 percent of the external shipping came from England and 31.5 percent from the United States.

20. Socolow, *The Merchants of Buenos Aires, 1778–1810,* 16–19; Brading, *Miners and Merchants in Bourbon Mexico, 1763–1810,* 104–19, esp. 112. Humboldt reported that, in contrast, merchants from southern Spain and the Canary Islands dominated in modern-day Venezuela (*Personal Narrative of Travels,* 395). Further in-depth analysis would be required for comparison with Socolow on Buenos Aires and Brading on Mexican merchants, including data on the ages of the merchants at marriage, the ages of their wives at marriage, and the family backgrounds of their wives. See Socolow, *Merchants of Buenos Aires,* 39–40, and Brading, *Miners and Merchants in Bourbon Mexico,* 104–14.

21. Socolow, *Merchants of Buenos Aires,* 18–25.

22. Socolow, *Merchants of Buenos Aires,* 57; Brading, *Miners and Merchants in Bourbon Mexico,* 103.

23. Socolow, *Merchants of Buenos Aires,* 170, 177. Socolow does not state which merchants were investing in this manner, that is, whether they were Spanish-born, native-born, British, or even American.

24. This school is anchored by John Fisher and Barbara and Stanley Stein. See Fisher, "Commerce and Imperial Decline: Spanish Trade with Spanish America, 1797–1820," 459–79; *Commercial Relations between Spain and Spanish America in the Era of Free Trade, 1778–1796*; and Stein and Stein, *Edge of Crisis*.

25. This school includes Jeremy Adelman, Susan Migden Socolow, Carlos Marichal, and Fabricio Prado. See Adelman, *Sovereignty and Revolution in the Iberian Atlantic*; Socolow, *Merchants of Buenos Aires, 1778–1810*; Marichal, *Bankruptcy of Empire*; and Prado, *Edge of Empire*. Within this school, Adelman stressed that the colonies remained loyal to the Bourbons for quite long despite the financial and military failures of Charles IV (*Sovereignty and Revolution in the Iberian Atlantic*, 101). Marichal agreed that continual "war demands and skyrocketing royal debts" created a "financial maelstrom" from which Charles IV himself could not recover (*Bankruptcy of Empire*, 265) but also argued that the overseas empire "experienced a remarkable resurgence" in that very period (6). Similarly, both Socolow and Prado noted that trans-imperial trade and cooperation permitted Spanish colonial trade in the Rio Plata to thrive despite the Bourbon king (Socolow, *Bankruptcy of Empire* 67, 125–32; Prado, *Edge of Empire*, esp. 2–8, 58–82). The quote is from Adelman, *Sovereignty and Revolution in the Iberian Atlantic*, 101.

26. Prado, *Edge of Empire*, 8.

27. Clark seems to have ignored the economic spheres of agriculture, raw material production (especially lumber), real estate speculation, slave-trading, transport, and the law ("Business Elite").

28. Clark, "Business Elite," 96–98, 101–2. Clark identified twenty-one such merchants, but the list he provided is of twenty-two men. Clark's list appears as appendix 2 of this work, with a column for ethnicity for comparison with the previous appendix 1 on the city's Spanish-era merchants.

3. TRADE IN SPANISH NEW ORLEANS

1. Marichal, *Bankruptcy of Empire*, 265. See also Fisher, "Commerce and Imperial Decline: Spanish Trade with Spanish America, 1797–1820," 459–79.

2. Marichal, *Bankruptcy of Empire*, 262.

3. Prado, *Edge of Empire*, 58–59.

4. AGI, Papeles de Cuba, 597, microfilm E-87, roll 116, pp. 64–65. Harshaw was a member of a Masonic Lodge at Fells Point, in Baltimore, in the late 1790s (Schulz, *History of Freemasonry in Maryland*, 234).

5. AGI, Papeles de Cuba, 597, microfilm E-87, roll 117, p. 672.

6. AGI, Papeles de Cuba, 597, microfilm E-87, roll 116, pp. 45–48 (draft), pp. 49–51 (final version, with minor changes in spelling, abbreviations, and so forth), letter of Enrique Darcantel, countersigned by Juan Ventura Morales, dated 19 March 1789. Darcantel did not realize that Gálvez had been replaced in that position due to illness over a year earlier, in 1787.

7. *Financial Report*, Francisco Blache, City Treasury, New Orleans, January 1–December 1786, in New Orleans Municipal Papers, per Clark, *New Orleans, 1718–1812*, 228. AGI, Papeles de Cuba, 514, microfilm E-78, roll 38, pp. 146–94, Entradas—1789 (from Entrada y Salidas); AGI, Papeles de Cuba, 514, microfilm E-78, roll 38, pp. 198–228.

8. Additional vessel-arrival records were kept, not at New Orleans itself, but at the Balize, an

isolated customs post at the mouth of the Mississippi River, from 1784 to 1793. These records were utilized by Jean-Pierre Le Glaunec in an essay on slave routes. Le Glaunec reported them to be in AGI, Papeles de Cuba, 10, 11, 13, 14, 16, 25A, 25B, 26, 112, and 602B. See Le Glaunec, "Slave Migrations and Slave Control in Spanish and Early American New Orleans," 204–38, esp. 205 and 230.

9. AGI, Papeles de Cuba, 514, microfilm E-78, roll 38, pp. 229–329. This register was oddly maintained, with entries across months, broken up, and out of order. Consequently, the numbers used here are the total of entry signatures that de Texada made that month (for each of those, he wrote only his last name), minus his monthly compilation and signature (which he signed with his full name). The statistics for 1799 were January, 8; February, 29; March, 32; April, 49; May, 45; June, 48; July, 36; August, 31; September, 25; October, 14; November, 23; and December, 17. Fortunately, Texada's 1799 book did use digits, amounts taxed, and clear dates in each entry.

10. AGI, Papeles de Cuba, 514, microfilm E-78, roll 38, p. 329. The actual revenues in Spanish reales for 1799 were: January, 20,577; February, 68,445; March, 42,421.7; April, 80,027.7; May, 99,927.7; June, 166.417.7; July, 83,809; August, 57,668; September, 21,523.7; October, 16,317; November, 39,431; December, 39,056.7; total 735,621.7. These figures seem to be off by 7—presumably a transcription error by the author.

11. AGI, Papeles de Cuba, 514, microfilm E-78, roll 38, pp. 229–329. For the departure list, see Papeles de Cuba, 514, microfilm E-78, roll 38, pp. 198–228. The actual numbers were 56 *bergantines*, 14 frigates, 13 *goletas*, 5 *baladuas*, 3 *paquebots del rey* (Royal packet boats), 5 *polacres*, 1 *ongarre*, and 1 *calandra*. *Bergantines* (in English, brigantines) were two-masted, square-rigged ships with extra sails fore and after and a single deck (about 110 feet), built to run fast but carry substantial cargo—in this way, they were a predecessor to the later clipper ships, which were much longer (about 240 feet) with three to five masts. Frigates were large three-masted, square-rigged ships with two decks, about 210 feet long. *Goletas* were schooners, two-masted ships with variations in their rigging, typically longer than brigantines (about 140 to 150 feet), which could be easily enough built, were shallow enough to move in coastal waters, and were not meant for speed and so required fewer sailors than other vessels. *Polacres* were carryovers from seventeenth-century European vessels, similar to the North African *xebec*, with three masts, including a large triangular lateen sail in the bow and square rigging on the midmast. *Baladuas* were probably a misspelling/translation of *belandres/balandras* (in English, bilanders), flat-bottom boats used to transport coal along the coast, rivers, and canals. These are more frequently seen as picturesque barges on French rivers and canals, but were sometimes rigged with sails for coastal trade. It is unclear what type of vessels were referred to as an *ongarre* or a *calandra*; *ongarre* may refer to a boat used for guard or coastal duty ("en garde") and *calandra* may simply be a misspelling of *belandre/balandra*.

12. *Ano de 1800, Libro Real Comun y Gral. de Cargo y Data*, in National Archives of Colombia. Of the American vessels, the brigantine *La Maria*, captained by William Ald, arrived on 17 May 1800, carrying a full load of *galletas* (biscuits). Ten days later, on 27 May, the brigantine *La Margarita*, captained by Henry Reed, arrived from Cádiz. On 19 September, the frigate *Flora*, captained by James Lovett, arrived in the city from New York City. The *Flora* was the only large vessel to arrive in Cartagena that year, and it carried a vast load of mixed cargo. Consequently, the *Flora's* cargo brought in far more into the Cartagenan tax coffers than many other vessels combined and, like the two earlier American ships, required two different tax computations. (Lovett's voyages to Cartagena are documented in the New York Supreme Court case *Blagge v. New York Insurance*

Company. The *Flora* would later be seized by the British and held in Jamaica, and Lovett would be represented in that case by Alexander Hamilton. See *The Law Practice of Alexander Hamilton*. *La Luisa*, captained by Diego Mantell, arrived in Cartagena on 29 November from Philadelphia.

13. *Anchorage Fees Report*, 1801, in New Orleans Municipal Papers, per Clark, *New Orleans, 1718–1812*, 228; *Moniteur de le Louisiane*, per Clark, *New Orleans, 1718–1812*, 228; AGI, Papeles de Cuba, 631, microfilm E-141, roll 2, *Libro de registro del depósito de las mercancías compra das por los americanos en Nueva Orleans, anos 1798–1802*, folio #1, microfilm pp. 1–284; *Libro de registro del depósito de las mercancías compra das por los americanos en Nueva Orleans, año 1803*, folio #2, microfilm pp. 285–324. These records were supplemented by registers/logbooks for the Guarda Almacén, on the same roll, pp. 349–409, for early 1796 (entries 1–239, signed by Juan Ventura Morales), pp. 410–634 (entries 2–1462, from April 1796 to 31 December 1798). Similarly, three massive volumes of correspondence on trade issues from Martin Navarro, labeled as being from the Guarda Almacén, can be found in AGI, Papeles de Cuba, 633, microfilm roll E-141, roll 2.

14. Laussat, *Memoirs of My Life*, 73. Laussat wrote five days earlier, on 24 November, that he had received a dispatch from his own minister, via the US government, informing him of the Louisiana Purchase. It is doubtful that the North Americans on the ground, such as Daniel Clark, would have kept the news secret from anyone, much less their Spanish friends and frequent allies.

15. This estimate is arrived at by considering that 200 flatboats (20–30 tons of each, for 6,000–8,000 tons of total cargo) from upriver were subject to Guarda Almacén regulation/taxation in 1799. By contrast, 367 ships, probably most brigantines (60 tons each), left New Orleans, probably carrying total cargo of 22,020 tons. The total percentage of cargo probably arriving in the city from upriver subject to Spanish taxation would have been 27 to 36 percent; the remaining 73 to 64 percent would not have been so subject.

16. The easiest method to measure the Spanish economy during the subject period is by the number of actual pages of business transactions for each year. It is probably a safe assumption that the number of pages of business transactions in a given year reflects, more or less, the amount of economic activity in that year. Admittedly, some transactions (contracts, wills, and so forth) may be quite long and yield a disproportionate number of pages, but such transactions spread themselves over the course of years, and should not statistically invalidate a simple page count. And in fact, as figure 3.6 demonstrates, the method is actually reasonably accurate, and, in fact, notarial pages may be a more useful measure than notarial transactions!

17. Notarial records were clearly poorly kept in New Orleans before 1771, in a single book from 1764 to 1767, with only sixty-one pages and fifty-nine entries, and a single book for 1768–70. In addition, at least two of the handwritten ledgers were not transcribed by the WPA in the 1930s, in part because of their poor condition. These untranscribed volumes were Almonaster 9 (A9) from 1777 and Almonaster 01 (A01) from 1779. In both cases, some analysis is possible using photocopies. Amusingly, in both documents, Almonaster's work was indexed by the first name of transactors, not their surnames, that is, all of the transactors named Francisco are indexed together, all of the Juans, and so forth.

18. Subsequent to the American Revolution, the Bourbon government closed the Mississippi River to American shipping at least between Natchez and New Orleans, and the American attempt to negotiate better terms via the Jay-Gardoqui Treaty failed to earn approval of the then merely confederated American states in 1786. A prominent if dated work on the treaty is Bemis,

Pinckney's Treaty. It is likely that any closure of the river to American shipping, at least above New Orleans, was mitigated because most planters then shipping downriver were Spanish *vecinos* or, in the case of the prominent William Dunbar and Daniel Clark Sr., arguably still British subjects.

19. NONA, Pedesclaux, v, 43, 44, and 45 (1803). Merieult's activity in 1803 began with a sale of property and a single receipt in January 1803, then suddenly several receipts and sales issued on 4–10 March. The issuance of receipts and sales dribbled on until 28 May, when they exploded until December. In all, Merieult sold at least two hundred slaves in the six months between late May and late November 1803. All were sold during the Spanish administration—the only two transactions during the three weeks of French rule were a receipt and a protest for payment.

20. George Pollock and his wife, Catherine Yates Pollock, were painted by famed portraitist Gilbert Stuart around 1793–94; the works are in the National Gallery of Art. Their daughter Marie Louise Pollock Chiapella married the son of Geromo La Chiapella. (Portrait can be seen at the National Gallery of Art, www.nga.gov/Collection/art-object-page.1112.html [accessed 24 January 2018].) On the distant relationship between Oliver Pollock and George Pollock, see Claiborne, *Interim Appointment*, 438–40.

21. Le Glaunec, "Slave Migrations and Slave Control in Spanish and Early American New Orleans," 204–38.

22. The comprehensive *Trans-Atlantic Slave Trade Database,* sponsored by Emory and Harvard universities and the National Endowment for the Humanities, www.slavevoyages.orgvoyage/search (accessed 18 November 2017). The voyage identification numbers are *Thetis,* #32343; *Guipuscano,* #41845; *Africain,* #33596; *Sally,* #14138; and *Confiance,* #33608. The ship name *Guispuscano* indicates the ship was owned by a Basque from Gipuzkoa. However, the data on *Sally* and *Confiance* seem to be interchanged, at least compared with its original source, Le Glaunec, "Slave Migrations and Slave Control in Spanish and Early American New Orleans."

23. NONA, Broutin, vol. 7; Pedesclaux, vols. 9–10, 11; Perdomo, vols. 15–16.

24. ADNO, vol. 5 (1791–95), entries for "Pedesclaux," "Jorda," "Mayronne."

25. Le Glaunec, "Slave Migrations and Slave Control in Spanish and Early American New Orleans," 195; NONA, multiple entries for "John/Juan McDonough/McDonogh/McDonugh & Co." as early as Perdomo, vol. 9 (1787), and Pedesclaux, vol. 5 (1789). None of these entries appear in 1788, the year the *Santa Catalina* arrived in New Orleans. See NONA, multiple entries for "Alexandro/Alejandro Baudin," beginning for Baudin in Perdomo, vol. 5 (1785), but for both "Baudin" and "Geromo La Chiapella" esp. in Perdomo, vols. 11–12 (1788) and Pedesclaux, vols. 2, 3, and 4 (1788).

26. Le Glaunec, "Slave Migrations and Slave Control in Spanish and Early American New Orleans," 204–38.

27. Faber, *Building the Land of Dreams,* 356–57nn, based upon Clark, *New Orleans, 1718–1812.*

28. The fire of 1788 destroyed 856 buildings in the city, several months before the economic downturn. Perhaps the greatest reported losses for a single merchant were those of Pablo Segond, who reported he had lost 100,044 pesos 3.5 reales (NOPR, Black Books 136: 33). These losses, if accurate, would indicate that Segond had significant capital as compared to other locations in the Spanish empire. By comparison, Brading reported that, in 1781, the very prominent Fago-aga merchant house's inventory listed 164,148 pesos in stock and 202,891 in cash. (*Miners and Merchants in Bourbon Mexico, 1763–1810,* 123.) Juan Lacoste reported that he suffered the damage of

two large houses; some moveable property had been saved into the warehouse of Colonel Gilbert Antonio Maxent, but this was destroyed in a second fire on 8 April of the same year (NOPR, Black Books 136: 58).

29. Bergad, Garcia, and Barcia, *The Cuban Slave Market, 1790–1880*, 162–64, table B1. See also Kotlikoff, "Quantitative Description of the New Orleans Slave Market, 1804 to 1862," in Fogel and Engerman, *Without Consent or Contract* 1: 31–53.

30. AGI, Papeles de Cuba, 597, microfilm E-87, roll 116, pp. 45–48 (draft), pp. 49–51 (final version, with minor changes in spelling, abbreviations, and so forth), letter of Enrique Darcantel, countersigned by Juan Ventura Morales, dated 19 March 1789.

31. Charles Vivant himself would form a smaller company with some success, and Juan Dupuy, too, lingered in the notarial record, but neither was ever so successful as before 1789.

32. Din, *Spaniards, Planters, and Slaves*, 130; Coutts, "Boom and Bust: The Rise and Fall of the Tobacco Industry in Spanish Louisiana, 1770–1790," 306–9.

33. Carondelet was actually not Spanish; he was born in Cambrai, France, in 1747 but had served in the Spanish military since he was fifteen years old. He would eventually marry a Spanish woman, and after his service in Louisiana, he would head the *Audiencia* in Quito (*DLB*, "Carondelet, Luis Francisco Héctor de"). On his trade practices, see Holmes, *A Guide to Spanish Louisiana, 1762–1806*, 19–22.

34. AGI, Papeles de Cuba, 1442B, microfilm E-145, roll 22–23, p. 594 (modern number-stamped in the margin as #637), Carondelet to Captain General of Cuba Luis de Las Casas (his brother-in-law), 31 August 1794. Perhaps by a typographical error, Din reported this hurricane as occurring in August 1793 (Din and Harkins, *New Orleans Cabildo*, 32 and 141), but the original documents clearly prove the correct date was in 1794.

35. AGI, Papeles de Cuba, 1442B, microfilm E-145, roll 22–23, p. 594 (modern number-stamped in the margin as # 637), Carondelet to Captain General of Cuba Luis de Las Casas, 31 August 1794.

36. The extent of the flooding is based upon the author's geospatial analysis of contemporary and current city maps. For the *cabildo's* request, see Din and Harkins, *New Orleans Cabildo*, 280, citing *Actas del Cabildo* 3, no. 3: 167–69 of 10 October 1794.

37. Carondelet was a driving force behind the cathedral in Quito's dome being completed, and he is buried in that cathedral. His quarters in Quito so impressed Simón Bolívar that he dubbed the building "El Palacio de Carondelet," and so it is still named, now serving as the Presidential Palace of Ecuador. On Gayoso, see Pitot, *Observations on the Colony of Louisiana from 1796 to 1802*, 15.

38. AGI, Papeles de Cuba, 212B, microfilm E-106, roll 68, pp. 28–33. My following translation introduces more modern punctuation and occasional clarifying words for readability. The full text in English and Spanish is provided as appendix 1. I have left most of the misspellings, mindful that the petition was written as the Spanish language was evolving and that the petition was written by bilingual petitioners. Some words are also unintelligible in the original, but may be well supposed.

39. AGI, Papeles de Cuba, 212B microfilm 106 roll 68, pp. 28–33, dated 31 August 1796.

40. AGI, Papeles de Cuba, 597, microfilm E-87, roll 116, pp. 212–15, petition dated 22 February 1797. The full list of names is: Cavalier et Petit, M. Fortier, J. Lanvier (or Lauvier?), P. Sauve, Laburther, Francisco Mayronne, Geromo La Chiapella, Labatut, C F Girod, Dhabeen(?), Domingo de Lemos, James Kennedy, J. Bautista Sarpy, Reaud, Jean Paillet, illegible (perhaps Ferraro), Jh. Martineng, Beaugaud, Gairal, D. Prevost, Jacques Monton, and Vivant Duclos y Soule.

41. AGI, Papeles de Cuba, 1493, *Hoja de servicios y listas de revista, Regiment of Luisana.*

42. Din, *An Extraordinary Atlantic Life,* ix–xv.

43. AGI, Papeles de Cuba, 1550; see Indices of 27 December 1799, Letters 1 and 3 of 20 September 1799 (voyage and arrival); #2 of 20 September (destruction of San Carlos), and #5: 10, 12, and 14, of 27 October 1799 on his military considerations.

44. Archivo Histórico Nacional, Madrid, Estado, legajo 3892 bis, exped. 1, letter of Morales to Miguel Cayetano Soler, no. 354, 30 November 1799, with attachments, and Casa-Calvo's letter of 10 October 1799. See also Din, *Extraordinary Atlantic Life,* 191–92.

45. Din and Harkins, *New Orleans Cabildo,* 292–93n4. The Din quote is from AGI, PC, legajo 1553, Salcedo to Someruelos, no. 90, 17 March 1802, with a note attached from Someruelos.

46. Pitot, *Observations on the Colony of Louisiana from 1796 to 1802,* xx–xxi. On the book itself, see xi–xii.

47. Pitot, *Observations on the Colony of Louisiana from 1796 to 1802,* 35.

48. Pitot, *Observations on the Colony of Louisiana from 1796 to 1802,* 58–59.

49. Pitot, *Observations on the Colony of Louisiana from 1796 to 1802,* 59.

50. AGI, Papeles de Cuba, 597, microfilm E-87, roll 116, pp. 64–65; AGI, Papeles de Cuba, 597, microfilm E-87, roll 117, p. 672.

51. Pitot, *Observations on the Colony of Louisiana from 1796 to 1802,* 59; AGI, Papeles de Cuba, 514, microfilm E-78, roll 38, pp. 229–329.

52. Pitot, *Observations on the Colony of Louisiana from 1796 to 1802,* 46, 22–23, and 47. Pitot did not accuse any officials of corruption by name but did note "the person whom Spain bribed several years before to condition favorably the sentiments of the Kentucky inhabitants," that is, General James Wilkinson, by 1802 the senior officer in the US military, and implied that Wilkinson's friend, the now-dead Governor Gayoso, was corrupt as well (16, 15, 18). The Guarda Almacén records also reveal important seasonal variations in New Orleans commerce associated with the arrival of flatboats, but Pitot did not note any such variations, a rather surprising omission for a merchant.

53. Pitot, *Observations on the Colony of Louisiana from 1796 to 1802,* 36–37, 58, 80–86, 93–95.

54. Pitot, *Observations on the Colony of Louisiana from 1796 to 1802,* 41; for the quote, 42–48. Pitot wondered of that memoir and Gayoso, "Did he send it? I do not know, but what is certain is that since then only one cédula or royal order has arrived from the court . . . which resulted in the ruin of the colony during the remainder of the war (1796–1801); and if New Orleans has taken several more steps towards her future grandeur, it is only through the effect of her fortunate position on the American continent." The Spanish archives, in fact, do not indicate any such memoir from Pitot reaching Spanish authorities in either Cuba or Spain. However, a 1797 letter from Pitot and J. B. Labatut to the Intendant Morales as "diputados del comercio" does appear in AGI, Papeles de Cuba, 603A and B, and may contain or reference Pitot's memoir.

55. Pitot also wrote that "during my first four years (1796–1799) in New Orleans there was hardly enough trade to justify a chamber of commerce" (*Observations on the Colony of Louisiana from 1796 to 1802,* 37).

56. Pitot, *Observations on the Colony of Louisiana from 1796 to 1802,* 48.

57. Smith, "Shipping in the Port of Veracruz, 1790–1821," 5–20. Maritime movement between Veracruz and New Orleans was probably not linked to the viceroyalty's support of the colony.

Instead, any financial support provided by the viceroyalty would probably have first been sent to Havana—not directly to New Orleans. Similarly, naval vessels would probably proceed from Veracruz to Havana, not New Orleans, given the difficulties of sailing upriver to the city.

58. Pitot, *Observations on the Colony of Louisiana from 1796 to 1802*, xxi. Pitot's predecessors as mayor were Étienne Boré and Cavalier Petit (who only held the post for ten days). Pitot served as mayor only for one year, from 6 June 1804 to 26 July 1805.

4. SPANISH ATTEMPTS TO CONTROL TRADE

1. See, for example, Brading, *Miners and Merchants in Bourbon Mexico, 1763–1810*; Marichal, *Bankruptcy of Empire*; Paquette, *Enlightenment, Governance, and Reform in Spain and Its Empire, 1759–1808*; Stein, *Apogee of Empire*. Bernardo de Gálvez's father, Matías, made such efforts when he governed Guatemala. However, these efforts were actually "At the Mercy of the World Market": "While Bourbon authority expanded, the world economy invaded. Together the two forces transformed the colony" (Wortman, *Government and Society in Central America, 1680–1840*, 157–71). Wortman was writing of Central America, but the "World Market" was just as important in New Orleans.

2. For a somewhat dated but accurate treatment, see Bemis's 1962 work, *Pinckney's Treaty*.

3. AGI, Papeles de Cuba, 631, Microfilm E-141, roll 2, *Libro de registro del depósito de las mercancías compra das por los americanos en Nueva Orleans, anos 1798–1802*, folio 1–284, ano 1803, folio 285–324.

4. Beckert, *Empire of Cotton*, 209–11.

5. AGI, Papeles de Cuba, 514, microfilm E-78, roll 39, pp. 146–228.

6. AGI, Papeles de Cuba, 2366, microfilm E-145, roll 49, p. 419, British ship discharge for Bahamas; AGI, Papeles de Cuba, 597, microfilm E-87, roll 117, p. 672, Port of Philadelphia form for ships clearing dated 6 May 1793.

7. A detailed ledger sheet, in modern terms a true spreadsheet, can be found in the Seville archives, documenting the complete numbers for all Spanish military forces in Louisiana and the Floridas. See AGI, Papeles de Cuba, 597, microfilm E-87, roll 116, pp. 194–95. A similar spreadsheet was used for the 1795 "chimney census."

8. AGI, Papeles de Cuba, 1493, *Hoja de servicios y listas de revista, Regiment of Luisana*. This legajo, which includes many military records for other colonial units in the region, especially Havana itself, is fragile. Carondelet used a printed format to document important data on his individual military commissioned and non-commissioned officers, including their name, service location, ranks and years/months/days served in each rank, with totals, a text block on regiments served in, another block for campaigns and military actions in which served, a block entitled *Notas* requiring very brief comment grades signed by the unit's senior military officer, and a final block, *Informe del Inspector* (Inspector's Report), which permitted a brief comment signed by Carondelet himself.

9. Private conversation with the author, 12 September 2017, at the AGI. These military forms were a model of efficiency and a clear predecessor of the modern military fitness report, which in recent memory was still contained in one printed page. The modern researcher must wonder if the Spanish developed the form independently or copied it from another military. The broader

empire was slowly catching up with the use of printed documents and forms—but very slowly indeed. The Spanish court and governors only began printing royal *cédulas* and treaties by 1790, and in 1793 printed both the declaration of war against France and a permit for Louisiana to conduct free trade with all friendly nations. However, some of these printed copies were then laboriously copied by hand for further distribution. The Havana postal officials used only a few forms. See AGI, Papeles de Cuba, 184A, microfilm E-106, roll 8, pp. 447 (royal decree, 1790); pp. 500–505 (free trade permitted to Louisiana, 1793); pp. 148 (declaration of war, 1793), AGI, Correos, 307 (1796). The British and North Americans had been printing state documents much longer: when General Anthony Wayne wrote to Carondelet on 15 October 1796 on the terms of the 1796 San Lorenzo Treaty, he included a printed copy of the treaty for Carondelet's reference (AGI, Papeles de Cuba, 212B, microfilm E-106, roll 69, p. 275).

10. More research would be useful on the Grand Isle/Barataria route. Francisco Mayronne, the successful slave trader during the Spanish era, relocated to Grand Isle sometime during the American era, as did Santiago LeDuf. This was the route famously used by the Lafittes during the American era. Mayronne's property is shown on Lafon's Map, a hand-drawn map of Barataria dated May 31, 1813, Library of Congress, Brueman #40G-35 #2, G 3862.C6, 1776, p. 3. The map shows that Mayronne, spelled "Merone" on the map, owned only Grand Terre then.

11. NOPR, Black Books 126: 52 (Fortier), 54 (Delagroue), 118 (Miraval); #128: 46 (Terrasson).

12. NOPR, Black Books 130: 78–79 (Dupeaux); 129, 93–94 (Legret); 123 (LeMoyne); 125 (Dousset); 132: 41 (Gallart); 126: 90 (Lafita/Lafite).

13. NOPR, Black Books 128: 12 (*Hercules* to Guárico), 33–34 (duplicates) (*La Matilde* to Philadelphia); 132: 103–5 (*San Antonio* to New Orleans); 136: 59 (*La Petit Julia* to Marseilles).

14. Prado, *Edge of Empire*, 64–65.

15. Ermus, "Reduced to Ashes: The Good Friday Fire of 1788 in Spanish Colonial New Orleans," 311–12; Lopez Armesto letter of 13 July, citing royal decree of 23 March 1791, Briscoe Center for American History, University of Texas, Austin, www.cah.utexas.edu/db/dmr/image_lg.php?-variable=e_eap_0233 (accessed 2 December 2017).

16. For only a few early examples of Spanish cases involving such losses, see NOPR, Black Books 124: 58 (shipwreck); 125: 6–2 (piracy), 32 (ship damages); 49 (dry goods damaged on a ship); 98 (piracy); 126: 25 (storm damage to cargo); 128: 72 (shipwreck), 129: 127 (on careenage of vessel), 130: 48 (ship loss, including load of flour); 131: 49 (ship appraisals); 132: 165 (sale of shipwreck pieces). For inspector's position, see NOPR, Black Books 126: 33 (Visoso replaces Magnon); 127: 7 and 50.

17. NOPR, Black Books 128: 62–63 (Loison).

18. NOPR, Black Books 134: 44 (Boyaval), 76 (Acher, denied travel for debts); 147: 63 (White, granted travel despite alleged debt). For comparison, see NOPR, Black Books 150: 8 (French passport for Cadroy), 22 (French passport for Dubisson with multiple entries), 70 (French passport entry for Dubuisson, dentist).

19. Le Glaunec, "Slave Migrations in Spanish and Early American Louisiana," 188–97.

20. Laussat, *Memoirs of My Life*, 36, which refers to rumors by 19 June, p. 44, implying the rumors were circulating by 13 June, and p. 56, on the official confirmation. The treaty was signed on 30 April that same year; news of the treaty clearly reached New Orleans well within two months, but official French confirmation reached Laussat, then, four months after the event. Famously,

the US Senate authorized President Jefferson to take possession of the territory on 21 October, six months after its signature! The US flag was finally raised over New Orleans two months later, on 20 December 1803, nearly eight months after the treaty's signature.

21. New Orleans received regular Spanish packets several times a month, and ships arrived every few days from the eastern United States. Accordingly, a Bourbon governor in New Orleans could be well informed of events in Europe, as compared to his colleagues in other Spanish colonies. However, despite this actual closeness in communication, the governors in Louisiana seem to have exercised great personal responsibility without close royal supervision. These governors were mostly protégés of Colonial Minister Gálvez, and could also draw upon the Captain General in Cuba for advice and guidance, without resorting to the royal court.

22. AGI, *Correos*, individual *Cuentas de la Administración de La Habana.* Generally, each year of postal records is found in a single large legajo, about 12 inches in thickness, set aside for that specific year.

23. AGI, Correos, 308 (1797).

24. AGI, Correos, 306 (1795), "Isla de Cuba, Reunión de los Ramos de Embarcaciones, Estafeta, e Impresos, Hasta 31 Diciembre 1795." The New Orleans accounts are not ordered by when the vessel actually arrived, but when the masters of the ships were paid for mail received. In 1795, New Orleans received fifty-five mail shipments, whether by a contracted packet boat or other vessels—again, roughly weekly, although there were a few two-week gaps in service, which may have been based on weather, but also perhaps on ship availability. A number of vessels of all sizes were used: brigantines, goletas, polacres, and avisos. The latter more often than not claimed their reimbursement for mail delivery upon return to Havana, perhaps a month after sailing away. The most commonly paid vessel was the *Liebra*, captained by Don Antonio Acosta.

25. Sellers-Garcia, *Distance and Documents at the Spanish Empire's Periphery*, 88–91, 96–98, esp. map 3.2.

26. AGI, Correos, 307 (1796). The full data on the *gazeta* distribution was: Luisiana y las Floridas, 894; Mexico, 638; Campeche, 31; Veracruz, 384; Guatemala, 93; Cartagena, 125; Panama, 12.5; Portovelo, 7.5; Santa Fe, 93; Quito 7.5; Caracas, 15; Guayra, 9.5; Puerto Rico, 26; Santo Domingo, 26. The *Gaceta* (or *Gazeta*) *de Madrid* was first published in 1661 as a monthly, then in 1697 as a weekly, but was eventually placed under royal control in 1762 under Charles III. The first Spanish daily, the *Diario de Madrid*, appeared in 1758. These two newspapers were the only two permitted by the Spanish government to be published between 1789 and 1808, under Charles IV ("Gazeta, colección histórica: ayuda y contenido," www.boe.es/buscar/ayudas/gazeta_ayuda.php). In 1796, issue 71 was dated 2 September, and issue 78 was dated 23 September.

27. AGI, Correos, 309 (1798).

28. AGI, Correos, 309, Estafeta Nueva Orleans.

29. Llovet, *Cartas a Vera Cruz, Comerce América*, 13, 23; McGroarty, "Diary of Captain William Buckner," 173–207, see. 199, gen. note; ADNO, vol. 7: 270, "Relf."

30. AGI, Papeles de Cuba, 212B, microfilm 106, roll 68, pp. 28–33 (author's translation); AGI, Papeles de Cuba, 631, microfilm E-141, roll 2, *Libro de registro del depósito de las mercancías compradas por los americanos en Nueva Orleans, anos 1798–1802*, folio 1–284, año 1803, folio 285–324; AGI, Estado, 2.N.33 on Evan Jones as consul, camera copy only (not on microfilm), in which the Marqués de Someruelos, governor of Cuba, himself referred to "los Americanos." On Rumsey, one

of the most active business transactors in New Orleans in 1777, see NONA, Almonaster, vol. 9 (1777); Garic, vol. 8 (1777). On the difficulties of the Spanish economic system, see Grafe, *Distant Tyranny*. The most comprehensive historical work on the early US Postal Service is Richard R. John's *Spreading the News*; see esp. 3–7, which indicate the US Postal Service far surpassed those of Great Britain and France by 1800 in number of post offices, employees, and services provided.

31. Pitot, *Observations on the Colony of Louisiana from 1796 to 1802*, 48–49.

32. AGI, Estado, 2.N.17, camera copy only, 27 September 1799.

33. AGI, Estado, 2.N.33, camera copy only, 24 October 1799, but attached to the letter dated 29 November 1799. See also AGI, Estado, 2.N.33, camera copy only, dated 24 October 1799, but attached to the letter dated 29 November 1799, which indicates that the interim military governor (the Marqués de Casa-Calvo) convinced Someruelos to rescind his directions on accepting Jones.

34. AGI, Papeles de Cuba, 597, microfilm E-87, roll 116, pp. 83–84; Laussat, *Memoirs of My Life*, 19.

35. Klein, *The American Finances of the Spanish Empire*, esp. 8.

36. Klein, *The American Finances of the Spanish Empire*, 110.

37. Miles Wortman wrote, "Regional Creole economics relied upon the church's credit institutions to defend against natural catastrophes and to support local subsistence economies." However, my own research has found no indication that the church actively provided credit to any New Orleans *vecinos*. See Wortman, *Government and Society in Central America, 1680–1840*, 133.

38. Pitot, *Observations on the Colony of Louisiana from 1796 to 1802*, 47; AGI, Papeles de Cuba, 212B, microfilm E-106, roll 68, pp. 28–33. Translation is my own.

39. AGI, Papeles de Cuba, 597, microfilm E-87, roll 116, pp. 212–15, petition dated 22 February 1797.

40. Clark, "The Business Elite of New Orleans before 1815," 95–97, 102–3. The actual level of investment within the corporations or from outside sources remains unclear.

5. LITERACY IN A SPANISH IMPERIAL CITY

1. Research refutes the earlier French, Franco-American, and American accounts that Spanish New Orleans was notably illiterate. French accounts may be found in Robin, *Voyage to Louisiana, 1803–1805*, 57; Pitot, *Observations on the Colony of Louisiana from 1796 to 1802*, 32; and Berquin-Duvallon, *Vue de la colonie espagnole de Mississipi, ou des provinces de Louisiane et Floride Occidentale, en l'année 1802*, 205–7, 279, 283, 291, 295–96. John Davis's rough translation of Berquin-Duvallon was in the same harsh vein. See Davis, *Travels in Louisiana and the Floridas in the Year, 1802*; for comparison with the original French, see 32, 42, 50–53, 59–60. The seminal French-American account is in Martin, *History of New Orleans from the Earliest Period* 1: 256; the similar American account is in Sibley et al., *Account of Louisiana*, 38.

2. Sibley et al., *Account of Louisiana*, 38.

3. *Terr Papers* 9, 38.

4. For a recent example, see Faber, *Building the Land of Dreams*, 6 and esp. 75, for his repetition of the harsh critiques of Berquin-Duvallon and Treasury Secretary Albert Gallatin. By comparison, Kastor's 2004 work on the Louisiana Purchase, which is in some discourse with Faber's, casts no aspersions about literacy or education in New Orleans, noting instead the importance of private

one-room schools (*The Nation's Crucible,* 215). It should hardly be surprising that such critiques originated with French and continued with US sources, each prone to promote its own nationalisms/imperialisms at the expense of Spanish imperialism. However, at least one famous historian, Angel Rama, insisted that, throughout the Spanish empire and the subsequently independent Spanish America, administrators, lawyers, notaries, doctors, and priests composed a small circle of *letrados,* surrounded by "downwardly mobile Creoles and Europeans, along with all the inhabitants of darker complexion" (Rama, *Lettered City,* 29–32). Similarly, historian Jorge Dominguez calculated that "not more than 10–12 percent of adult Cubans (fifteen years and older) would have been literate before 1820" (Jensen, *Children of Colonial Despotism,* 21).

5. Houdaille, "Trois paroisses de Saint-Domingue au XVIIIe siècle," 93–110; "Reconstitution des familles de Saint-Domingue (Haïti) au XVIIIe siècle," 29–40. Calvo, "Politics of Print," 277–305. This last article is a comprehensive bibliography of books in pre–twentieth-century Spanish America. A number of original sources and historical works have also focused upon literacy in Spanish America *after* independence; these include most famously the works of Bello and Sarmiento and Benedict Anderson's *Imagined Communities,* but also Acree, *Everyday Reading,* esp. 17–20; and Lanning, *Academic Culture in the Spanish Colonies,* 53–54. At least one degreed individual was prominent in New Orleans: Dr. Nicolas Maria Vidal received a *bachiller, maestro,* and *doctor* in canon and civil law in Cartagena de Indias (modern-day Cartagena, Colombia), was a professor of canon and civil law at the Royal Seminary of San Carlos, and the *auditor de guerra* (judge advocate/lieutenant governor) in both Cartagena and New Orleans.

6. Dart, "Public Education in New Orleans in 1800," 241–52; McDermott, *Private Libraries in Creole Saint Louis.* See also McCutcheon, "Books and Booksellers in New Orleans, 1730–1830," 606–18; "First English Plays in New Orleans," 183–199; Leonard, "Frontier Library, 1799," 21–51; Holmes, "The Moniteur de la Louisiane in 1798," 230–53; "Louisiana in 1795," 133–51; Din and Harkins, *New Orleans Cabildo,* 19–21; Din, "Death and Succession of Francisco Bouligny," 314–15.

7. Laussat, *Memoirs of My Life,* 98.

8. While definitions of basic, advanced, and scientific literacy are somewhat subjective, I have applied a definition similar to that used in US government language testing. Basic literacy, for these purposes, may be considered to be the ability to write one's signature, manage accounts, write brief notes and letters, and read short newspaper articles in a particular language (similar to levels 1 and 2 in US language testing; advanced literacy is the ability to read and analyze sophisticated written works, including literature and theory (similar to levels 3, 4, and 5 in US language testing); scientific literacy is the ability to read, analyze, and write sophisticated scientific works (again, similar to levels 3, 4, and 5). However, given the science of the late 1790s, it might be argued that there was little difference between this literacy and the more middling advanced literacy postulated above. A more relativist view of literacy may be found in Newman, "Early Americanist Grammatology," 76–92.

9. Grubb, "Growth of Literacy in Colonial America," 452. For a more recent example of the use of signature analysis for literacy, see Murray, "Family, Literacy, and Skill Training in the Antebellum South," 773–99. Other methods of measuring literacy are of limited use for Spanish America, where primary and secondary education was mostly via Catholic schools, private schools, and contracted tutors; student lists have generally not been published. Spanish imperial colleges and universities were notably active; Lanning estimated that 150,000 students graduated from over

thirty universities spread across the imperial empire from the 1550s to 1810 (*Academic Culture in the Spanish Colonies*, 216). However, lists of students and student theses (in Latin) have not been compiled or published. Lastly, while newspapers and journals were an everyday part of British and perhaps French life, the Spanish Crown tightly monitored the publication and dissemination of newspapers and journals until the late Bourbon era.

10. Lanning, *Academic Culture in the Spanish Colonies*, 53–54. By comparison, the United States had twenty-five colleges in 1789; the oldest, Harvard, was founded as early as 1636, but two more (William & Mary and St. John's) were established only in the 1690s. The remaining twenty-two oldest colleges were all established in the 1700s; the first public college (North Carolina) and the first Jesuit college (Georgetown) were founded in 1789. See "The 25 Oldest Colleges in America," www.niche.com/blog/the-25-oldest-colleges-in-america/ (accessed 28 July 2018).

11. However, statistics on public education (schools, teachers, student enrollments) and newspapers/subscriptions may foreground northern European cultural perceptions of the importance of literacy for free commerce and trade, individual religious salvation, secular education at all levels, and a free and often partisan press in northern Europe and North America. Such cultural perceptions conflict with those which might be considered southern European perceptions, including the importance of literacy for restricted commerce and trade, collectivist Catholic education, and a late-blooming, restricted press.

12. Calvo, "The Politics of Print," 281–91. The most famous work analyzing Spanish American book lists is Irving A. Leonard's *Books of the Brave*.

13. APS *Proceedings*, online entries for "Elected Members/Member Directory" until 1803.

14. NONA, Mazange, vol. 1 (1780): 1–150; Perdomo, vol. 6 (1785): 348–54.

15. AGI, Papeles de Cuba, 212B, microfilm E-106, roll 68, pp. 28–33.

16. Houdaille, "Trois paroisses de Saint-Domingue au XVIIIe siècle," 104. Twenty-five years later, Houdaille issued updated statistics indicating that more than 89 percent of the white males, 77 percent of white females, 49 percent of free mulatto males, 14 percent of free black males, 20 percent of free mulatto females, and 3 percent of free black females were literate in St. Domingue. See Houdaille, "Reconstitution des familles de Saint-Domingue (Haïti) au XVIIIe siècle," 32; Garrigus, *Before Haiti*, 124–27; McClellan, *Colonialism and Science*. McClellan points out that one St. Domingue newspaper, the *Affiches Américain*, published up to a thousand pages annually from 1764 to 1791—an astonishing amount of journalism then available to some New Orleans residents.

17. McDermott, *Private Libraries in Creole Saint Louis*, 12–13; Grubb, "Growth of Literacy in Colonial America," 452–58. Scholars of Spanish American literacy have often focused on recovering indigenous, precolonial literacies; see, for example, Rappaport and Cummin's *Beyond the Lettered City* and Johnson's *Translating Maya Hieroglyphs*. However, a few works have moved beyond the contradictions evident in the works of Benedict Anderson and Angel Rama to more carefully consider the flow of information within colonial Latin America. These include Julie Greer Johnson's *The Book in the Americas*, Jonathan Carlyon's *Andres Gonzalez de Barcia and the Creation of the Colonial Spanish American Library*, and Cristina Soriano's *Tides of Revolution*.

18. Garrigus, *Before Haiti*, 291–96; The full list of names with these markings is Jean Baptiste Benoit St. Clairy and Alexandre Baure (1780), Pedro Bissadan, J. B. Condorcet, Pedro H. Pedesclaux, Pedro LeBourgeois, Louis Darby, Louis Blanc, Jean Baptiste Poeyfarre, Julien Vienne, Albert Bonne, Angel Babiny, and Louis Cornu (1785). Pedesclaux was a lodge officer in the American

era. An additional indication of early Masonic influence in Spanish New Orleans may be found in José Salazar's well-known painting of Dr. Joseph Montegut and his family, in which Dr. Montegut holds a small triangle, a clear symbol of Masonic participation.

19. Uribe-Uran, "The Birth of a Public Sphere in Latin America during the Age of Revolution," 440–45.

20. Holmes, "Louisiana in 1795," 133–51; "The Moniteur de la Louisiane in 1798," 230–53.

21. Emily Clark, *Masterless Mistresses*, 140n19; Din and Harkins, *New Orleans Cabildo*, 19–20. Din was also insistent that many elite French families learned Spanish, partly for social and military promotion: "shopkeepers, merchants, and others, including prostitutes . . . acquired at least a functional use of Spanish. Slaves owned by Spaniards learned it, too. Berquin-Duvallon admitted in the early nineteenth century that the use of Spanish and English in the city was fairly universal" ("Carondelet, the Cabildo, and Slaves," 9). For educational contracts, see NONA, Mazange, vol. 5, prominent merchant Juan Bautista Jourdain, prominent merchant Mauricio Conway; vol. 6 (1782), Juan Bertrand, Aubin Hallys; Rodriguez, vol. 3 (1784), Pedro Le Bourgeois with Pablo LeBlanc; vol. 4, Antonio Sauber, Bely Esterquil, Francisco Robin; vol. 5 (1785), free African Pedro Violette with free African Miguel, Matheo Hottard, Guillermo Gros; vol. 8 (1786), free mulatto Pedro deSalles/Sales with Amelot; vol. 9 (1786), Marie Pradeau Hognon with Nancy Laffond; vol. 10 (1786), William Quays with Francois Mayronne; vol. 11, Bertrand Dingirart with Arnaldo Magnon (canceled later also); vol. 12 (1787), Luisia Roquigny with Estevan Roquigny, prominent merchant Santiago/James Fletcher with Raymundo Gaillard; Pedesclaux, vol. 12 (1791), Francisco Otono. On women's education in the United States, it should be remembered that, when the American Philosophical Society was approached by Reverend Timothy Alden "on the tuition of ladies," the society replied that the contents of the communication did not come "within the objects of the Society." See APS, Correspondence, 16 April 1813. The Ursuline convent in Charlestown, Massachusetts, was burned and sacked by a crowd in 1834 (Clark, *Masterless Mistresses*, 258–59).

22. Goudeau, "Booksellers and Printers in New Orleans, 1764–1885," 6.

23. McDermott, *Private Libraries in Creole Saint Louis*, 43–44. Duralde appears in multiple NONA volumes from 1785 to 1799: Rodriguez 5, 12; Perdomo 9, 15; Pedesclaux 11, 12, 35; Ximenes 1; Broutin 15, 30, 47. One of Duralde's daughters married Henry Clay's brother; his son married Clay's daughter; another daughter married Louisiana governor W. C. C. Claiborne. Oddly enough, Clay himself referred to Duralde as "a French gentleman," although Duralde was born in Spain and had worked for Spain for two decades (Kastor, *Nation's Crucible*, 105).

24. McDermott, *Private Libraries in Creole Saint Louis*, 49–52, 65–71. Didier's choices may reveal something about his sermons—the works tended toward the rhetorical, as represented by Bossuet, Massillon, Cicero, and Marcus Aurelius. For Chouteau, see McDermott, *Private Libraries in Creole Saint Louis*, 22, 128–29.

25. McDermott, *Private Libraries in Creole Saint Louis*, 21.

26. NOPR, Succession Pedro Philippe de Marigny, file 99, dated 24 May 1800. The elder de Marigny had famously hosted the then-exiled but future King Louis Philippe I of France and his brother in New Orleans in 1798, served as an aide-de-camp to Gálvez at Pensacola, and sent his son Bernard to be educated as a Spanish militia cadet, a merchant under the British firm Panton & Leslie in Pensacola, and then to London. For the storekeeper's inventory, see NOPR, Black Books 1790, May–June files (file 1802), settlement for J. B. Durel, 4 June 1790. For examples of an elite member or officer's death, see NOPR, Succession of Estevan Lolo/Lalo, June–December

1786, file 178, dated 20 July 1786; Succession of Cosme Christobal (2nd pilot), June–December 1786, file 175, dated 15 October 1786; and Succession of Lieutenant Lorenzo Rigoleme at Natchez, August–October 1788, file 128, dated 25 October 1788. Rigoleme's succession contains his original commission, in Dutch, signed by William, Prince of Orange—perhaps the only document I have seen in New Orleans archives not in Spanish, French, or English.

27. Leonard, "Frontier Library, 1799," 26–27.

28. It would be difficult to prove that the purchasers of these colonial-era books actually read them without discovering personal copies with emendations. Such a difficulty is hardly unique to Bourbon New Orleans: many academic friends of mine have acquired hundreds of books without reading all of them, and yet it is safe to assume that, if the friend is able to read merely one of those books, he or she is probably able to read most if not all. One suspects the same was true of the eighteenth-century owners of books.

29. Leonard, "Frontier Library, 1799," 27–34.

30. The Texeyros do not appear in the WPA indices of the New Orleans Notarial Archive from 1780 to 1799. However, a Juan Francisco Teyseyre does appear in 1786, submitting a will (NONA, Rodriguez, vol. 9), and may be related.

31. NONA, Pedesclaux, vol. 27. Francisco Ramon Canes/Cane/Canet appears throughout the notarial archives from 1786 through at least 1799. A search for these works within the convent library might reveal that Gayoso's books still survive there.

32. This analysis is based on a copy of the original source in Leonard, "Frontier Library, 1799," 36–51. Leonard, unlike McDermott, did not further study the purchasers of Gayoso's library or potential rationales for their purchases. The practice of reading aloud in nineteenth-century England and America has been most recently detailed in Abigail Williams's *The Social Life of Books*. Closer to Spanish New Orleans, a work on reading in New Spain (Mexico) reports that "Spanish and poor Creoles, mestizos and even Indians were instructed using proverbs, folk tales, ballads, songs and social gatherings, meetings where some novelistic passage or a moral commentary was read aloud" (Teodoro Hampe Martínez, "La historiografía del libro en America hispana," in *Leer en Tiempos de la Colonia*, 55–72, esp. 59; my translation).

33. This analysis is based on the copy of the original source in Din, "The Death and Succession of Francisco Bouligny," 314–15. This source did not identify the purchasers of Bouligny's library; his biography is on p. 307.

34. "Frontier Library," 37–38, 160; NONA, Ximenes, 7, 13; Pedesclaux, 25, 27, 31, 32, 33, 34. Castillón was identified as "Don" in the 1799 Gayoso book sale, but was more specifically identified in *Old Families of Louisiana* as "the dapper young French consul in New Orleans" who married the forty-six-year-old second wife of well-known Andres Almonaster y Roxas and so received rough treatment via charivari from disapproving residents on his wedding night (Arthur and Huchet de Kernion, *Old Families of Louisiana*, 29, 395, and 431). If this identification is correct, Castillón certainly numbered among the elite, but it is odd that Laussat, Robin, and Pitot fail to mention him at all—and Laussat was very good indeed at naming residents, especially of French ancestry, in whom he felt he might repose trust. Of the works Castillón purchased in 1799 from Gayoso's estate—a two-volume French-Italian dictionary by Alberti, a twelve-volume Spanish translation of *Lives of the Emperors*, and a four-volume *Don Quixote* in Spanish, only the Alberti, although not listed as such, appears in his 1810 inventory.

35. Adelman, *Sovereignty and Revolution in the Iberian Atlantic,* 174.

36. Book lists from other Bourbon ports might also indicate unsuspected reading in "republicanism."

37. Poydras, "La prise du morne du Baton Rouge."

38. Poydras, "La prise du morne du Baton Rouge," lines 69–72, 85–91, and 95–98 (my translation).

39. Poydras, "La prise du morne du Baton Rouge," lines 1–22.

40. For background on this Spanish scientific explosion in the late eighteenth century, the most revelatory works include Bleichmar, *Visible Empire;* Wilson and Gomez Duran, *Kingdom of Ants;* Barrerá-Osorio, *Experiencing Nature;* Kendrick, *Alejandro Malaspina;* and Glick, "Science and Independence in Latin America," 307–33.

41. Science in the late 1700s often included what we would now consider a variety of social sciences and even philosophy.

42. Nolan's 1797 will can be found in NONA, Pedesclaux, vol. 30.

43. Notaries in colonial Peru would often scrawl caricatures in the covers and spare pages of their archives (Burns, *Into the Archive,* 68–75). However, I have seen no such drawings in the notarial archives of New Orleans and only three or four in the Bourbon-era records in Seville— all by two governors themselves. At the bottom of a signed letter by Carondelet on military and building matters appears a drawing of a fish with no explanation or comment (AGI, Papeles de Cuba, 1442, microfilm E-145/22–23, roll 23, p. 544).

44. APS *Membership,* "Daniel Clark."

45. APS *Transactions* 1 (1769–70): xiii–xxii.

46. Ellicott, *Journal of Andrew Ellicott,* 188, 194–95. Ellicott arrived on 4 January 1799 and remained until 3 March that year. Ellicott does not appear in the New Orleans Notarial Archives indices in 1799, although it was not unusual for visitors to the city to procure powers of attorney for routine personal business. Given that Daniel Clark and William Dunbar were both assisting him at that point, perhaps one of them handled the Ellicott expedition business. On the telescope, see APS *Transactions,* 19 August 1796.

47. Ellicott, *Journal,* 22; Ellicott, "Astronomical, and Thermometrical Observations," 189; Ferrer, "Astronomical Observations," 158–64. Ferrer's observations in New Orleans are clearly from June 1801, but it is unknown how long he remained in the city. He updated his work and compared it to the calculations of other well-known astronomers in APS *Transactions* 6 (1809): 345–68. See also APS *Transactions* 6 (1809): 264, and Galliano, *Biografía Del Astrónomo Español,* esp. 27, which indicates that first among Ferrer's accomplishments on his tombstone was his membership in the APS. Ferrer lives on in the modern world in an odd fashion—his visual double, Rafael Joaquin de Ferrer, also from the Basque Province of Guipuzcoa, is a New Orleans–based scientist and assassin in the very popular computer game *Assassin's Creed.*

48. Dunbar, "Observations on the Comet of 1807–8." NONA, Mazange, vols. 2, 3; Rafael Perdomo, vols. 5 and 13; Rodriguez, vol. 11; Pedesclaux, vols. 2, 12, 13, 14, 17, 21, 23, 27; Ximenes, vols. 1, 3, 6, 9B, 15, 40. APS *Membership,* "William Dunbar." Dunbar and Hunter, *Forgotten Expedition, 1804–1805,* xvi–xix, xxxii. For election to the APS, see APS *Transactions,* 17 January 1800.

49. APS *Transactions,* 15 August 1800, 7 December 1798. Given this was a period of numerous fossil discoveries, it is possible Wilkinson's donation was of fossilized bones.

50. APS *Transactions,* 16 September 1803, 18 March 1803.

51. Laussat, *Memoirs of My Life,* 98.

52. Of these languages, Spanish was logically eclipsed with the 1803 annexation; French, on the wane in 1803, might have also been shrugged off, but was revived by the 1808–10 influx of thousands of French Caribbean refugees.

6. THE JUDICIAL SYSTEM IN SPANISH NEW ORLEANS

1. Most of the later probate records, unfortunately, do not appear in the New Orleans archives, and are apparently lost.

2. Din and Harkins, *New Orleans Cabildo,* 57.

3. Din and Harkins, *New Orleans Cabildo,* 69. The full listing in alphabetical order, with duplicates removed: Almonaster, Amelot, Argote (two), Boré, Caisergues, Chabert, D'Aunoy, de La Chaise, de la Ronde, Desneville (presumably Derneville), Deverges, Doriocourt, Dufossat, Duplessis, Forstall, Foucher, Huchet de Kernion, Lanusse, Le Breton, Livaudais, de Lovio, Marigny, Merieult, Morales, Navarro, de Ortega, de Orue, Panis, de la Pena, Perez, Piernas, Poeyfarre, de Pontalba, de Reggio, de Riano, Serrano, Trudeau, and de Villere.

4. Author's compilation from NOPR, Black Books. The data for 1790 is partial; the files end in July 1790 but were consistent with the number of cases and files the previous year.

5. Author's compilation from NOPR, Black Books. Figure 6.2 represents the first statistical analysis of the individual caseloads of Spanish judges from Bourbon New Orleans, and may be the first such analysis on any colonial court in the Spanish empire.

6. Din and Harkins, *New Orleans Cabildo,* 69. De Reggio was *de primer voto* in 1784, Forstall in 1785, Orue in 1786, Chabert in 1787, and Ortega in 1789; Argote was *de segundo voto* in 1788 and Almonaster in 1789–90. For Postigo's position and training, see Din and Harkins, *New Orleans Cabildo,* 162.

7. Din and Harkins, *New Orleans Cabildo,* 68–70.

8. NOPR, Black Books 129: 119 (natural death of Silba), 120–21 (murder of sailor Joseph); 143: 1 (inquest on death of slave Josef Nepomuseno on ship); 145: 56 (drowning of sailor Pedro).

9. NOPR, Black Books 123: 144 (coiffures lost in hurricane); 125: 19 (handkerchiefs); 130: 74–75 (a billiard table, admittedly a source of income).

10. Premo, *Enlightenment on Trial,* esp. her compelling conclusion, "Why Not Enlightenment?" 224–36.

11. NOPR, Black Books 125: 27–28 (*Fanchon v. Demaziller*); 128 (Linda); 131: 6 (Christoval Francisco, a free mulatto whose free parents resided in New York); 132: 138–39 (*Baptista Corce v. Francisca*); 133: 70 (Juan Smith from a three-year bondage imposed by Gálvez, evidently to serve the church or Charity Hospital).

12. NOPR, Black Books 132: 89 (Agustin) and 110; 127: 117–18 (*Valentin v. Succession of Jung*); 137: 21 (Mangloan); 145: 23–24 (price for Barbara's daughter). It is possible that the Cristobal Francisco who assisted Mangloan was the same one who had earlier documented his own freedom in NOPR, Black Books 131: 6. Mangloan's emancipation appears in NONA, Perdomo, vol. 11, under the name Juan Santiago Mangloar; he does not appear in any other New Orleans notarial index during the Spanish era. It is also possible that his last name was actually Magloire, a common St.

Dominguan/Haitian surname—at least one and perhaps two free men of color appear in Spanish New Orleans with that name, but without a first name.

13. NOPR, Black Books 143: 59 (Morzu and Bourguinon); 147: 2–4 (Morzu rewins freedom). Some historians believe that American references to "Black Islands," as in George Washington's 1789–91 diary, is a garbling of Illinois with "Isles noires." The Spanish referred to the "Islas Negras" as well, which may indeed indicate a garbling of French references to the "Illinois" tribe.

14. NOPR, Black Books 123: 93 (Leonon [sic] Monsanto), 112 (de Villiers v. de Volsay).

15. NOPR, Black Books 133: 48–49 (Fontenelle v. Fontenelle). Despite his claims of nobility, the quarreling Fontenelles only appeared in the New Orleans Notarial Archives in the same year as they fought in court, in 1787 (NONA, Perdomo, vol. 9; Rodriguez, vol. 11). Also see ADNO, vol. 5 (1791–95): 167, although her family name is spelled as Barrois.

16. Din and Harkins, New Orleans Cabildo, 99.

17. For works on the fuero militar, especially its importance for free men of color, see Vinson, Bearing Arms for His Majesty, and Kuethe, Cuba, 1753–1815.

18. NOPR, Black Books 127: 85–86 (v. Smith); 134: 50–51 (v. Barba and Malos).

19. NOPR, Black Books 132: 63–64 (v. Badia and de Flores). Badia was active in New Orleans Notarial Archives at least from 1786 to 1799; de Flores was from 1792 to at least 1800.

20. NOPR, Black Books 123: 138 (Baronnier v. Blanc—see also Louisiana Historical Quarterly 16 [July 1933]: 521); 134: 95 (Riquer the disguised husband). Riquer appears in NONA as Juan Riguero or Riquero from 1781 to 1788. On the Collat case, see NOPR, Black Books 129: 70–71 (v. Roche). Collat was presumably Pablo Collet, who only appears in the late notarial record in 1782.

21. NOPR, Black Books 143: 38–40 (Cezar's injury).

22. NOPR, Black Books 130: 52–53 (Dapremont v. slave Julia for attempted poisoning); 146: 86–89 (v. Dominque for theft and murder); 139: 98–99 (v. Bidou); 127: 54–55 (Josef Dorquine arrested, sentenced), 59–60 (Dorquiny escape). Bidou never appeared in the notarial indices and was clearly not very active in the city's economy. It is likely that Dorquiny was actually surnamed Dorgenois/Dorgenoy.

23. NOPR, Black Books 129: 120–21 (murder by Juan Oliveros); 125: 54–55 (murder of agent) and 84–86 (de los Santos for homicide).

24. Laussat, Memoirs of My Life, 82–84.

25. Robin, Voyage to Louisiana, 208–22, 224–32.

26. Territory of Orleans, Criminal Cases Tried by Orleans County Court (1805–1807) and City Court (1807–1812), entries 3, 16, 68, 73, 85, 94, 197, 205, 212, 220, 222. More cases probably were against free persons of color, based on the number of cases against persons listed with only one name, but many of these may have also been against slaves.

27. Levasseur and Feliu, Moreau Lislet, 28–35, esp. 35 for this quotation.

28. However, the very well-educated American lawyer Edward Livingston, with Pierre Derbigny and Etienne Masureau, would eventually translate Las siete partidas into both French and English (Kastor, Nation's Crucible, 216–17).

29. Levasseur and Feliu, Moreau Lislet, 54–57.

30. Eberhard Faber makes a convincing argument that this legislation was a mélange of French, Spanish, and American law, including the French Code Noir of 1724, a Spanish provision, and the cabildo's attempt at a Code Noir of 1777. However, he also wrote, "But beyond any French or

Spanish antecedents, the legislation of 1806 also incorporated large swaths of slave law from the United States" (*Building the Land of Dreams*, 232–36, esp. 235).

7. POLITICAL DISCOURSE AND PRACTICES IN SPANISH NEW ORLEANS

1. Calderón de la Barca, *El Alcade de Zalamea*, 30 (my translation).

2. The British, Dutch, and French systems all permitted the appointment of military governors in colonies and forms of law that seem decidedly nonrepresentative—thus the American and St. Dominguan revolutions.

3. Kastor, *Nation's Crucible*, esp. 56–60, on the remonstrance of May 1804, and 220 on the attitudes of Jeffersonian policymakers toward Louisiana.

4. Pitot, *Observations on the Colony of Louisiana from 1796 to 1802*, 36.

5. Pitot, *Observations on the Colony of Louisiana from 1796 to 1802*, 91–92.

6. Pitot, *Observations on the Colony of Louisiana from 1796 to 1802*, 12–13.

7. Laussat, *Memoirs of My Life*, 20, for the insults, and 18 for his quote.

8. Laussat, *Memoirs of My Life*, 101–2; for Clark's view on Laussat, see *Terr Papers 9*, 120–21.

9. Robin, *Voyage to Louisiana*, 59–60.

10. Pitot, *Observations on the Colony of Louisiana from 1796 to 1802*, 109, 37–52. Elsewhere and more even-handedly, Pitot noted that the *cabildo* included "aldermen, judges, an attorney general, and clerks," but reported that many of the daily operations of the city of New Orleans were actually managed by the governor general himself but should have been delegated to subordinates, including, presumably, the *cabildo*. Pitot himself served as mayor of New Orleans, but only from June 1804 to July 1805. He served afterwards as probate court judge for the Orleans Territory and state of Louisiana until 1831, filling judicial responsibilities filled for so long by Spanish governors and leading *cabildo* members.

11. Laussat, *Memoirs of My Life*, 75–76. The appointees were Boré (mayor), Derbigny, Destrehan, Sauve, Labatut, and councilmen Livaudais Sr., Petit-Cavelier, Villeray (Villere), Johns (Evan Jones), Fortier Sr., Donaldson, Faurie, Allard Jr., Tureaud, and Watkins. Given the declining percentage of French-surnamed white residents in 1803, an election might have placed a well-known Anglophone like Daniel Clark as the mayor of a French colony, an amusing turn of events indeed. And an election would have raised two truly difficult questions for Laussat: Could Spanish-surnamed individuals vote? More controversially, could free men of color vote? Surely he would have said no to each question, but the mere questions would have amplified existing tensions.

12. Laussat, *Memoirs of My Life*, 78, 92–96. Laussat attempted to appoint a fourth American to the council, Benjamin Morgan, who declined because he spoke neither French nor Spanish.

13. AGI, Papeles de Cuba, 212B, microfilm B-106, roll 68, pp. 494–95. Gayoso spoke English well, owned numerous English works in his private library, and was married to two Anglophone sisters in succession (Arthur, *Old New Orleans*, 281).

14. AGI, Papeles de Cuba, 2366, microfilm E-145, roll 48, pp. 25–27. Clarksville was founded by Clark Sr., who had previously commanded a Pennsylvania regiment in the British Army and been granted thousands of acres in then British West Florida in 1768. Clark remained active in Mississippi while the younger Clark handled operations in New Orleans. The "town" never had more than a few white residents, and was clearly merely a plantation. See US Army Corps of Engi-

neers, New Orleans District, *Cultural Resources Survey of Fort Adams Reach Revetment,* 41–44, 46 (on ownership by Wade Hampton), and 87 (on lack of any remaining extant artifacts during the 1993 Corps of Engineers survey.

15. AGI, Papeles de Cuba, 597, microfilm E-87, roll 116, pp. 45–48 (draft), pp. 49–51 (final version, with minor changes in spelling, abbreviations, etc.), letter of Enrique Darcantel, countersigned by Juan Ventura Morales, dated 19 March 1789.

16. Herzog, *Defining Nations,* 164–200.

17. Herzog, *Defining Nations,* 164–200.

18. Faber, *Building the Land of Dreams,* 91–92; AGI, Estado, 2.N.17 dated 27 September 1799, and AGI, Estado, 2.N.33, dated 24 October 1799 but attached to the letter dated 29 November 1799; *Louisiana Gazette,* 19 July 1805, 16 February 1808.

19. Socolow, *The Merchants of Buenos Aires, 1778–1810,* 19. The New Orleans *censos* may also indicate how ambivalent Spanish authorities in the city were about the difference between *vecinos* and residents they could have easily labeled "foreign." In Buenos Aires and Montevideo, during this period, census takers enumerated *vecinos* and foreigners, but in New Orleans, neither the 1791 nor the 1795 census takers noted whether residents were *vecinos* or foreigners. See Prado, *Edge of Empire,* 50; Johnson and Seibert, "Estimaciones de la población de Buenos Aires en 1744, 1778 y 1810," 115, table 4, right-hand column; Goldberg, "La Población Negra y Mulata de la Ciudad de Buenos Aires, 1810–1840," 79–80. By comparison, the much larger city of Buenos Aires had 481 foreigners, comprising about 1 percent of the city's population; over half of that small number was Luso-Brazilian, with another quarter of that small number consisting of Italians. Similarly, an 1807 British census of Montevideo listed 165 foreigners, again only about 1 percent of the entire city's population, with similar numbers of Portuguese and Italians as in Buenos Aires.

20. NOPR, Black Books 124: 26 (Carlota Fazende), for the language quoted above; 127: 90 (Antonio Mendes, native Havana) and 104 (Mendes becoming city attorney); 132: 29 (Amorant) and 36 (Layssard); 134: 23 (Juana Maria Josefa de Grand Pre, wife of the former military counsellor and general assessor of the colony); 135: 29 (for Antonio Ramis—Bosque etc. reported they knew him well); 136: 22 (even Gilberto Antonio St. Maxent, Gálvez's father-in-law). Other Spanish imperial records beyond New Orleans refer to *limpieza de sangre.*

21. Ducasse, *Cartas de cabildos hispanoamericanos (Audiencia de Guatemala); Cartas de cabildos hispanoamericanos (Audiencia de Quito); Cartas de cabildos hispanoamericanos (Audiencia de Santa Fe de Bogotá—Siglos XVI–XIX); Cartas de cabildos hispanoamericanos (Audiencia de Lima).*

22. See Din and Harkins, *New Orleans Cabildo.* Other less notable works have been published specifically on *cabildos* in English, including Wilson and Huber's *The Cabildo on Jackson Square;* John Preston Moore's 1954 *The Cabildo in Peru under the Hapsburgs* and 1966 *The Cabildo in Peru under the Bourbons;* and Stephen Webre's 1980 dissertation, "The Social and Economic Bases of Cabildo Membership in Seventeenth-Century Santiago de Guatemala." The comprehensive list of functions used here is taken from the table of contents of Din and Harkins, *New Orleans Cabildo.*

23. While some would argue that the *cabildo* often represented the interests of the city's elite, this can be said as well of perhaps every city and town in every civilization. For comparison with other Spanish *cabildos,* see Bayle, *Los cabildos seculares en la America espanola.*

24. Din and Harkins, *New Orleans Cabildo,* 57.

25. Din and Harkins, *New Orleans Cabildo,* 60–61.

26. Din and Harkins, *New Orleans Cabildo,* 69. The full listing includes the following names in alphabetical order, with duplicates removed: Almonaster, Amelot, Argote (two), Boré, Caisergues, Chabert, D'Aunoy, de La Chaise, de la Ronde, Desneville (presumably Derneville), Deverges, Doriocourt, Dufossat, Duplessis, Forstall, Foucher, Huchet de Kernion, Lanusse, Le Breton, Livaudais, de Lovio, Marigny, Merieult, Morales, Navarro, de Ortega, de Orue, Panis, de la Pena, Perez, Piernas, Poeyfarre, de Pontalba, de Reggio, de Riano, Serrano, Trudeau, and de Villere.

27. Din and Harkins, *New Orleans Cabildo,* 72–75.

28. Din and Harkins, *New Orleans Cabildo,* 56, 71.

29. Din and Harkins, *New Orleans Cabildo,* 41–43, 90; King, 118; Arthur, *Old New Orleans,* 333; Burson, *Stewardship of Don Esteban Miró,* 8, from ADNO, Baptismal Records, vol. 1: 210, no. 549, dated 15 July 1781; Arthur, *Old New Orleans,* 281.

30. Din and Harkins, *New Orleans Cabildo,* 87–93.

31. Din and Harkins, *New Orleans Cabildo,* 179–80. For the actual petition, see "Letters, Petitions, and Decrees of the Cabildo," documents 361–63 (pp. 161–86). The *cabildo* members in favor of reopening the maritime slave trade were de La Ronde, de la Barre, Forstall, Ducros, and Riaño. Those opposed were Poeyfarre, de la Roche, Jorda (a slave-ship investor), Andry, Castanedo, and Fonvergne.

32. Casey, "Masonic Lodges in New Orleans," 1–20. Why Carondelet felt comfortable approving a Masonic establishment in the colony, presumably without royal permission, is not evident.

33. Mackey, *History of Freemasonry* 6: 1445–47.

34. AGI, Papeles de Cuba, 597, microfilm E-87, roll 116, pp. 212–15, petition dated 22 February 1797. The 1796 petition included the signatures of J. B. Labatut, J. B. Tricou, Viennes y Hamelin (a partnership), J. L. Lagroue, and A. P. (Wahn/Vahn?); the 1797 petition included those of (Dhabeen?) and Vivant Duclos y Soule (actually a partnership of three merchants).

35. AGI, Papeles de Cuba, 212 B, microfilm E-106, roll 68, pp. 212–43, including letter dated 18 August 1796 (St. Amant, in a Spanish letter); pp. 244–49 (Andry); pp. 561–66 (Beauregard, in a French letter); p. 600 (Filhiol); Papeles de Cuba, 212A, microfilm E-106, roll 67, pp. 306–7 (Blanc). In contradiction of my assessment that the dots and bar signified Masonic membership, one might mention the 1799 signature of Thomas Power in a letter written in Spanish from Pensacola. Power's signature had no bar and dots—but it had six dots inside the flourish (Papeles de Cuba, 2366, microfilm E-145, roll 48, p. 343). Similarly, the signatures of Jacob Myers used two dots inside and following his signature in an earlier 1793 letter to Gayoso (Papeles de Cuba, 212A, microfilm E-106, roll 67, pp. 152–55, letter dated 2 December 1793). De Lafour signed a letter to Carondelet with two bars on the sides of his signature but no dots within those bars, another oddity (Papeles de Cuba, 212A, microfilm E-106, roll 67, p. 136, letter dated 12 June 1797).

36. Historical New Orleans Collection, *Bibliography of New Orleans Imprints, 1764–1864,* Florence M. Jumonville, 1989, 38–63; Casey, "Masonic Lodges in New Orleans," 1–20.

37. King, *New Orleans,* 151–53. Louis Philippe d'Orléans, Antoine Philippe (the titular Duke of Montpensier), and Louis Charles (the titular Count of Beaujolais) had fled France in 1793, although Louis Philippe had been a liberal supporter of the early French Revolution. Louis Philippe had traveled widely in exile, including working four years in the United States, but, upon learning of the coup of 18 Fructidor in 1797, he and his brothers traveled to New Orleans, with the intent to sail thence to Havana and then Spain. The trip was in vain; the brothers were stopped at sea by

the British Navy, deposited in Cuba, expelled from that colony a year later, and made their way to England via the Bahamas, Nova Scotia, and New York only in 1800.

38. AGI, PC, legajo 71A, letters from Casa-Calvo to Vidal, 4 February 1800, and Vidal to Casa-Calvo, 3 February 1800.

39. AGI, Papeles de Cuba, 597, microfilm E-87, roll 116, pp. 45–48 (draft), pp. 49–51 (final version, with minor changes in spelling, abbreviations, etc.), letter of Enrique Darcantel, countersigned by Juan Ventura Morales, dated 19 March 1789.

40. AGI, Papeles de Cuba, 212B, microfilm E-106, roll 68, pp. 28–33. My translation, with more modern punctuation and occasional clarifying words inserted for readability—these are in parentheses. The full text in English translation and Spanish is provided as appendix 1 of this work. I have left most of the misspellings, mindful that the petition was written in a time when the Spanish language was evolving and that the petition was written by bilingual petitioners.

41. Laussat, *Memoirs of My Life,* 75–76.

42. AGI, Papeles de Cuba, 597, microfilm E-87, roll 116, pp. 212–15, petition dated 22 February 1797.

43. By way of counterpoint, see Adelman, *Sovereignty and Revolution in the Iberian Atlantic,* 174: "Rights to property did not lead automatically to, or harken back to, rights to representation. Colonial injunctions did not include political demands, and if they did, they were couched not as 'rights' for themselves but as claims that were good for the sovereign. . . . at no point did any of the letrado vindications accuse the sovereign of public corruption." For a more thorough discussion of how American colonists first attempted to negotiate with their king while respecting his sovereignty, see McConville, *The King's Three Faces.*

44. AGI, Papeles de Cuba, 1550, Casa-Calvo letter 15, dated 27 December 1799, with copy of Vidal ordinance dated 26 October 1799, and letter from *alcades ordinaries* dated 21 November. Vidal comes off as a bit of a prude in this correspondence. In October 1803, as judge advocate, he directed the post commander at Pointe Coupee to prevent the conduct of any *charivari.* Din and Harkins, *New Orleans Cabildo,* 25, based on AGI, PC, legajo 73, Vidal to Casa-Calvo, October 8, 1803.

45. Morazan, "Quadroon Balls in the Spanish Period," 310–11; *Actas del Cabildo* 4, no. 1: 88–89, 22 January 1796; revised to meet Carondelet's wishes, 90–91, 29 January 1796.

46. Din and Harkins, *New Orleans Cabildo,* 174–75.

47. "Letters, Petitions, and Decrees of the Cabildo of New Orleans, 1800–1803," trans. Morazan, 204–10, Document 367, dated 24 Oct 1800. The full translation may be found in appendix 3 of the present work. Morazan's footnotes indicate that Saraza/Scarasse departed with the Spanish troops in 1803 to Florida but eventually returned to New Orleans and operated an upholstery shop at 89 Dauphin Street; Galafate/Calpha worked as a lamplighter, lived at 67 Toulouse Street, and served in the War of 1812 in the Third Regiment; Pedro José Tomas resided at 41 Rue St. Ann; and Bacusa (Bacuse) was born in Gonaives, St. Domingue, and resided at 7 Levee North ("Letters, Petitions, and Decrees of the Cabildo of New Orleans, 1800–1803," 204nn). Notarial records indicate the Saraza/Scarasse was Juan Bautista Saras, a free mulatto; Pedro/Pierre Tomas does not appear in the notarial record; Pierre Galafate/Calpha was presumably linked to Juan Calafate and Carlos Simon Calpha (the latter referred to as a free mulatto or *grifo*); and Jean Baptise Bacuse was probably Bautista Bacus (a free African) and related to Luis and Nicolas Bacus/Bachus (both

also free Africans)—he may have also been the Juan Bautista Bacus/Bachus reported in notarial records but not noted as a free man of color.

48. Charles IV's birthday was actually not on 4 November; it was on 11 November.

49. *Terr Papers* 9, 174–75. The names were printed in the source material in a slightly different manner, in two columns, with numerous capital letters omitted and misspellings, some presumably by the signatories and some perhaps from my unfamiliarity with French cursive writing. I have corrected capitalization and, based upon notarial records, the misspellings of names. The names appear in the source as follows, with the names in column format, the correct spelling, and notation if the name appears in the NONA database for the years 1780 to 1799. Any corrections and notations are in brackets. Of the fifty-five signatories, few appear in the New Orleans notarial archives from 1780 to 1799, indicating a limit to their economic mobility. However, almost all of the names are common to colonial New Orleans, and the surnames suggest some were the sons of white males in the city, the vast majority French. Several appear in the notarial records without their race being noted; it is possible these were their fathers or, more likely, the notary simply didn't note them as mulattoes in the notarial indexes.

Louis Simon [Luis Simon, free mulatto]

Leonard Pomet [not in NONA]

Noel Banrepan [not in NONA, perhaps Bonrepos]

Valfroy Trudeaux [not in NONA, but certainly Valfroi Trudeau]

Jn Bte Depres [not in NONA]

V le Dut [not in NONA, perhaps Leduf]

Baptiste Rousaire [perhaps Juan Bautista Rougier/Rougie, no race noted]

Barthelemi Ducret [not in NONA]

Louis Brion fils [not in NONA]

Philippe Auguste [not in NONA]

Jacque Auguste [not in NONA]

Henry Hugont [not in NONA, but probably Hugon]

E__ Sarriey [not in NONA]

Baptiste Pierre [not in NONA]

Jathainte Charle [not in NONA]

Charles Poree [Carlos Poree, no race noted]

Jn Saseier [not in NONA, perhaps Saucier]

___ alin [unknown, but perhaps Malineau, Mallia, or Mallines]

Baltazard Demazelliere [not in NONA, certainly Demazilliere]

Henry Bricou [Henry Bricou, no race noted]

Entoine Populuse [not in NONA, but mulatto Antoine Populus]

Charle Caveux [Carlos/Charles Cayeux, no race noted]

Voltairre Fonvergne [not in NONA]

Fransoi Caves pere [Francisco Cavet, no race noted]

Celestin Populus [not in NONA, but mulatto Celestin Populus]

Louis Daunoy fils [Luis Daunoy, free mulatto]

Nobert fortier [Norberto Fortier, no race noted]

Eugene Demasiliere [not in NONA, certainly Demazilliere]

Jn Louis Dolliote [probably Luis Dolioule, no race noted]

Pierre Bailly [Pedro Bailly, free mulatto]

Pierre Bailly fils [Pedro Bailly, free mulatto]

Louis Aurit [not in NONA, but certainly Louis Aury]

Honoree Frechinet [not in NONA, probably Frassinet]

Pierre Bouye [not in NONA]

Antoine Foucher [Antonio Foucher, no race noted]

Maurice Populos [Mauricio Populus, free mulatto]

Charles Simon [Carlos Simon, no race noted]

Baptiste Maidesingue [not in NONA, but perhaps Mentzinger]

Celestin Matata [not in NONA]

Baptiste d aigles [Juan B. Daigle,] race noted

Voltaire Auguste [not in NONA]

Miniere Rosemone [not in NONA, probably related to mulatto Rosemon]

Noel Hes [not in NONA]

Charles D'ecoup [perhaps Carlos Decu, but no race noted]

Etienne Saulet [not in NONA]

Louis Ferdinand [not in NONA]

Louis Liotant [Luis Liotau, no race noted]

Louis Hardy [not in NONA]

Baptiste Hardy [not in NONA]

Joachim Hardy [not in NONA]

Jean Pierre Cennois [not in NONA, probably no Cenas]

Josephe J. Bte Voisin [Juan Bautista Voisin, free mulatto]

Charles Boidore [not in NONA, but certainly Boisdore]

50. AGI, Papeles de Cuba, 212B, microfilm B-106, roll 68, pp. 494–95, which uses the term "Your Excellency" in English. Some historians have claimed that Clark's later duel with Claiborne was over Clark's fervent *disapproval* of using free men of color in a militia. This seems odd, given that it was Claiborne who spurned the free militia and attempted to disband it

CONCLUSION: THE TRANSITION BETWEEN TWO EMPIRES

1. *Terr Papers* 9, 23–24, emphasis added. To further contextualize Bourbon New Orleans and Louisiana within the Spanish empire, one should examine Mahoney, *Colonialism and Postcolonial Development*. Mahoney argues that Spanish colonialism sorted the colonies into different levels of development, including mercantilist colonies and liberal colonies, some of which he labeled "rising peripheries" (124–41, 203). Although Mahoney did not address Louisiana at all (sadly, like so many historians of Spanish America), it may be safely assumed that Louisiana would have fallen squarely in Mahoney's list of rising peripheries, just as did the Rio Plata and Venezuela.

BIBLIOGRAPHY

ARCHIVAL AND PRINTED ORIGINAL RESOURCES

Archdiocese of New Orleans Sacramental Records.

Archivo General de Indias, Sevilla.

 Audiencia de Santo Domingo.

 Correos.

 Indiferente General.

 Papeles de Estado.

 Papeles Procedentes de la Isla de Cuba.

 Secretaria del Despacho de Guerra.

Archivo Histórico Nacional, Madrid.

"Letters, Petitions, and Decrees of the Cabildo of New Orleans, 1800–1803: Edited and Translated (Volumes I and II)." Ed. and trans. Ronald Rafael Morazan. PhD diss., Louisiana State University, 1972. digitalcommons.lsu.edu/gradschool_disstheses/2300.

Louisiana Census, 1810.

Louisiana First Judicial District Court (Orleans Parish). Index to Suit Records, 1813–35.

Louisiana Soldiers in the War of 1812. Compiled by Marion John Bennett Pierson. Louisiana Genealogical and Historical Society, 1963.

Natchez Court Record Abstracts.

National Archives of Colombia. *Ano de 1800, Libro Real Comun y Gral. de Cargo y Data.*

New Orleans Cemetery Records

 St. Louis Cemetery I, II, Girod Street.

New Orleans Census, 1791. WPA translation held by Louisiana State Museum Library, New Orleans. Rpt. in *New Orleans Genesis* 1: 33–37, 156–60, 253–57.

New Orleans City Directory and Census, 1805. New Orleans: Pelican Gallery, Inc., 1936.

New Orleans City Directory, 1811.

New Orleans City Directory, 1822.

New Orleans City Directory, 1832.

New Orleans Crew Lists.

New Orleans Indenture Records.

New Orleans Notarial Archives. These archives are divided by names of notaries. Abbreviations are those used by the author in the WPA index-based database, in the order of their historical appearance:

Fernandez, Joseph, 1760–69.

Garic, Juan B., 1739, 1760–69, 1771–78.

Almonaster y Roxas, Andres (*A*), 1771–82.

De Quinones, Estevan, no notarial records—only court cases.

Pedesclaux, Pedro (*P*), 1778 into American era.

Mazange, Leonardo (*M*), 1779–83.

Perdomo, Rafael (*RP*), 1783–90.

Rodriguez, Fernando (*R*), 1783–87.

Broutin, Francisco (*B*), 1790–99.

Ximenes, Carlos (*X*), 1791–1803.

Broutin, Narcisse (*NB*), 1799 into American era.

Hernandez, Fermin, no notarial records—only court cases.

Bermudez, A. F., 1801–2.

New Orleans Probate Records. The actual probate court documents for the entire Louisiana colony, as administered in New Orleans, indexed in several systems over the years.

New Orleans Probate Records Indexes. Indexed and selectively translated in outline form in bound (and now online) works generally referenced as the Black Books.

New Orleans Public Library.

Actas del Cabildo, 1769–1803. 10 vols. Microfilm of WPA transcripts in Spanish.

Miscellaneous Spanish and French Documents, 1789–1816. 4 vols., 1937. Trans. Joseph Albert Gutierrez for the WPA.

Petitions, Letters and Decrees of the Cabildo. 3 vols.

"New Orleans Trip Journal, 1811." Manuscript. Library of Congress, 81-91660.

Passenger Arrivals at the Port of New Orleans.

Poydras, Julien. "La prise du morne du Baton Rouge par Monseigneur de Galvez." Bibliothèque Tintamarre. french.centenary.edu/poydras.htm (accessed 11 March 2017).

Tepper, Michael H., gen. ed. *Passenger Arrivals at the Port of Philadelphia, 1800–1819.* Baltimore: Genealogical Publishing Co.

Territorial Papers of the United States. Vol. 9: *The Territory of Orleans, 1803–1812.* Ed. Clarence Edwin Carter and John Porter Bloom. US Government Printing Office, 1940.

Territory of Orleans. Criminal Cases Tried by Orleans County Court (1805–7) and City Court (1807–12).

Territory of Orleans, Superior Court. Index to Suit Records, 1804–13.

University of Notre Dame Archives. Catholic Archives of America, archives.nd.edu/search/index.html.

US Army Corps of Engineers, New Orleans District. *Cultural Resources Survey of Fort Adams Reach Revetment, Mile 312.2 to 306.0-L, Mississippi River, Wilkinson County, Mississippi.* Baton Rouge: Museum of Geoscience, Louisiana State University, August 1993, Final Report. Reports #AD-A271 114 or COELMN/PD-91/04.

US Census, 1790.
Kentucky.
Maryland.
South Carolina.
Works Progress Administration. Transcripts in English.
  "Alphabetical and Chronological Digest of the Acts and Deliberations of the Cabildo,
  1769–1803: A Record of the Spanish Government in New Orleans." In introduction
  to WPA English translation of the *Actas del Cabildo*.
  "Confidencial Dispatches of Don Bernardo de Galvez."
  "Dispatches of the Spanish Governors of Louisiana: Messages of Francisco Luis
  Hector, El Baron de Carondelet."
  Dispatches of the Spanish Governors, 1766–1792. 7 vols.
Ship Registers and Enrollments of New Orleans, Louisiana. University: Louisiana State
  University Library, 1941–42.

BOOKS

Acosta Rodríguez, Antonio. *La Población de Luisiana Española (1763–1803)*. Madrid:
  Ministerio de Asuntos Exteriores, 1979.
Acree, William Garrett, Jr., *Everyday Reading: Print Culture and Collective Identity in the
  Rio de la Plata, 1780–1910*. Nashville: Vanderbilt University Press, 2011.
Adelman, Jeremy. *Sovereignty and Revolution in the Iberian Atlantic*. Princeton, NJ: Princ-
  eton University Press, 2006.
Allan, William. *The Life and Work of John McDonogh*. 1886. Jefferson Parish, LA: Jeffer-
  son Parish Historical Commission, 1983.
Anderson, Benedict. *Imagined Communities: Reflections on the Origin and Spread of Nation-
  alism*. Rev. ed. New York: Verso, 2006.
Aron, Stephen. *American Confluence: The Missouri Frontier from Borderland to Border
  State*. Bloomington: Indiana University Press, 2009.
Arthur, Stanley Clisby. *Old New Orleans: A History of the Vieux Carre, Its Ancient and
  Historical Buildings*. Westminster, MD: Heritage Books, 1936.
Arthur, Stanley Clisby, and George Campbell Huchet de Kernion. *Old Families of Loui-
  siana*. 1931. Gretna, LA: Pelican Publishing Co., 1998.
Barbier, Jacques, and Allan J. Kuethe, eds. *The North American Role in the Spanish Imperial
  Economy, 1760–1869. Manchester, UK: Manchester University Press, 1984*.
Barrerá-Osorio, Antonio. *Experiencing Nature: The Spanish American Empire and the Early
  Scientific Revolution*. Austin: University of Texas Press, 2006.
Baudry des Lozières, Louis Narcisse. *Second Voyage à la Louisiane, faisant suite au premier
  de l'auteur de 1794 à 1798*. 2 vols. Paris, 1803.
Bayle, Constantino. *Los cabildos seculares en la America española*. Madrid: Sapnientia, 1952.

Beckert, Sven. *Empire of Cotton: A Global History.* New York: Alfred A. Knopf, 2015.

Beers, Henry Putney. *French and Spanish Records of Louisiana: A Bibliographical Guide to Archive and Manuscript Sources.* Baton Rouge: Louisiana State University Press, 1989.

Bello, Andrés. *Selected Writings of Andrés Bello.* Trans. Frances M. López-Morillas. New York: Oxford University Press, 1997.

Bemis, Samuel Flagg. *Pinckney's Treaty: America's Advantage from Europe's Distress, 1783– 1800.* New Haven, CT: Yale University Press, 1962.

Bergad, Laird W., Fe Iglesias Garcia, and Maria del Carmen Barcia, *The Cuban Slave Market, 1790–1880.* New York: Cambridge University Press, 1995.

Berlin, Ira. *Many Thousands Gone: The First Two Centuries of Slavery in North America.* Cambridge, MA: Harvard University Press, 1998.

Berquin-Duvallon, Pierre-Louis. *Travels in Louisiana and the Floridas in the Year, 1802, Giving a Correct Picture of Those Countries.* Trans. John Davis. New York: I. Riley & Co., 1806.

———. *Vue de la colonie espagnole du Mississipi, ou des provinces de Louisiane et Floride Occidentale, en l'année 1802, par un observateur résident sur les lieux.* Paris: l'Imprimerie Expéditive, 1803.

Berry, Trey, Pam Beasley, and Jeanne Clements, eds. *The Forgotten Expedition, 1804–1805: The Louisiana Purchase Journals of Dunbar and Hunter.* Baton Rouge: Louisiana State University Press, 2006.

Bibliography of New Orleans Imprints, 1764–1864. Ed. Florence M. Jumonville. New Orleans: Historical New Orleans Collection, 1989.

Bleichmar, Daniela. *Visible Empire: Botanical Expeditions and Visual Culture in the Hispanic Enlightenment.* Chicago; University of Chicago Press, 2012.

Borucki, Alex. *From Shipmates to Soldiers: Emerging Black Identities in the Rio de la Plata.* Albuquerque: University of New Mexico Press, 2015.

Brading. D. A. *Miners and Merchants in Bourbon Mexico, 1763–1810.* Cambridge, UK: Cambridge University Press, 1971.

Braudel, Fernand. *The Identity of France.* Vol. 1: *History and Environment.* Trans. Sian Reynolds. New York: Harper & Row, 1989.

Burns, Kathryn. *Into the Archive: Writing and Power in Colonial Peru.* Durham, NC: Duke University Press, 2010.

Burson, Caroline Maude. *The Stewardship of Don Esteban Miró, 1782–1792: A Study of Louisiana Based Largely on the Documents in New Orleans.* New Orleans: American Printing Co., 1940. Rpt. from collection of University of Michigan Library.

Calderón de la Barca, Pedro. *El Alcalde de Zalamea.* 26th ed. Madrid: Catedra, Edicion de Ángel Valbuena-Briones, 2016.

———. *The Painter of Dishonour.* Trans. David Johnston and Lawrence Boswell. Bath, UK: Absolute Press, 1995.

———. *Three Plays.* Bristol: Longdunn Press Ltd. Rpt. 1992.

Campillo y Cossío, José del. *Nuevo Sistema de gobierno económico para la América: Con Los Males y Danos que Le Causa El que Hoy Tiene de los que Participa Copiosamente España, y Remedios Universales para que la Primera Tenga Considerables Ventajas y la Segunda Mayores Intereses.* Madrid: La Imprenta de Benito Cano, 1789.

Caneque, Alejandro. *The King's Living Image: The Culture and Politics of Viceregal Power in Colonial Mexico.* New York: Routledge, 2004.

Carlyon, Jonathan. *Andres Gonzalez de Barcia and the Creation of the Colonial Spanish American Library.* Toronto: University of Toronto Press, 2005.

Carroll, Patrick J. *Blacks in Colonial Veracruz: Race, Ethnicity, and Regional Development.* Austin: University of Texas Press, 2001.

Carvajal, Miguel de. *The Josephine Tragedy: The Story of Joseph in Spanish Golden Age Drama.* Trans. Michael McGaha. Lewisburg, PA: Bucknell University Press, 1998.

Claiborne, W. C. C. *Interim Appointment: W. C. C. Claiborne Letter Book, 1804–1805.* Ed. Jared William Bradley. Baton Rouge: Louisiana State University Press, 2002.

Clark, Daniel. *Proofs of the Corruption of General James Wilkinson, and of His Connexion with Aaron Burr.* 1809. Freeport, NY: Books for Libraries Press, 1970.

Clark, Emily. *Masterless Mistresses: The New Orleans Ursulines and the Development of a New World Society, 1727–1834.* Chapel Hill: University of North Carolina Press, 2007.

Clark, John G. *New Orleans, 1718–1812: An Economic History.* Baton Rouge: Louisiana State University Press, 1970.

Coggeshall, George. *Second Series of Voyages to Various Ports of the World, Made between the Years 1802 and 1841.* New York: D. Appleton & Co., 1852.

Cusick, James G. *The Other War of 1812: The Patriot War and the American Invasion of Spanish East Florida.* Athens: University of Georgia Press, 2007.

Cutler, Carl C. *Greyhounds of the Sea: The Story of the American Clipper Ship.* New York, Halcyon House, 1930.

Davis, John. *Travels in Louisiana and the Floridas in the Year, 1802, Giving a Correct Picture of Those Countries.* New York: I. Riley & Co, 1806.

Davis, William C. *The Pirates Laffite: The Treacherous World of the Corsairs of the Gulf.* Orlando: Harcourt, Inc., 2005.

———. *The Rogue Republic: How Would-Be Patriots Waged the Shortest Revolution in American History.* Boston: Houghton Mifflin Harcourt, 2011.

Dessens, Nathalie. *From Saint-Domingue to New Orleans: Migration and Influences.* Gainesville: University Press of Florida, 2007.

De Ville, Winston. *The 1795 Chimney Tax of New Orleans: A Guide to the Census of Proprietors and Residents of the Vieux Carre.* Ville Platte, LA: Provincial Press, 1995.

Dictionary of Louisiana Biography online. https://www.lahistory.org/resources/dictionary-louisiana-biography/.

Din, Gilbert C. *An Extraordinary Atlantic Life: Sebastián Nicolás Calvo de la Puerta y O'Farrill, Marqués de Casa-Calvo.* Lafayette: University of Louisiana at Lafayette Press, 2016.

———. *Spaniards, Planters, and Slaves: The Spanish Regulation of Slavery in Louisiana, 1763–1803.* College Station: Texas A&M University Press, 1999.

Din, Gilbert C., and John E. Harkins. *The New Orleans Cabildo: Colonial Louisiana's First City Government, 1769–1803.* Baton Rouge: Louisiana State University Press, 1996.

Ducasse, Javier Ortiz de la Tabla. *Cartas de cabildos hispanoamericanos (Audiencia de Guatemala).* Sevilla: CSIC, 1986.

———. *Cartas de cabildos hispanoamericanos (Audiencia de Quito).* Sevilla: CSIC, 1991.

———. *Cartas de cabildos hispanoamericanos (Audiencia de Santa Fe de Bogotá—Siglos XVI–XIX).* Sevilla: CSIC, 1996.

———. *Cartas de cabildos hispanoamericanos (Audiencia de Lima).* Sevilla: CSIC, 1999.

Dunbar, William, and George Hunter. *The Forgotten Expedition, 1804–1805: The Louisiana Purchase Journals of Dunbar and Hunter.* Ed. Trey Berry, Pam Beasley, and Jeanne Clements. Baton Rouge: Louisiana State University Press, 2006.

Duval, Kathleen. *Independence Lost: Lives on the Edge of the American Revolution.* New York: Random House, 2015.

Ellicott, Andrew. *The Journal of Andrew Ellicott.* Philadelphia: William Fry, 1814.

Escalle, Elisabeth, and Mariel Gouyon-Guillaume. *Francs-Maçons des Loges Françaises "aux Amériques," 1770–1850.* 1993. Tulane University Library, Latin America Room, Rare Books Section.

Faber, Eberhard L. *Building the Land of Dreams: New Orleans and the Transformation of Early America.* Princeton, NJ: Princeton University Press, 2016.

Farriss, Nancy Marguerite. *Maya Society under Colonial Rule: The Collective Enterprise of Survival.* Princeton, NJ: Princeton University Press, 1984.

Fisher, John R. *Commercial Relations between Spain and Spanish America in the Era of Free Trade, 1778–1796.* Manchester, UK: Manchester Free Press, 1985.

Flannery, Matthew, comp. *New Orleans in 1805: A Directory and a Census Together with Resolutions Authorizing Same Now Printed for the First Time.* New Orleans, 1805.

Flores, Dean L. ed. *Southern Counterpoint to Lewis & Clark: The Freeman & Custis Expedition of 1806.* Norman: University of Oklahoma Press, 1984.

Galliano, Antonio Alcala. *Biografía Del Astrónomo Español Don José Joaquín De Ferrer Y Cafranga.* Madrid: J. Martin Alegría, 1858.

García Carraffa, A. *El Soler Catalán, Valenciana y Balear.* Vol. 1. San Sebastian, Spain: 1918.

Garrigus, John D. *Before Haiti: Race and Citizenship in French Saint-Domingue.* New York: Palgrave Macmillan, 2006.

Gayarré, Charles. *Fernando de Lemos: Truth and Fiction, a Novel.* 1872.

———. *History of Louisiana: The French Domination.* 2nd ed. New York: William J. Widdelton, 1867.

———. *History of Louisiana: The Spanish Domination,* 2nd ed. New York: William J. Widdelton, 1867.

Glasco, Sharon Bailey. *Constructing Mexico City: Colonial Conflicts over Culture, Space, and Authority.* New York: Palgrave Macmillan, 2010.

Gould, Emerson W. *Fifty Years on the Mississippi, or Gould's History of River Navigation.* St. Louis: Nixon Jones Printing Co., 1889.

Grafe, Regina. *Distant Tyranny: Markets, Power, and Backwardness in Spain, 1650–1800.* Princeton, NJ: Princeton University Press, 2012.

Hamilton, Alexander, and Alastair Hamilton. *The Law Practice of Alexander Hamilton: Documents and Commentary.* Ed. Julius Goebel Jr. 2nd ed. New York: Colombia University Press, 1969.

Hanger, Kimberly S. *Bounded Lives, Bounded Places: Free Black Society in Colonial New Orleans, 1769–1803.* Durham, NC: Duke University Press, 1997.

Hart, Stephen Harding, and Archer Butler Hulbert, eds. *The Southwestern Journals of Zebulon Pike, 1806–1807.* Albuquerque: University of New Mexico Press, 2006.

Hatcher, William F. *Edward Livingston: Jeffersonian Republican and Jacksonian Democrat.* Baton Rouge: Louisiana State University Press, 1940.

Herzog, Tamar. *Defining Nations: Immigrants and Citizens in Early Modern Spain and Spanish America.* New Haven, CT: Yale University Press, 2003.

Hodson, Christopher. *The Acadian Diaspora: An Eighteenth-Century History.* New York: Oxford University Press, 2012.

Holmes, Jack D. L. *A Guide to Spanish Louisiana, 1762–1806.* New Orleans: A. F. Laborde, 1970.

Humboldt, Alexander von. *Ensayo político sobre el reino de la Nueva-España.* Trans. Vicente Gonzalez Arnao. Paris: Casa de Rosa, 1822.

Humboldt, Alexander von, and Aime Bonpland. *Personal Narrative of Travels to the Equinotical Regions of America during the Years 1799–1804.* Vol. 1. London, 1870.

Hunt, Charles Haven. *The Life of Edward Livingston.* New York: D. Appleton & Co., 1864.

Ingersoll, Thomas N. *Mammon and Manon in Early New Orleans: The First Slave Society in the Deep South, 1718–1819.* Knoxville: University of Tennessee Press, 1999.

Jamieson, Ross W. *Domestic Architecture and Power: The Historical Archaeology of Colonial Ecuador.* Berlin: Springer Science+Business Media, 2002.

Jenkins, Earnestine, and Darlene Clark Hine, eds. *A Question of Manhood: A Reader in U.S. Black Men's History and Masculinity.* 2 vols. Bloomington: Indiana University Press, 1999.

Jensen, Larry R. *Children of Colonial Despotism: Press, Politics, and Culture in Cuba, 1790–1840.* Tampa: University of South Florida Press, 1988.

Jobb, Dean. *The Cajuns.* Hoboken, NJ: Wiley Publishing, 2005.

Johnson, Julie Greer. *The Book in the Americas: The Role of Books and Printing in the Development of Culture & Society in Colonial Latin America.* Providence, RI: Brown University/John Carter Brown Library, 1988.

Johnson, Lyman L. *Workshop of Revolution: Plebeian Buenos Aires and the Atlantic World, 1776–1810.* Durham, NC: Duke University Press, 2011.

Johnson, Scott A. *Translating Maya Hieroglyphs*. Norman: University of Oklahoma Press, 2014.

Johnson, Walter. *River of Dark Dreams: Slavery and Empire in the Cotton Kingdom*. Cambridge, MA: Harvard University Press, 2013.

———. *Soul by Soul: Life Inside the Antebellum Slave Market*. Cambridge, MA: Harvard University Press, 1999.

Kastor, Peter J. *The Nation's Crucible: The Louisiana Purchase and the Creation of America*. New Haven, CT: Yale University Press, 2004.

Kendrick, John. *Alejandro Malaspina: Portrait of a Visionary*. Montreal: McGill-Queen's University Press, 1999.

King, Grace. *New Orleans; The Place and the People*. New York: Macmillan Co., 1917.

Kinsbruner, Jay. *The Colonial Spanish-American City: Urban Life in the Age of Atlantic Capitalism*. Austin: University of Texas Press, 2005.

Klein, Herbert S. *The American Finances of the Spanish Empire: Royal Income and Expenditures in Colonial Mexico, Peru, and Bolivia, 1680–1809*. Albuquerque: University of New Mexico Press, 1998.

Korn, Bertram Wallace. *The Early Jews of New Orleans*. Waltham, MA: American Jewish Historical Society, 1969.

Kuethe, Allan J. *Cuba, 1753–1815: Crown, Military, and Society*. Knoxville: University of Tennessee Press, 1986.

Kukla, John. *A Wilderness So Immense: The Louisiana Purchase and the Destiny of America*. New York: Anchor House, 2003.

Lamikiz, Xabier. *Trade and Trust in the Eighteenth-Century Atlantic World: Spanish Merchants and Their Overseas Networks*. London: Royal Historical Society/Boydell Press, 2002.

Lanning, John Tate. *Academic Culture in the Spanish Colonies*. London: Oxford University Press, 1940.

Laussat, Pierre Clément de. *Memoirs of My Life*. Trans. Agnes-Josephine Pastwa. Baton Rouge: Louisiana State University Press, 1978.

Leonard, Irving A. *Books of the Brave: Being an Account of Books and of Men in the Spanish Conquest and Settlement of the Sixteenth-Century World*. 1949. Berkeley: University of California Press, 1992.

Levasseur, Alain, and Vicenc Feliu. *Moreau Lislet: The Man behind the Digest of 1808*. Baton Rouge: Claitor's, 2008.

Lineage Book of the Daughters of the American Revolution. Vol. 28. Washington, DC: National Society, Daughters of the American Revolution. Multiple years published for vols. 1–152.

Llovet, Joaquim. *Cartes a Veracruz, Comerç americà: guerra napoleònica en las correspondència de Cabanyes, Cortecans, Pasqual i C.ª (1804–1813)*. Mataró, Spain: Caixa d'Estalvis Laietana, 1974.

Mackey, Albert Gallatin. *The History of Freemasonry*. Vol. 6. New York: Masonic History Co., 1898.

Mahoney, James. *Colonialism and Postcolonial Development: Spanish America in Comparative Perspective*. Cambridge, UK: Cambridge University Press, 2010.

Mapp, Paul W. *The Elusive West and the Contest for Empire, 1713–1763*. Chapel Hill: University of North Carolina Press, 2011.

Marichal, Carlos. *Bankruptcy of Empire: Mexican Silver and the Wars Between Spain, Britain, and France, 1760–1810*. New York: Cambridge University Press, 2007.

Marotti, Frank, Jr. *Heaven's Soldiers: Free People of Color and the Spanish Legacy in Antebellum Florida*. Tuscaloosa: University of Alabama Press, 2013.

Martin, François-Xavier. *The History of New Orleans from the Earliest Period*. Vol. 1. New Orleans: Lyman and Beardslee, 1827.

———. *The History of New Orleans from the Earliest Period*. Vols. 1 and 2, with appended *Annals of Louisiana (1815–1861)* by John F. Condon. New Orleans: James A. Gresham, 1882.

McClellan, James E., III. *Colonialism and Science: Saint Domingue in the Old Regime*. 1992. Chicago: University of Chicago Press, 2010.

McConville, Brendan. *The King's Three Faces: The Rise and Fall of Royal America, 1688–1776*. Chapel Hill: University of North Carolina Press, 2006.

McDermott, John Francis. *Private Libraries in Creole Saint Louis*. Baltimore: Johns Hopkins Press, 1938.

Mehl, Eva Maria. *Forced Migration in the Spanish Pacific World: From Mexico to the Philippines, 1765–1811*. Cambridge, UK: Cambridge University Press, 2016.

Meyer, Douglas K. *Making the Heartland Quilt: A Geographical History of Settlement and Migration in Early Nineteenth-Century Illinois*. Carbondale: Southern Illinois University Press, 2000.

Moore, John Preston. *The Cabildo in Peru under the Bourbons: A Study in the Decline and Resurgence of Local Government in the Audiencia of Lima, 1700–1824*. Durham, NC: Duke University Press, 1966.

———. *The Cabildo in Peru under the Hapsburgs: A Study in the Origins and Powers of the Town Council in the Viceroyalty of Peru, 1530–1700*. Durham, NC: Duke University Press, 1954.

Nolte, Vincent. *Fifty Years in Both Hemispheres, or Reminiscences of the Life of a Former Merchant*. Trans. from German. New York: Redfield, 1854.

Norton, Marcy. *Sacred Gifts, Profane Pleasures: A History of Tobacco and Chocolate in the Atlantic World*. Ithaca, NY: Cornell University Press, 2008.

Onuf, Peter S. *Jefferson's Empire: The Language of American Nationhood*. Charlottesville: University of Virginia Press, 2000.

Oxford Desk Dictionary and Thesaurus. Ed. Elizabeth J. Jewell. New York: Oxford University Press, 2002.

Paquette, Gabriel B. *Enlightenment, Governance, and Reform in Spain and Its Empire, 1759–1808*. New York: Palgrave Macmillan, 2008.

Parrish, Susan Scott. *American Curiosity: Cultures of Natural History in the Colonial British Atlantic World*. Chapel Hill: University of North Carlin Press, 2006.

Pecor, Charles J. *The Ten-Year Tour of John Rannie: A Magician-Ventriloquist in Early America*. Glenwood, IL: David Meyer Magic Books, 1998.

Pitot, James, *Observations on the Colony of Louisiana from 1796 to 1802*. Trans. Henry C. Pitot. Baton Rouge: Louisiana State University Press, 1979.

Potter, Dorothy Williams. *Passports of Southeastern Pioneers, 1770–1823*. Baltimore: Gateway Press, 1982.

Prado, Fabricio. *Edge of Empire: Atlantic Networks and Revolution in Bourbon Rio de la Plata*. Oakland: University of California Press, 2015.

Premo, Bianca. *The Enlightenment on Trial: Ordinary Litigants and Colonialism in the Spanish Empire*. New York: Oxford University Press, 2017.

Rama, Angel. *The Lettered City*. Trans. John Charles Chasteen. Durham, NC: Duke University Press, 1996.

Rappaport, Joanne, and Thomas B. F. Cummins. *Beyond the Lettered City: Indigenous Literacies in the Andes*. Durham, NC: Duke University Press, 2011.

Richter, Daniel K. *Facing East from Indian Country: A Native History of Early America*. Cambridge, MA: Harvard University Press, 2001.

Robichaux, Albert, ed. *Louisiana Census and Militia Lists, 1770–1789*. New Orleans: Polyanthos, 1977.

Robin, C. C. *Voyage to Louisiana, 1803–1805*. Abridged ed. Trans. Stuart O. Landry Jr. Gretna, LA: Pelican Press, 2000.

Rodriguez, Antonio Acosta. *La Población de Luisiana Española (1763–1803)*. Madrid: Ministerio de Asuntos Exteriores, 1979.

Rowland, Dunbar, ed. *Official Letter Books of W. C. C. Claiborne, 1801–1816*. Vols. I and II. Jackson: Mississippi State Department of Archives and History, 1917.

Sarmiento, Domingo F. *Facundo, or Civilization and Barbarism*. Trans. Mary Mann. New York: Penguin Books, 1998.

Schavelzon, Daniel. *The Historical Archaeology of Buenos Aires: A City at the End of the World*. Trans. Alex Lomonaco. New York: Kluwer Academic/Plenum Publishers, 2000.

Schulz, Edward Thomas. *History of Freemasonry in Maryland*. Vol. 1. Baltimore: J. J. Medairy & Co., 1884.

Sellers-Garcia, Sylvia. *Distance and Documents at the Spanish Empire's Periphery*. Stanford, CA: Stanford University Press, 2014.

Sibley, John, et al. *An Account of Louisiana, Being an Abstract of Documents in the Offices of the Departments of State, and of the Treasury*. Philadelphia: Deane, 1803.

Smyth, Samuel Gordon, comp. *A Genealogy of the Duke–Shepherd–Van Metre Family*. Lancaster, PA: New Era Printing Co., 1909.

Socolow, Susan Migden. *The Merchants of Buenos Aires, 1778–1810: Family and Commerce.* New York: Cambridge University Press, 1978.

———. *The Women of Colonial Latin America.* New York: Cambridge University Press, 2000.

Soriano, Cristina. *Tides of Revolution: Information, Insurgencies, and the Crisis of Colonial Rule in Venezuela.* Albuquerque: University of New Mexico Press, 2018.

Stein, Barbara H., and Stanley J. Stein. *Apogee of Empire: Spain and New Spain in the Age of Charles III, 1759–1789.* Baltimore: Johns Hopkins University Press, 2003.

———. *Edge of Crisis: War and Trade in the Spanish Atlantic, 1789–1808.* Baltimore: Johns Hopkins University Press, 2009.

Tabla, Javier Ortiz de la. *Comercio Exterior de Vera Cruz, 1778–1821: Crisis de Dependencia.* Seville: Ducasse Escuela de estudios hispano-americanos, 1978.

Usner, Daniel H., Jr. *Indians, Settlers, & Slaves in a Frontier Exchange Economy: The Lower Mississippi Valley before 1783.* Chapel Hill: University of North Carolina Press, 1992.

Vinson, Ben, III. *Bearing Arms for His Majesty: The Free-Colored Militia in Colonial Mexico.* Stanford, CA: Stanford University Press, 2001.

Viqueira Alban, Juan Pedro, et al. *Propriety and Permissiveness in Bourbon Mexico.* Trans. Sonya Lipsett-Rivera and Sergio Rivera Ayala. Lanham, MD: SR Books, 1999.

Voss, Barbara L. *The Archaeology of Ethnogenesis: Race and Sexuality in Colonial San Francisco.* 2008. Rev. ed. Gainesville: University of Florida Press, 2015.

Warren, Adam. *Medicine and Politics in Colonial Peru: Population Growth and the Bourbon Reforms.* Pittsburgh: University of Pittsburgh Press, 2010.

Weeks, Charles A. *Paths to a Middle Ground: The Diplomacy of Natchez, Boukfouka, Nogales, and San Fernando de las Barrancas, 1791–1795.* Tuscaloosa: University of Alabama Press, 2010.

Williams, Abigail. *The Social Life of Books: Reading Together in the Eighteenth-Century Home.* New Haven, CT: Yale University Press, 2017.

Wilson, Edward O., and Jose M. Gomez Duran. *Kingdom of Ants: José Celestino Mutis and the Dawn of Natural History in the New World.* Baltimore: Johns Hopkins University Press, 2010.

Wilson, Samuel, and Leonard Victor Huber. *The Cabildo on Jackson Square: The Colonial Period, 1723–1803.* Gretna, LA: Pelican Publishing, 1970.

Winzerling, Oscar. *Acadian Odyssey.* Baton Rouge: Louisiana State University Press, 1955.

Wortman, Miles L. *Government and Society in Central America, 1680–1840.* New York: Columbia University Press, 1982.

ARTICLES AND ESSAYS

Arena, C. Richard. "Philadelphia–Spanish New Orleans Trade in the 1790s." *Louisiana History* 2 (1961): 429–45.

Beerman, Eric. "'Yo Solo' not 'Solo': Juan Antonio de Riano." *Florida Historical Quarterly* 58, no. 2 (October 1979): 174–84.

Borah, Woodrow. "Trends in Recent Studies of Colonial Latin American Cities," *Hispanic American Historical Review* 64, no. 3 (August 1984): 535–54.

Brown, Everett S., ed. "The Orleans Territory Memorialists to Congress, 1804." *Louisiana Historical Quarterly* 1 (1918): 99–102.

Calvo, Hortensia. "The Politics of Print: The Historiography of the Book in Early Spanish America." *Book History* 6 (2003): 277–305.

Casey, Powell A. "Masonic Lodges in New Orleans." *New Orleans Genesis* 20, no. 77 (January 1981): 1–20.

Clark, John G. "The Business Elite of New Orleans before 1815." *Nebraska Journal of Economics and Business* 8, no. 3 (Summer 1969): 94–103.

Couch, R. Randall. "The Public Masked Balls of Antebellum New Orleans: A Custom of Masque outside the Mardi Gras Tradition." *Louisiana History* 35, no. 4 (Autumn 1994): 403–31.

Coutts, Brian E. "Boom and Bust: The Rise and Fall of the Tobacco Industry in Spanish Louisiana, 1770–1790." *The Americas* 42, no. 3 (January 1986): 289–309.

———. "An Inventory of Sources in the Department of Archives and Manuscripts, Louisiana State University, for the History of Spanish Louisiana and Spanish West Florida." *Louisiana History* 19, no. 2 (Spring 1978): 213–50.

Dart, Henry P. "Public Education in New Orleans in 1800." *Louisiana Historical Quarterly* 11 (1928): 241–52.

———, ed. "Spanish Procedure in Louisiana in 1800 for Licensing Doctors and Surgeons." Trans. Laura L. Porteous. *Louisiana Historical Quarterly* 17 (1933): 294–305.

De Grummond, Jane Lucas. "Cayetana Susana Bosque y Fangui, 'A Notable Woman.'" *Louisiana History* 23, no. 3 (Summer 1982): 277–94.

Din, Gilbert C. "Carondelet, the Cabildo, and Slaves: Louisiana in 1795." *Louisiana History* 38, no. 1 (Winter 1997): 5–28.

———. "Empires Too Far: The Demographic Limitations of Three Imperial Powers in the Eighteenth-Century Mississippi Valley." *Louisiana History* 50, no. 3 (Summer 2009): 261–92.

———. "The Death and Succession of Francisco Bouligny." *Louisiana History* 22, no. 3 (Summer 1981): 307–15.

———. "The Immigration Policy of Governor Esteban Miró in Spanish Louisiana." *Southwestern Historical Quarterly* 73, no. 2 (October 1969): 155–75.

Donaldson, Gary A. "Bringing Water to the Crescent City: Benjamin Latrobe and the New Orleans Waterworks System." *Louisiana History* 28, no. 4 (Autumn 1987): 381–96.

Dunbar, William. "Observations on the Comet of 1807–8." *Transactions of the American Philosophical Society* 6 (1809): 368–74.

Ellicott, Andrew. "Astronomical, and Thermometrical Observations, Made at the Confluence of the Mississippi, and Ohio Rivers." *Transactions of the American Philosophical Society* 5 (1802): 162–202.

Ermus, Cindy. "Reduced to Ashes: The Good Friday Fire of 1788 in Spanish Colonial New Orleans." *Louisiana History* 54, no. 3 (Summer 2013): 292–331.

Everett, Donald E. "Emigres and Militiamen: Free Persons of Color in New Orleans, 1803–1815." *Journal of Negro History* 38, no. 4 (October 1953): 377–402.

Ferrer, José Joaquín de. "Astronomical Observations Made by José Joaquín de Ferrer, Chiefly for the Purpose of Determining the Geographical Position of Various Places in the United States, and Other Parts of North America." *Transactions of the American Philosophical Society* 6 (1809): 158–64.

———. "Notes: With Corrections, to Be Applied to the Geographical Situations Inserted from Page 158 to Page 164, in the First Part of the Present Volume of Transactions, by J. J. de Ferrer. . . ." *Transactions of the American Philosophical Society* 6 (1809): 360–68.

———. "Observations on the Comet Which Appeared in September 1807, in the Island of Cuba: Made by J. J. de Ferrer. Continuation of the Astronomical Observations, Made by Him at the Same Place. . . ." *Transactions of the American Philosophical Society* 6 (1809): 345–59.

Fisher, John R. "Commerce and Imperial Decline: Spanish Trade with Spanish America, 1797–1820." *Journal of Latin American Studies* 30 (1998): 459–79.

Fossier, A. E. "The Funeral Ceremony of Napoleon in New Orleans, December 19, 1821." *Louisiana Historical Quarterly* 13 (1930): 246–52.

Glick, Thomas F. "Science and Independence in Latin America (with Special Reference to New Granada)." *Hispanic American Historical Review* 71, no. 2 (May 1991): 307–33.

Goldberg, Marta B. "La Población Negra y Mulata de la Ciudad de Buenos Aires, 1810–1840." *Desarrollo Económico* 16, no. 61 (April–June 1976): 75–99.

Goudeau, John M. "Booksellers and Printers in New Orleans, 1764–1885." *Journal of Library History* 5, no. 1 (January 1970): 5–19.

Greenleaf, Richard. "The Inquisition in Spanish Louisiana, 1762–1800." *New Mexico Historical Review* 50 (1975): 45–72.

Grubb, F. W. "Growth of Literacy in Colonial America: Longitudinal Patterns, Economic Models, and the Direction of Future Research." *Social Science History* 14, no. 4 (Winter 1990): 451–82.

Hampe Martínez, Teodoro, "La historiografía del libro en América hispana: un estado de la cuestión." In *Leer en Tiempos de la Colonia: Imprenta, Bibliotecas y Lectores en la Nueva España*, comp. Idalia García and Pedro Rueda Ramírez. Mexico City: Universidad Nacional Autónoma de México, 2010.

Hilton, Sylvia. "Movilidad y expansión en la construcción política de los Estados Unidos: 'estos errantes colonos' en las fronteras españolas del Misisipi (1776–1803)." *Revista Complutense de Historia de América* 28 (2002): 63–96.

Holmes, Jack D. L. "Louisiana in 1795: The Earliest Extant Issue of the 'Moniteur De La Louisiane.'" *Louisiana History* 7, no. 2 (Spring 1966): 133–51.

——. "The Moniteur de la Louisiane in 1798." *Louisiana History* 2, no. 2 (Spring 1961): 230–53.

——. "A New Look at Spanish Louisiana Census Accounts: The Recent Historiography of Antonio Acosta." *Louisiana History* 21, no. 1 (Winter 1980): 77–86.

——. "The 1794 New Orleans Fire: A Case Study of Spanish Noblesse Oblige." *Louisiana Studies* 15 (1976): 21–43.

——. "Vidal and Zoning in Spanish New Orleans, 1797." *Louisiana History* 14, no. 3, (Summer 1973): 270–82.

Houdaille, Jacques. "Reconstitution des familles de Saint-Domingue (Haïti) au XVIIIe siècle." *Population* 46, no. 1 (January–February 1991): 29–40.

——. "Trois paroisses de Saint-Domingue au XVIIIe siècle." *Population* 18, no. 1 (January–March 1963): 93–110.

Hurwitz, Samuel J., and Edith F. Hurwitz, "A Token of Freedom: Private Bill Legislation for Free Negroes in Eighteenth-Century Jamaica." *William and Mary Quarterly,* 3rd ser., vol. 24, no. 3 (July 1967): 423–31.

Ingersoll, Thomas N. "The Slave Trade and the Ethnic Diversity of Louisiana's Slave Community." *Louisiana History* 37, no. 2 (Spring 1996): 133–61.

Johnson, Lyman L., and Sibila Seibert. "Estimaciones de la población de Buenos Aires en 1744, 1778 y 1810." *Desarrollo Económico* 19, no. 73 (April–June 1979): 107–19.

Kotlikoff, Laurence J. "Quantitative Description of the New Orleans Slave Market, 1804 to 1862." In *Without Consent or Contract: Markets and Production, Technical Papers* 1, ed. Robert William Fogel and Stanley L. Engerman, 31–53. New York: Norton, 1992.

Lachance, Paul F. "The 1809 Immigration of Saint-Domingue Refugees to New Orleans: Reception, Integration and Impact." *Louisiana History* 29, no. 2 (Spring 1988): 109–41.

La Vere, David. "Edward Murphy: Irish Entrepreneur in Spanish Natchitoches." *Louisiana History* 32, no. 4 (Autumn 1991): 371–91.

Le Gardeur, Rene J., Jr., and Henry C. Pitot. "An Unpublished Memoir of Spanish, Louisiana, 1796–1802." In *Frenchmen and French Ways in the Mississippi Valley,* ed. John Francis McDermott. Urbana: University of Illinois Press, 1969.

Le Glaunec, Jean-Pierre. "Slave Migrations and Slave Control in Spanish and Early American New Orleans." In *Empires of the Imagination: Transatlantic Histories of the Louisiana Purchase,* ed. Peter J. Kastor and François Weil, 204–38. Charlottesville: University of Virginia Press, 2009.

——. "Slave Migrations in Spanish and Early American Louisiana: New Sources and New Estimates." *Louisiana History* 46, no. 2 (Spring 2005): 185–209.

Leonard, Irving. "A Frontier Library, 1799." *Hispanic American Historical Review* 23 (1943): 21–51.

McCutcheon, Roger Philip. "Books and Booksellers in New Orleans, 1730–1830." *Louisiana Historical Quarterly* 20 (1937): 606–18.

———. "The First English Plays in New Orleans." *American Literature* 11 (May 1939): 183–99.

McGroarty, William Buckner. "Diary of Captain Philip Buckner." *William & Mary Quarterly* 6, ser. 2, no. 3 (July 1926): 173–207.

Morazan, Ronald R. "Don Andres Almonaster y Rojas Estrada, Benefactor of Nueva Orleans." *Louisiana History* 13, no. 4 (Autumn 1972): 387–89.

Murray, John E. "Family, Literacy, and Skill Training in the Antebellum South: Historical-Longitudinal Evidence from Charleston." *Journal of Economic History* 63, no. 3 (September 2004): 773–99.

Nasatir, Abraham P., ed. "Government Employees and Salaries in Spanish Louisiana." *Louisiana Historical Quarterly* 29 (1946): 885–1040.

Newman, Andrew. "Early Americanist Grammatology: Definitions of Writing and Literacy." In *Colonial Mediascapes: Sensory Worlds of the Early Americas*, ed. Matt Cohen and Jeffrey Glover, 76–92. Omaha: University of Nebraska Press, 2014.

Noble, Stuart Grayson. "Schools of New Orleans During the First Quarter of the Nineteenth Century, *Louisiana Historical Quarterly* 14 (January 1931): 65–78.

Padgett, James A. "The Ancestry of Edward Livingston of Louisiana: The Livingston Family." *Louisiana Historical Quarterly* 19 (1936): 900–937.

Pfaff, Caroline S. "Henry Miller Shreve: A Biography." *Louisiana Historical Quarterly* 10 (April 1927): 192–240.

Pintard, John. "New Orleans, 1801: An Account by John Pintard." Ed. David Lee Sterling. *Louisiana Historical Quarterly* 34 (1951): 217–33.

Riley, Martin Luther. "The Development of Education in Louisiana." *Louisiana Historical Quarterly* 19 (1936): 594–634.

Sibley, John. "The Journal of Dr. John Sibley, July–October, 1802." *Louisiana Historical Quarterly* 10 (1927): 474–97.

Smith, Robert Sidney. "Shipping in the Port of Veracruz, 1790–1821." *Hispanic American Historical Review* 23, no. 1 (February 1943): 5–20.

Stewart, Whitney Nell. "Fashioning Frenchness: *Gens de Couleur Libres* and the Cultural Struggle for Power in Antebellum New Orleans." *Journal of Social History* 51, no. 3 (2018): 526–56.

Uribe-Uran, Victor M. "The Birth of a Public Sphere in Latin America during the Age of Revolution." *Comparative Studies in Society and History* 42, no. 2 (April 2000): 425–57.

Usner, Daniel H., Jr. "American Indians in Colonial New Orleans." In *Powhatan's Mantle:*

Indians in the Colonial Southeast, ed. Gregory A. Waselkov, Peter H. Wood, Tom Hatley, 164–86. Lincoln: University of Nebraska Press, 2006.

Watson, Charles S. "A Democracy of the State of Spanish Rule: James Workman's 'Liberty in Louisiana' (1804)." *Louisiana History* 11 (1970): 245–58.

Wellford, Robert. "Diary of Dr. Robert Wellford." *William & Mary Quarterly* 11 (1903).

THESES AND DISSERTATIONS

Coutts, Brian E. "Martin Navarro: Treasurer, Contador, Intendant, 1766–1788: Politics and Trade in Spanish Louisiana." PhD diss., Louisiana State University, 1981.

Rodriguez, John E. "City of Chameleons: Spanish New Orleans and the Transition of Empires, 1766–1803." PhD diss., George Mason University, 2018.

Webre, Stephen. "The Social and Economic Bases of Cabildo Membership in Seventeenth-Century Santiago de Guatemala." PhD diss., Tulane University, 1980.

Wohlip, Michael Stephen. "A Man in the Shadow: The Life of Daniel Clark." PhD diss., Tulane University, 1984.

NEWSPAPERS

Baltimore Patriot, 1812–13, then *Baltimore Patriot & Evening Advertiser.*

Charleston Courier, 1803–52.

Courrier de la Louisiane/Louisiana Courier, 1804–59.

Courrier de Londres, 1803–4.

Jornal Económico Mercantil de Vera Cruz.

Louisiana Advertiser, 1820–42.

Louisiana Commercial Bulletin, 1832–71.

Louisiana Gazette, 1804–26.

Louisiana Union.

Moniteur de la Louisiane, 1794–1815.

National Intelligencer & Washington Advertiser/National Intelligencer, 1810–67.

New Orleans Democrat.

Philadelphia Aurora, 1794–1824.

Providence Gazette, 1795–1811.

Republican and Savannah Evening Ledger, 1809–16.

Virginia Herald and Fredericksburg Advertiser, 1787–95.

ONLINE SOURCES

American Philosophical Society

Membership (1769–present). search.amphilsoc.org//memhist/search.

Proceedings (1838–present). www.jstor.org/journal/procamerphilsoci.

Transactions (1769–present). www.jstor.org/journal/tranamerphilsoci.

U.S. COURT CASES

1 Cai. 549, *John Blagge v. New York Insurance Company* (1804).

2 Howard 44, *Gaines v. Chew.*

12 Howard, *Gaines v. Chew.*

43 US 2, *Gaines v. Chew* (2 How.) (1844).

6 Wallace 573–723, *Gaines v. Delacroix; City of New Orleans v. Gaines* (1884).

15 Peters, *Gaines v. Relf* (1841).

53 US (12 How.) 472 *Gaines v. Relf et al.* (1852).

INDEX